THE GILGAMESH EPIC AND
OLD TESTAMENT PARALLELS

THE
GILGAMESH EPIC
AND
OLD TESTAMENT
PARALLELS

By ALEXANDER HEIDEL

Phoenix Books

THE UNIVERSITY OF CHICAGO PRESS

CHICAGO & LONDON

SBN: 226-32397-8 (clothbound); 226-32398-6 (paperbound)

The University of Chicago Press, Chicago 60637
The University of Chicago Press, Ltd., London

PREFACE

The present volume is a companion to my monograph <u>The Baby-</u>
<u>lonian Genesis</u> and as such follows the same pattern. The trans-
lations of the Babylonian and Assyrian texts here offered were made
originally for the Assyrian Dictionary files of the Oriental Institute of the University of Chicago. Like my publication on the Babylonian creation stories, this book is intended not primarily for
the professional Assyriologist but for a somewhat wider circle of
readers. With this purpose in mind, I have again published the
texts in translation only and have endeavored to confine my dis-
cussions chiefly to matters which will be of a somewhat more general interest, striving at all times to treat everyone's view with
due consideration and to present the material <u>sine ira et studio</u>,
though it be in a straightforward manner.

In the preparation of the material here presented I again enjoyed the unstinted co-operation of the members of the Oriental Institute staff, particularly of Assistant Professor F. W. Geers,
Associate Professor Thorkild Jacobsen, and Mr. Pinhas Delougaz. The
work of translating the more objectionable passages into Latin has,
for the most part, been done by a friend who prefers to remain anon-
ymous. I wish to express my appreciation also to the director of the
Oriental Institute, Professor John A. Wilson, for providing the necessary subsidy to make this publication possible. It goes without
saying that as a co-worker on the Assyrian Dictionary of the Oriental Institute I had full access to the Dictionary files.

ALEXANDER HEIDEL

Oriental Institute
University of Chicago

TABLE OF CONTENTS

LIST OF SYMBOLS AND SPECIAL CHARACTERS

( )   in translations enclose elements not in the original but desirable or necessary for a better understanding in English.

(?)   indicate that the meaning is uncertain.

[ ]   enclose restorations in the cuneiform text.

⌈ ⌉   enclose a word, a phrase, or a line which is partially damaged.

....   (1) in translations of cuneiform material indicate that the text is unintelligible to the translator;

          (2) elsewhere indicate omission.

[....] or ⌈....⌉   indicate that the text is wholly or partially damaged and therefore unintelligible.

⁻ or ^   indicates a long vowel.

˘   indicates a short vowel.

ʾ   = א.

ʿ   = ע.

ḫ   = ח.

ṣ   = צ.

ś   = שׂ.

ṭ   = ט.

CHAPTER I

THE GILGAMESH EPIC

The Gilgamesh Epic, the longest and most beautiful Babylonian poem yet discovered in the mounds of the Tigro-Euphrates region, ranks among the great literary masterpieces of mankind. It is one of the principal heroic tales of antiquity and may well be called the _Odyssey_ of the Babylonians. Though rich in mythological material of great significance for the study of comparative religion, it abounds with episodes of deepest human interest, in distinct contrast to the Babylonian creation versions; and, although composed thousands of years before our time, the Gilgamesh Epic will, owing to the universal appeal of the problems with which it is concerned and the manner in which these are treated, continue to move the hearts of men for ages to come. To Bible students in particular it will be of special interest because of its eschatological material and because it contains the best preserved and most extensive Babylonian account of the deluge.

The Discovery of the Tablets

During the seventh century B.C., to which the greater part of the available tablets date back, the Gilgamesh Epic consisted of twelve large tablets, each of which contained about three hundred lines, with the exception of the twelfth, which had only about half as many lines. Most of the material of this epic was _found_ by Austen H. Layard, Hormuzd Rassam, and George Smith at about the middle of the last century among the ruins of the temple library of the god Nabû (the biblical Nebo) and the palace library of the Assyrian king Ashurbanipal (668-ca. 633 B.C.), both of which were located in Nineveh, the later capital of the Assyrian empire. Since then numerous other tablets and fragments belonging to the Gilgamesh series have come to light. At the turn of the century Bruno Meissner acquired a fragment of considerable size from a dealer in Baghdad. This piece, found among the ruins of ancient Sippar (the modern Abu Ḥabba), contains part of an Old Babylonian version of the tenth tablet. In 1914 the University of Pennsylvania secured by purchase from a dealer in antiquities a large and fairly complete six-column tablet containing an Old Babylonian recension of Tablet II. At about the

1

same time Yale University had the good fortune to obtain from the same
dealer a tablet which forms a continuation of the Pennsylvania tablet and is inscribed with an Old Babylonian version of Tablet III.
Shortly before the outbreak of hostilities in 1914 the German excavations at Ashur, the old capital of Assyria, produced a considerable fragment of the Assyrian edition of the sixth tablet.
And in 1928/29 the Germans discovered at Uruk two rather small
pieces, which supposedly belong to Tablet IV. Numerous Sumerian
portions of material bearing on the Gilgamesh Epic have been recovered from the mounds of Nippur, Kish, and Ur. Of these, the
portions belonging to Tablet XII agree almost verbatim with the
Semitic recension, while the others, not utilized in the present
translation of the epic, differ very considerably from the Semitic version. Finally, from distant Ḫattusas (modern Boghazköy),
the ancient Hittite capital, have come a Babylonian fragment containing a rather brief and widely deviating version of Tablets V
and VI, about a dozen of fragments inscribed in Hittite, and even
a few pieces of a Hurrian translation.[1] Despite all these discov-
eries, the text of some of the tablets is still rather incomplete;
but the general trend of the story is quite clear.

The Publication of the Tablets

The story of the publication of the Gilgamesh material is
rather long and need not be related in detail at this time. Suffice it to recapitulate some of the more salient points. The
first arrangement and translation of the tablets discovered among
the remains of Nineveh was made by George Smith, of the British
Museum, who, on December 3, 1872, read a paper before the Society
of Biblical Archaeology entitled "The Chaldean Account of the Deluge,"[2] in which he presented a translation and a discussion of a
number of fragments of the Gilgamesh Epic, particularly of the
deluge episode. Fragmentary as this material was, it created a
tremendous enthusiasm throughout Europe and gave a great impetus
to the study of cuneiform inscriptions in general. The first com-

---

[1] On the Hurrian material see J. Friedrich, Kleinasiatische
Sprachdenkmäler (Berlin, 1932), pp. 32-34, and the references
given there.

[2] Published in the Transactions of the Society of Biblical
Archaeology, II (1873), 213-34.

plete edition of the known cuneiform texts of the epic was put out
by Paul Haupt, Das Babylonische Nimrodepos (Leipzig, 1884-91),[3]
with Tablet XII in Beiträge zur Assyriologie, I (1890), 49-65.
Some years thereafter Peter Jensen published a transliteration and
translation of the extant material, together with an extensive commentary, in his Assyrisch-Babylonische Mythen und Epen (Berlin,
1900), pages 116-265 and 421-531. This work marked a great ad-
vance over all previous translations and is still a mine of useful information. Another important work from the earlier days of
the decipherment of our epic was issued by Arthur Ungnad and Hugo
Gressmann, Das Gilgamesch-Epos (Göttingen, 1911), which contains
a translation of the epic and a detailed discussion of its contents. The most recent edition of the cuneiform text is found
in R. Campbell Thompson, The Epic of Gilgamish (Oxford, 1930).
While Thompson has published the cuneiform text of only the Assyrian recension, he has given us a complete transliteration of
all the Semitic Gilgamesh material known to him at the time, and,
unless otherwise indicated, the present rendering of the Semitic
version of this epic is based on Thompson's edition of the cuneiform original. The latest translations are those by Erich
Ebeling in Gressmann's Altorientalische Texte zum Alten Testament
(Berlin and Leipzig, 1926), pages 150-98; Thompson, The Epic of
Gilgamish (London, 1928); Albert Schott, Das Gilgamesch=Epos
(Leipzig [1934]); G. Contenau, L'Épopée de Gilgamesh (Paris, 1939);
and F. M. Th. Böhl, Het Gilgamesj-Epos (Amsterdam, 1941).[4] Men-
tion may be made also of a rendition in free rhythms by W. E.
Leonard, Gilgamesh, Epic of Old Babylonia (New York, 1934).

The Hero of the Epic

The central figure of our poem is a youthful ruler named
Gilgamesh, originally a historical personage whom the Sumerian
king list assigns to the First Dynasty of Uruk, allowing him a
reign of one hundred and twenty-six years, and with whose illus-
trious name scores of myths and legends of quite distinct origin

_____

[3]Haupt called our poem the "Babylonian Nimrod epic" because
in former days Gilgamesh was identified with Nimrod (Gen. 10:8-10),
although without sufficient evidence.

[4]I regret that, because of present conditions, Böhl's translation is not available to me.

were associated in the course of time. Claudius Aelianus,[5] a
Roman author of the second century A.D., records the following
curious story concerning the birth and childhood of Gilgamesh:

"When Seuēchoros[6] reigned over the Babylonians, the Chaldeans
said that the son who would be born of his daughter would wrest
the kingdom from the grandfather. At this he was alarmed and, to
express it jocularly, became an Acrisios[7] to the girl; for he
guarded (her) very closely. But without his knowledge—for fate
was more ingenious than the Babylonian—the girl became a mother
by an obscure man and bore a child. (Her) guards, in fear of the
king, threw it from the acropolis; for it was there that the aforementioned girl was imprisoned. But an eagle very quickly saw the
child's fall, and before the infant was dashed upon the ground got
underneath it and received (it) on (his) back, and carrying (it)
to an orchard, he set (it) down very cautiously. The caretaker
of the place, seeing the beautiful child, loved it and reared (it);
it was called Gilgamos, and reigned over the Babylonians."

According to our epic and an inscription of the Sumerian king
Utuḫegal of Uruk, Gilgamesh was the son of the goddess Ninsun, the
wife of the god Lugalbanda. His father, however, was not Lugalbanda, as would be expected, but rather an unknown mortal whom the
Sumerian king list calls "the high priest of Kullab," a district
in the city of Uruk.[8] This circumstance is of importance because
it explains why Gilgamesh, according to the epic, was part god and
part man. One of his famous accomplishments was the building of
the wall of Uruk, which is mentioned in the epic and in a Sumerian
inscription of Anam (a later ruler of this city), who calls the
wall of Uruk, which he rebuilt, "an ancient work of Gilgamesh."[9]

_____

[5]De natura animalium xii. 21. Translated by Hugo Gressmann,
Mose und seine Zeit (Göttingen, 1913), pp. 11-12, and A. M. Harmon
in A. T. Clay, A Hebrew Deluge Story in Cuneiform (New Haven, 1922),
p. 48, n. 15.

[6]On the identification of this king with Enmekar, king of Uruk,
see Thorkild Jacobsen, The Sumerian King List (Chicago, 1939), p. 87.

[7]King of Argos, of whom a similar story is told in Greek literature.

[8]Cf. A. Poebel, Historical Texts (Philadelphia, 1914), p. 75;
Jacobsen, op. cit., pp. 90-91.

[9]F. Thureau-Dangin, Die sumerischen und akkadischen Königsinschriften (Leipzig, 1907), p. 222.

In the course of time Gilgamesh became a god of the lower
world. In a Sumerian inscription, the Ur-Nammu composition, he is
designated as "king of the underworld," where he pronounces judgment.[10] And in an incantation text, in which the sign for deity is
prefixed to his name, he is addressed in these terms: "Gilgamesh,
perfect king, [judge of the Anunnaki], wise prince, bra[ce(?) of
mankind, who surveys the regions of the world], ruler of the earth,
[lord of the underworld]! Thou art the judge, like a god thou per-
ceivest (everything). Thou standest in the underworld (and) givest
the final deci[sion]. Thy judgment is not changed, [thy] word is
not forgotten. Thou dost inquire, examine, judge, perceive, and
lead aright. Shamash has entrusted into thy hand judgment and decision. Kings, rulers, and princes lie prostrate before thee."[11]

A Summary of the Epic

Like the Odyssey, the Aeneid, and the Nibelungenlied, the
Gilgamesh Epic opens with a brief résumé of the deeds and fortunes
of the hero whose praises it sings. It first extols the great
knowledge and wisdom of him who saw everything and knew all things;
who saw secret things and revealed hidden things; who brought information of the days before the flood; who went on a long journey
(in quest of immortality), became weary and worn; who engraved on
a tablet of stone an account of all that he had done and suffered;
and who built the walls of Uruk and its holy temple Eanna.

After these lines the text in the Assyrian edition, of which
alone the proem has been preserved, breaks off. But, to judge from
the first two lines of the next column and from the Hittite recension, the epic went on from here to relate the story itself. When
the text again becomes fairly connected, the epic has already
turned to the oppressive reign of Gilgamesh.

In his exuberant strength and vigor, his arrogant spirit and
undisciplined desires, Gilgamesh apparently carries the maidens
of the city off to his court and drives the young men to such
heavy labors on the city walls and the temple Eanna that the

---

[10]S. Langdon, Sumerian Liturgical Texts (Philadelphia, 1917),
Pls. XIX:11 and XXI:16-17 (cf. S. N. Kramer in the Bulletin of the
American Schools of Oriental Research, No. 94 [April, 1944], p. 6).

[11]Erich Ebeling, Tod und Leben nach den Vorstellungen der
Babylonier (Berlin and Leipzig, 1931), p. 127:7-15 (cf. W. von
Soden in Zeitschrift für Assyriologie, XLIII [1936], 266).

inhabitants at length invoke the gods to relieve them of their
unbearable burden. At last the gods listen to the cry of the op-
pressed and tyrannized population and decide to create a counterpart
to Gilgamesh to divert the latter's attention to other matters, by
having the two constantly strive, or wrestle, with each other.

The resultant creation is a wild-looking human being of ti-
tanic strength called Enkidu. His whole body is covered with hair;
the hair of his head is long like that of a woman, and the locks of
the hair on his head sprout like grain. He knows nothing about land
or people and is garbed like Sumuqan, the god of cattle and agri-
culture. With the game of the field he ranges at large over the
steppe, eats grass and drinks water from the drinking-places of the
open country, and delights in the company of the animals.

First through dreams, and then through a trapper, Gilgamesh
learns of this unique individual and sends out a courtesan to en-
chain Enkidu with her charms and to bring him to Uruk. There
Gilgamesh and Enkidu meet, at the entrance to the community house.
This place was to be the scene of one of Gilgamesh's nocturnal or-
gies. But Enkidu is so repelled by this unseemly affair that he
tries to block the passage to prevent Gilgamesh from entering the
house. Thereupon a bitter struggle ensues. The two fight with
each other like infuriated bulls. They shatter the doorpost of
the community house and cause the wall to shake. They fight in
the doorway of the community house and they fight on the street.
Finally Gilgamesh succeeds in forcing Enkidu to the ground, whereupon the fury of Gilgamesh abates and he turns away. Enkidu ac-
knowledges Gilgamesh as his superior, and the two, admiring each
other's strength and prowess, form a friendship.

At first thought it might seem that the purpose of the gods
has been frustrated. But in reality it has not, for Gilgamesh
now devotes his attention to his newly won friend and dreams of
adventure, which is to insure everlasting fame for himself and his
companion. Soon the two, armed with gigantic weapons, are found
on a dangerous expedition against a terrible ogre, whose name appears as Huwawa in the Old Babylonian and Hittite versions and as
Humbaba in the Assyrian recension. This ogre had been appointed
by Enlil, the lord of the gods, as the guardian of a distant and
almost boundless cedar forest, but in the pride of his heart he
evidently overshot the mark and is therefore deserving of punishment. After a long journey the two companions arrive at the gate

of the forest, which is guarded by a fearful watchman placed there
by Ḫumbaba. The watchman is killed, and Enkidu opens the gate to
the beautiful cedar forest. But alas! the gate is enchanted, and
as Enkidu opens it, his hand is paralyzed, and he hesitates to
proceed. However, upon the urgent plea of Gilgamesh, who may have
resorted to magic and thus may have restored Enkidu's hand to its
former condition, Enkidu follows Gilgamesh, and the two go into the
depths of the forest together. After another long journey they arrive at the sacred cedar of Ḫumbaba. Gilgamesh takes the ax in his
hand and cuts down the cedar. The resounding noise of the strokes
of the ax brings fierce Ḫumbaba to the scene. At the sight of this
frightful ogre Gilgamesh is terror-stricken. He breaks into tears
and cries to Shamash, the sun-god. Shamash hears his prayer and
from all eight major points of the compass he sends mighty winds
against Ḫumbaba, so that he is neither able to go forward nor able
to turn back and has to surrender. Ḫumbaba pleads for mercy, but
no mercy is granted. Gilgamesh and Enkidu cut off his head and
victoriously return to Uruk.

Upon his arrival in Uruk, Gilgamesh washes his hair, polishes
his weapons, and garbs himself in festive attire. As he puts on
his tiara, Ishtar, the goddess of love, looks with admiration upon
the young and handsome king and, with many attractive promises, offers to be his wife. But Gilgamesh, knowing the wiles of Ishtar,
rejects her proposal in the most scathing terms. Enraged at this
crushing humiliation, Ishtar mounts up to heaven and goes before
Anu, her father, with the plea: "Create for me the bull of heaven
[that he may destroy Gilgamesh]!" After considerable hesitation,
Anu consents. The bull is created and sent down upon Uruk. A
whole army of men rush out to dispatch him, but it is of no avail.
One snort from the bull, and the king's men fall by the hundreds!
Another snort, and additional hundreds fall to the ground! Then
he rushes upon Enkidu, but Enkidu gets hold of the thick of his
tail, while Gilgamesh comes running along, thrusts his sword into
the nape of the bull, and kills him. Foiled in her plans, Ishtar
ascends the wall of Uruk and utters a curse upon Gilgamesh. But
Enkidu tears out the right thigh of the bull of heaven and tosses
it before her, amid vulgar taunts, while Gilgamesh dedicates the
bull's horns to his tutelary god, Lugalbanda. Thereupon Gilgamesh
and Enkidu wash their hands in the Euphrates, on whose former banks
Uruk was located, and then ride in triumph through the thronged and

lordly city, as Gilgamesh calls out in exultant gladness: "Who is
the (most) glorious among heroes? Who is the (most) eminent among
men?" and an enthusiastic crowd responds in joyful acclaim: "Gilgamesh is the (most) glorious among heroes! [Gilgamesh is the
(most) emine]nt among men!"

That night Enkidu has a dream foreboding his own speedy end.
He sees the gods assembled together, as they deliberate which of
the two who killed Ḫumbaba and the bull of heaven should perish.
The lot falls on Enkidu. Subsequently he takes ill and dies, at
the decree of the gods.

This has an overpowering effect on Gilgamesh. He cries "bitterly like unto a wailing woman." For seven days and seven nights
he weeps over his friend and refuses to give him up for burial,
hoping that he will rise after all at his lamentation. Finally
he reconciles himself to the fact that the life of his friend is
beyond recall, and Enkidu is buried with honors.

Steeped in sorrow at the death of his friend who has turned
to clay, Gilgamesh leaves Uruk and roams over the desert, lament-
ing: "When I die, shall I not be like unto Enkidu?" His grief-
stricken spirit is obsessed with the fear of death and finds no
comfort in the glory of his past accomplishments. His sole interest now lies in finding ways and means to escape the fate of mankind; he is willing to go through the greatest perils and the most
extraordinary hardships to gain immortal life! He thinks of faraway Utnapishtim, the Babylonian Noah, who, Gilgamesh has heard,
has received blessed immortality, and decides to hasten to him with
all possible speed to obtain from him the secret of eternal life.

But to reach the dwelling place of Utnapishtim, Gilgamesh
must go on a long and arduous journey fraught with many dangers.
He arrives at the towering mountain range of Mâshu, probably the
Lebanon and Antilebanon Range. Here is the gate through which the
sun passes on his daily journey. The gate is guarded by a terrifying pair of scorpion-people, "whose look is death" and "whose
frightful splendor overwhelms mountains." At the sight of them
the face of even a demigod like Gilgamesh becomes gloomy with fear
and dismay, and he falls prostrate before them. But the scorpion-
people, recognizing the partly divine nature of Gilgamesh, receive
him kindly and permit him to enter the gate and to traverse the
mountain range. After a journey of twelve double-hours of utter
darkness, which does not permit him to see what lies ahead of him

or what lies behind him, he comes out on the other side and stands
before a beautiful garden of precious stones, with trees and
shrubs, fruit and vines, all of glittering stone.

And there in the distance, at the edge of the sea, probably
the Mediterranean Sea on the Phoenician coast, dwells Siduri, the
divine barmaid! Gilgamesh hastens thither and inquires of her how
he can get to Utnapishtim, to obtain from him the secret of immortality. The barmaid at first tries to persuade him that his
quest is vain, for there is no escape from death. She therefore
advises him to enjoy life in full measure and to abandon his hazardous, yet hopeless, undertaking. Nevertheless, Gilgamesh per-
sists in his plan, and at last the barmaid directs him to Utnapishtim's boatman, who has come across from the other side of the sea,
where Utnapishtim dwells, and is now in the woods, in search of
something. "Him let thy face behold," she tells Gilgamesh. "[If
it is possi]ble, cross over with him; if it is not possible, turn
back (home)." Gilgamesh leaves the goddess and goes to the boatman, who at length agrees to take him along. With much difficulty
the two cross the sea and the waters of death and finally arrive
at the shores of the land of blessed Utnapishtim.

When Gilgamesh sees Utnapishtim and notices that this ancient
sage is not different from him but that there is, in fact, less
life and energy in Utnapishtim than there is in himself, his hope
of gaining immortality undoubtedly rises, and he asks Utnapishtim
how he entered into the company of the gods and obtained everlasting life. Thereupon Utnapishtim relates to him at great length the
story of the deluge, which we shall consider in detail in the final
chapter of this book, and tells him how he obtained the boon of immortal life. After that he turns to Gilgamesh and says to him, in
effect: "But now as for you, who will assemble the gods to you so
that they may confer immortality on you?" After a moment's reflection, Utnapishtim offers this suggestion: "Come, do not sleep
for six days and seven nights." The meaning of this line appears
to be that if he can master sleep, the twin brother of death, he
may then be able to master also death itself.[12] But hardly has
tired and exhausted Gilgamesh sat down when he falls asleep and
sleeps for six days, until Utnapishtim finally wakes him.

----

[12]A. Ungnad and H. Gressmann, Das Gilgamesch-Epos (Göttingen,
1911), p. 140; R. W. Rogers, Cuneiform Parallels to the Old Testament (New York and Cincinnati, 1926), p. 101.

There now seems to be nothing left for Gilgamesh but to return
home. However, just as he departs and his boat is already moving
away from the shore, Utnapishtim calls him back and reveals to
him a secret of the gods: There is a thorny plant of wondrous
power at the bottom of the sea; if he will obtain that plant and
eat it when he has reached old age, his life will be rejuvenated.
Gilgamesh descends to the bottom of the sea and obtains the plant.
In the joy of his heart he now sets out for Uruk, accompanied by
Utnapishtim's boatman, who evidently has been banished from the
land of Utnapishtim for having brought Gilgamesh to its shores.
However, on the way home Gilgamesh sees a pool of cold water and
goes bathing. While he is thus engaged, a serpent perceives the
fragrance of the plant, comes up from the water, snatches the plant
from him and eats it, and thus gains the power to shed its old skin
and thereby to renew its life. Gilgamesh sits down and weeps bitterly, for his last ray of hope has disappeared, his last chance
of gaining continued life is gone. But since there is nothing he
can do about it, he returns to Uruk; and since he cannot change the
course of destiny, he decides to be content with his lot and to rejoice in the work of his hands, the great city which he has built.

To this material was added in later days, as we shall see
shortly, a story which in some respects is quite incompatible with
what precedes. According to this tale, recorded on Tablet XII,
Gilgamesh makes two wooden objects of some kind, called pukku and
mikkû, respectively. One day they fall into the underworld, and
Gilgamesh is unable to get them up. Finally, Enkidu descends into
the underworld to bring them up for him. But, unfortunately, he
fails to follow the instructions which Gilgamesh has given him and
therefore is unable to return to the land of the living. Gilgamesh
then goes from one god to another in an effort to have Enkidu released from the realm of the dead so that he may commune with him
and find out the worst that is in store for man. At long last
Enkidu is permitted to ascend, and, in answer to the questions put
to him by Gilgamesh, he tells his friend a rather gloomy tale concerning the conditions in the dark abodes of death. On this sad
and somber note the Gilgamesh Epic ends.

The Central Theme of the Epic

The Gilgamesh Epic is a meditation on death, in the form of
a tragedy. To consider the matter in logical arrangement, the

epic is concerned, first of all, with the bitter truth that death
is inevitable. All men must die! For, when the gods created mankind, they allotted death to mankind, but immortal life they retained in their keeping.[13] The gods assemble and pass on life and
death. And from their decrees there is no escape.[14]

The inevitability of death is demonstrated in the life of
Gilgamesh and, to a lesser degree, in the life of his friend Enkidu
Gilgamesh was two-thirds god and only one-third man. Because of
his preponderantly divine nature, his energy was almost inexhaust-
ible; he rested neither day nor night, and no one could keep pace
with him. He built the mighty walls of Uruk, which no man can
equal. He worsted Enkidu, that savage man from the steppe. Together with Enkidu, he then killed fierce Ḫumbaba, the terrible
ogre who guarded the cedar forest. He spurned the love of so great
a divinity as Ishtar and, aided by Enkidu, met her challenge with
undoubted success, by killing the bull of heaven sent down by her.
Then Enkidu, whose strength was like that of "the host of heaven"
and—so we may infer—whose health mocked the doctor's rules, was
snatched away from him by divine decree in the prime of his manhood! Gilgamesh at first refused to bow to the inexorable law of
the gods and tried to call Enkidu back to life; but in the end he
had to submit and give his friend up for burial. In his subsequent
search for immortal life, Gilgamesh went through the most extraordinary hardships and performed superhuman feats. He succeeded in
passing through the very gate of the sun-god, which is guarded by
the terrifying scorpion-people, and traversed the dark mountain
range Mâshu. He crossed the wide and open sea and the waters of
death, a feat possible only to the sun-god and to deified Utnapishtim's boatman, who, according to Berossus, shared in the honors of
his master. He succeeded in coming into the very presence of immortal Utnapishtim, and for a while even had within his grasp the
magic plant that bestowed ever recurrent youth, which is virtually
synonymous with immortality. But in the end even he had to realize
that there is no escape from death and that man's most valiant
efforts avail him naught! If a superman and demigod like Gilgamesh
failed to attain everlasting life, or at least ever recurrent youth
how utterly futile it is for a mere mortal to aspire to such a

[13]Tablet X, col. iii, 1-5 (Old Babylonian version).

[14]Tablet X, col. vi, 36-39 (Assyrian version).

blessed estate and to hope to escape death! It is true, Utnapishtim and his wife obtained eternal life, but that was an exceptional case; and, furthermore, it was by divine favor, not through
their own efforts. The rule still holds good that all men must
die.

Next, in point of logic, the epic considers the question of
the life hereafter. The picture it draws on Tablet VII is extremely dismal. After the children of men have run their courses, all
must go to the land of no return, to the sad and dark abodes of
death, to "the house whose occupants are bereft of light, where
dust is their food and clay their sustenance." There dwell kings
and princes, high priests and acolytes, the powerful of the earth,
the wise, and the good. There the mighty rulers of the earth are
deprived of their crowns and have to play the roles of servants.
However, according to Tablet XII, the outlook is not quite so gloomy.
A man with two sons will be permitted to dwell in a brick structure and to eat bread; a man with three sons will drink water out
of the waterskins of the deep; a man with five sons will be an
honored scribe in the palace of the underworld; he who died a hero's
death on the field of battle will rest on a couch and drink pure
water; etc. But, even according to this tablet, man's heaven is
on earth.

Finally, the epic takes up the question as to what course a
man should follow in view of these hard facts. The solution it
offers is simple: "Enjoy your life and make the best of it!"
Gilgamesh, after his many fruitless adventures in quest of eternal
life, realized the wisdom of this course of action. Therefore he
returned to Uruk and again devoted his attention to his beloved
city and rejoiced in the work of his hands. "Climb upon the wall
of Uruk (and) walk about," he told the boatman with evident satisfaction. "Inspect the foundation terrace and examine the brickwork,
if its brickwork be not of burnt bricks, and (if) the seven wise
men did not lay its foundation! One shar is city, one shar orchards,
one shar prairie; (then there is) the uncultivated land(?) of the
temple of Ishtar. Three shar and the uncultivated land (?) comprise
Uruk" (Tablet XI:303-7). It is questionable whether the epic wants
to go so far as to champion the divine barmaid's hedonistic philosophy of life.[15] Such a philosophy would indeed be in full accord

---

[15]Tablet X (Old Babylonian version).

with the loose scenes in the epic, but it is more likely that this
is just one of the views on life held by the Babylonians and that
it was interwoven in this epic without an attempt at a complete
harmonization.[16] In the following section we shall note some
striking examples of contradictory ideas existing side by side in
the epic.

The Sources of the Epic

It has long been recognized that the Gilgamesh Epic constitutes a literary compilation of material from various originally
unrelated sources, put together to form one grand, more or less
harmonious, whole. The composite character of our poem is apparent from the following considerations.

To begin with, there can be no doubt that Tablet XII was
drawn from an independent source, for we now have the Sumerian
counterpart to it, showing unmistakably that the Gilgamesh Epic
used only the second half of the original story. In addition to
this, there is internal evidence that the material on this tablet
originally formed a separate tale. For it must be obvious even to
the casual reader that the final tablet is in some respects incompatible with what precedes. In the previous portions of the
epic the death of Enkidu has already been recorded on Tablet VII;
there he falls ill and dies at the decree of the gods because of
his part in the killing of Ḫumbaba and the bull of heaven. But in
the opening passage of Tablet XII he is still alive, and here he
descends into the underworld to recover the pukku and mikkû for
Gilgamesh but is deprived of life and kept in the lower world.
The tale recorded on Tablet XII was perhaps added not so much because it belongs to the Gilgamesh-Enkidu cycle of legends as because of the fact that it contains further material on the problem
of death, the main theme of the epic.

Moreover, also the Ḫumbaba episode (Tablets III-V) and the
deluge account (Tablet XI) have been found on Sumerian tablets
which have no connection with the Gilgamesh Epic. Another episode which has been discovered on Sumerian fragments forming a
separate composition is Ishtar's proposal to Gilgamesh and the
subsequent story of the bull of heaven (Tablet VI). Tablets VI:
97-100 and VII, columns iii, 6-22, and iv, 33-39, in the Gilgamesh

---

[16]Cf. Ungnad and Gressmann, op. cit., pp. 169-71.

Epic have in all probability been derived from the myth of Ishtar's
descent to the nether world, of which we have both a Sumerian and
a Semitic Babylonian version. The composite character of our epic
is thus established beyond any doubt.[17]

But the question as to the origin of the material of the
various episodes cannot as yet be answered with any certainty.
To judge from the Sumerian fragments of the epic which have so far
come to light and from the fact that the Semitic Babylonians became in general the heirs of Sumerian culture and civilization,
it appears reasonable to assume that also the other episodes in
the Gilgamesh Epic were current in Sumerian literary form before
they were embodied in the composition of this Semitic Babylonian
poem. From this, however, it does not necessarily follow that all
this material had its origin with the Sumerians, either in their
former home or after they had occupied the plains of the Tigro-
Euphrates Valley. Instead, the material itself may have originated,
at least in part, with the Semitic Babylonians, from whom the Sumerians may have taken it over, adapting it to their own views and
beliefs and giving it expression in their own script and language.
But irrespective of the origin of the raw material, the earliest
literary form of most, if not all, of the tales or episodes imbedded in the Gilgamesh Epic was doubtless Sumerian, as far as
available evidence goes. And these Sumerian literary pieces were
then utilized by the Babylonian Semites in the production of their
great national epic. The work of the Semites, however, did not
consist simply in translating the Sumerian texts and combining them
into one continuous story; rather, it constituted a new creation,
which in the course of time, as indicated by the different versions
at our disposal, was continually modified and elaborated at the
hands of the various compilers and redactors, with the result that
the Semitic versions which have survived to our day in most cases
differ widely from the available Sumerian material.

The Age of the Epic

When this process of compilation began, and when the "first
edition" of the Gilgamesh Epic appeared, cannot be stated with

-----

[17]For further information on this point see Kramer's discussion in the Journal of the American Oriental Society, LXIV (1944),
11-23.

certainty. The tablets of the Ninevite recension, which forms
the main base of our knowledge of the epic, date from the reign
of Ashurbanipal, i.e., from the seventh century B.C.; the fragment
from the city of Ashur is probably two or three hundred years older; while the pieces discovered at Hattusas belong approximately
to the middle of the second millennium B.C. The oldest portions
of the epic are the Meissner fragment and the two tablets now in
the museums of the University of Pennsylvania and Yale University;
these tablets are inscribed in Old Babylonian and therefore go
back to the First Babylonian Dynasty. But even these are probably
copies of older originals. The prominence given to the old Sumerian
ruler deities Anu and Enlil in our epic and the complete absence
of the name of Marduk, in sharp contrast with the main Babylonian
creation story, indicate that our epic was composed before Anu and
Enlil, in the days of Hammurabi, "committed the sovereignty over
all the people to Marduk,"[18] and before Hammurabi "brought about
the triumph of Marduk."[19] The date of the composition of the Gilgamesh Epic can therefore be fixed at about 2000 B.C. But the
material contained on these tablets is undoubtedly much older, as
we can infer from the mere fact that the epic consists of numerous
originally independent episodes, which, of course, did not spring
into existence at the time of the composition of our poem but must
have been current long before they were compiled and woven together
to form our epic.

This, however, does not imply that all the episodes now contained in this work were incorporated at the time when the Gilgamesh Epic was first composed, no matter how long some of them may
already have existed in literary form. Tablet XII, as attested by
the Sumerian fragments, consists of material which dates from about
the end of the third millennium or the beginning of the second millennium B.C. and which therefore existed in literary form already
at the time of the commonly accepted date of the composition of the
epic. Nevertheless, this tablet is without question a later supple-
ment to the adventures of Gilgamesh. For it will be noted that the
concluding passage of Tablet XI returns to the beginning of the
epic and closes with almost the same words with which the proem

---

[18]Cf. the opening lines of the Prologue to the Code of
Hammurabi.

[19]L. W. King, The Letters and Inscriptions of Hammurabi, Vols.
II and III (London, 1900), Pl. 185:1-7 and pp. 188 ff., respectively.

ends, indicating that the wreath of myths and legends is complete.
An instructive parallel to this is found in Psalm 8, which closes
with exactly the same words with which it opens—"O Lord, our Lord,
how glorious is Thy name in all the earth!" Others are contained
in the sections on the new, postdiluvian world order and the sign
of the covenant in Gen. 9:1-7 and 12-17, which close in much the
same way in which they begin. It will be recalled that also some
of our church hymns, ending with the same stanza with which they
begin, exhibit this feature.

Herewith we shall conclude our introductory comments and turn
to a perusal of the epic itself. As pieced together on the basis
of the various fragments of the different versions, the story reads
as follows.[20]

Tablet I
Column 1

1. [He who] saw everything [within the confi]nes(?) of the land;
2. [He who] knew [all things and was versed(?) in] everything;
3. [....] together [....];
4. [....] wisdom, who everything [....].
5. He saw [se]cret thing(s) and [revealed] hidden thing(s);
6. He brought intelligence of (the days) before the flo[od];
7. He went on a long journey, became weary and [worn];
8. [He engra]ved on a table of stone all the travail.
9. He built the wall of Uruk, the enclosure,
10. Of holy Eanna,[21] the sacred storehouse.
11. Behold its outer wall, whose brightness[22] is like (that of)
    copper!
12. Yea, look upon its inner wall,[23] which none can equal!

---

[20]With the entire translation are to be compared A. Schott's
notes in Zeitschrift für Assyriologie, XLII (1934), 92-143. Where
I feel especially indebted to Schott, it will be indicated.

[21]Eanna was a temple in Uruk and was dedicated to Anu, the
head of the Sumerian pantheon and the patron god of Uruk, and to
his daughter Ishtar, the goddess of love.

[22]Reading ni-ip-ḫ[u-shu]. On the meaning of this word see
Cuneiform Texts from Babylonian Tablets, etc., in the British Museum, Vol. XVIII (London, 1904), Pl. 6, obv. 9: shá-ru-ru = ni-ip-ḫu.

[23]Cf. Schott in Zeitschrift für Assyriologie, XLII, 93-94.

Tablet I

13. Take hold of the threshold, which is from of old!
14. Approach Eanna, the dwelling of Ishtar,
15. Which no later king, no man, can equal!
16. Climb upon the wall of Uruk (and) walk about;
17. Inspect the foundation terrace and examine the brickwork,
18. If its brickwork be not of burnt bricks,
19. (And if) the seven [wise men] did not lay its foundation![24]

At this point the Assyrian recension, to which we owe virtually all the material on this tablet, breaks off. To judge from the
length of the other columns of this tablet, about thirty lines are
missing. Some of this material, however, can be restored from the
opening passage of the Hittite version, which, after two almost
completely destroyed lines, reads as follows:

3. After Gilgamesh was created(?),
4. The valiant god [... perfected] his form .....
5. The heavenly Shamash granted him [comeliness];
6. Adad granted him heroism [....].
7. The form of Gilgamesh the great gods [made surpassing].
8. Eleven cubits [was his height]; the breadth of his chest was
     nine [spans].
9. The length of his [...] was three(?) [...].
10. [Now] he turns hither and thither [to see] all the lands.
11. To the city of Uruk he comes [....].[25]

After a few more fragmentary lines the Hittite text breaks
off. The second column of the Assyrian version, setting in before
line 10 of the Hittite fragment, continues the description of Gilgamesh.

---

[24]Cf. Tablet XI: 304-5.

[25]Translated by Friedrich in Zeitschrift für Assyriologie,
XXXIX (1930), 3-5 (cf. also Schott, Das Gilgamesch=Epos [Leipzig,
1934], pp. 15-16).

Tablet I
Column ii

1.   Two-(thirds) of him is god and [one-third of him is man].[26]
2.   The form of his body [none can match (?)].
3-8. (Almost completely destroyed.)
9.   The onslaught of [his] weapons has no [equ]al.
10. [His] fellows are .....
11. The men of Uruk fu[me] in [their] cha[mbers(?)]:
12. "Gilgamesh lea[ves] no son to [his] fath[er];
13. [Day] and [night his] outra[geousness] continues unrestrained.
14. [Yet Gilga]mesh [is the shepherd] of Uruk, the enc[losure].
15. He is [our] shepherd, [strong, handsome, and wise].
16. [Gilgamesh] leaves no [virgin to her lover],
17. The daughter of a war[rior, the chosen of a noble]!"
18. Their lament [the gods heard over and over again].
19. The gods of heaven [called] the Lord of Uruk:[27]
20. "[Aruru(?)] brought this furious wild ox into being.
21. [The onslaught of his weapons] has no equal.
22. [His fellows] are .....
23. Gilgamesh leaves no son to his father, day and ni[ght his outrageousness continues unrestrained];
24. And he is the shepherd of Uruk,[28] [the enclosure];
25. He is their shepherd, and (yet) [he oppresses them(?)].
26. Strong, handsome, (and) wise [....].
27. Gilgamesh leaves no virgin to [her lover],
28. The daughter of a warrior, the chosen of a no[ble]!"
29. When [Anu] heard their lament over and over again,
30. Great Aruru they called: "Thou, Aruru, didst create [Gilgamesh(?)];
31. Now create his equal, to the impetuosity of his heart let him be eq[ual].
32. Let them ever strive (with each other), and let Uruk (thus) have re[st]."
33. When Aruru heard this, she conceived in her heart an image of Anu;

---

[26]Cf. Tablet IX, col. ii, 16.

[27]This expression refers to Anu, the patron god of Uruk.

[28]I.e., the king of Uruk.

Tablet I

34. [A]ruru washed her hands, pinched off clay, (and) threw (it) on the steppe:[29]
35. [....] valiant Enkidu she created, the offspring .... of Ninurta.[30]
36. His whole body is [cov]ered with hair, the hair of (his) head is like (that of) a woman;
37. The locks of the hair of his head sprout like grain.
38. He knows nothing about people or land, he is clad in a garb like Sumuqan.[31]
39. With the gazelles he eats grass;
40. With the game he presses on to the drinking-place;
41. With the animals his heart delights at the water.
42. A hunter, a trapper,
43. Met him face to face at the drinking-place;
44. [One] day, a second, and a third (day) he met him face to face at the drinking-place.
45. The hunter saw him, and his face was benumbed with fear;
46. He went into his house with his game,[32]
47. [He was af]frighted, benumbed, and quiet.
48. His heart [was stirred], his face was overclouded;
49. Woe [entered] his heart;
50. His face was like (that of) [one who had made] a far [journey].

Column iii

1. The hunter opened [his mouth] and, addressing [his father], said:
2. "[My] father, there is a [unique] man who has co[me to thy field].
3. He is the [st]rong(est) [on the steppe]; stren[gth he has];
4. (And) [his strength] is strong [like (that of) the host] of heaven.
5. [He ranges at large] over thy field [.....];

---

[29]Cf. col. v, 3.

[30]God of war.

[31]God of cattle and vegetation.

[32]Lit.: he and his game.

Tablet I

6. [He ever eats grass] with the game;
7. [He ever sets] his [fo]ot toward the drinking-place.
8. [I am afraid and] do [not] dare to approach h[im].
9. [The p]its which I dug [he has filled in again];
10. The traps which I se[t he has torn up];
11. [He helps] the game (and) animals of the ste[ppe to escape out of my hands]
12. (And) [does not allow] me to catch the game of the steppe."[33]
13. [His father opened his mouth and,] addressing the hunter, [said]:
14. "[My son, in] Uruk [there lives] Gilgamesh;
15. [There is no one who] has prevailed against him;
16. His strength is str[ong like (that of) the host of heaven].
17. [Go, se]t thy face [toward Uruk];
18. [Tell Gilgamesh of] the strength of (this) man.
19. [Let him give thee a courtesan, a prostitute, and] lead (her) [with thee];
20. [Let the courtesan] like a strong one [prevail against him].
21. [When he waters the game at] the drinking-place,
22. [Deponat vestem] suam et [nudet venusta]tem suam.
23. [When he sees h]er, he will approach her.
24. (But then) his game, [which grew up on] his steppe, will change its attitude toward him."
25. [Listening] to the advice of his father,
26. The hunter went [to Gilgamesh].
27. He set out on (his) journey (and) st[opped] in Uruk.
28. [Addressing himself to] Gilga[mesh, he said]:
29. "There is a unique man who [has come to the field of my father].
30. He is the strong(est) on the steppe; [strength he has];
31. (And) [his strength] is strong like (that of) the host of heaven.
32. He ranges at large over the field [of my father];
33. He ever [eats grass] with the game;
34. He ever [sets] his foot toward the drinking-place.
35. I am afraid and do not dare to approach [him].

---

[33]Lit.: [He does not allow] me the doing of the steppe.

Tablet I

36. The pits which I d[ug] he has filled in (again);
37. The traps [which I set] he has torn up.
38. He helps the game (and) animals [of the steppe] to escape
    out of my hands
39. (And) does not allow me to catch the game of the steppe."
40. Gilgamesh said to him, [to] the hunter:
41. "Go, my hunter, take with thee a courtesan, a prostitute,
42. And when he w[aters] the game at the drinking-place,
43. Deponat vestem s[uam et nu]det venustatem suam.
44. When he sees her, he will approach her.
45. (But then) his game, which grew up on his steppe, will change
    its attitude toward him."
46. The hunter went and took with him a courtesan, a prostitute.
47. They set out on (their) journey (and) went straight forward;
48. On the third day they reached (their) destination.
49. The hunter and the courtesan sat down at (this) place.
50. One day, a second day, they sat opposite the drinking-place.
51. (Then) came the game to the drinking-place to drink.

Column iv

1. The animals came to the water, (and) their hearts were glad.
2. And as for him, (for) Enkidu, whose birthplace is the open
   country,
3. (Who) eats grass with the gazelles,
4. Drinks with the game at the drinking-place,
5. (Whose) heart delights with the animals at the water,
6. Him, the wild(?) man, the prostitute saw,
7. The savage man from the depths of the steppe.
8. "Is est, meretrix, nuda sinum tuum;
9. Aperi gremium tuum ut succumbat venustati tuae.
10. Noli cunctari ei appropinquare;[34]
11. Cum videt te, appropinquabit tibi.
12. Solve(?) vestem tuam, et sine eum incumbere in te.
13. Incita in eo libidinem(?), opus feminae.
14. (Tum) animalia quae aluntur in campo suo mutabunt habitum

---

[34]See B. Landsberger in *Zeitschrift für Assyriologie*, XLII,
100, n. 2.

Tablet I

suum in eum,

15. (Cum) amorem suum tibi impertiat."
16. Meretrix nudabat sinum suum, aperiebat gremium suum, et is succumbuit venustati eius.
17. Ea non cunctabatur ei appropinquare;
18. Ea solvit(?) vestem suam, et is incumbebat in eam;
19. Ea incitabat libidinem(?) in eo, opus feminae,
20. (Et) is impertiebat amorem suum ei.
21. Sex dies et septem noctes Enkidu coibat cum meretrice.
22. After he was sated with her charms,
23. He set his face toward his game.
24. (But) when the gazelles saw him, Enkidu, they ran away;
25. The game of the steppe fled from his presence.
26. It caused Enkidu to hestitate, rigid[35] was his body.
27. His knees failed, because his game ran away.
28. Enki[du] slackened in his running, no longer (could he run) as before.
29. But he had inte[lligence, w]ide was his understanding.
30. He returned (and) sat at the feet of the courtesan,
31. Looking at the courtesan,
32. And his ears listening as the courtesan speaks,
33. [The courtesan] saying to him, to Enkidu:
34. "[Wi]se art thou, O Enkidu, like a god art thou;
35. Why dost thou run around with the animals on the steppe?
36. Come, I will lead thee [to] Uruk, the enclosure,
37. To the holy temple, the dwe[lling] of Anu and Ishtar,
38. The place where Gilgamesh is, the one perfect in strength,
39. Who prevails over men like a wild ox."
40. As she speaks to him, her words find favor;
41. (For) he seeks a friend, one who understands his heart.
42. Enkidu says to her, the courtesan:
43. "Come, O prostitute, take me
44. To the holy temple, the sacred dwelling of Anu (and) Ishtar,
45. The place where Gilgamesh is, the one perfect in strength,
46. Who prevails over men like a wild ox.
47. I, I will summon him and [will] speak bold[ly];

---

[35]Lit.: bound.

Tablet I
Column v

1. [I will c]ry out in Uruk: 'I am the strong(est)!
2. [I, yea, I] will change the order of things!
3. [He who] was born on the steppe is the [strong(est)];
   strength he has!'"
4. ["Come, let us go, that he may see] thy face.
5. [I will show thee Gilgamesh, where] he is I know well.
6. [Go to Uruk], the enclosure, O Enkidu,
7. Whe[re peo]ple [array themselves in gorgeous] festal attire,
8. (Where) [each] day is a holiday.
9-12. (Badly damaged)
13. To thee, O Enkidu, [who rejoi]cest in life,
14. I will show Gilgamesh, a joyful man.
15. Look at him, behold his face;
16. Comely is (his) manhood, endowed with vigor is he;
17. The whole of his body is adorned with [ple]asure.
18. He has greater strength than thou.
19. Never does he rest by day or by night.
20. Enkidu, temper thine arrogance.
21. Gilgamesh—Shamash has conferred favor upon him,
22. And Anu, Enlil, and Ea have given him a wide understanding.
23. Before thou wilt arrive from the open country,
24. Gilgamesh will behold thee in dreams in Uruk."
25. Indeed, Gilgamesh arose to reveal dreams, saying to his
    mother:
26. "My mother, last night I saw a dream.
27. There were stars in the heavens;
28. As if it were the host of heaven[36] (one) fell down to me.
29. I tried to lift it, but it was too heavy[37] for me;
30. I tried to move it away, but I could not remove (it).
31. The land of Uruk was standing around [it],
32. [The land was gathered around it];
33. [The peop]le [pressed] to[ward it],
34. [The men th]ronged around it,

---

[36]The stars of heaven (cf. Isa. 34:4; Jer. 33:22; Ps. 33:6;
etc.).

[37]Lit.: too strong.

Tablet I

35. [....] while my [fell]ows kissed its feet;
36. I bent over it [as] (over) a woman
37. [And] put it at [thy] feet,
38. [And thou thyself didst put] it on a par with me."
39. [The wise, who] is versed in all knowledge, says to her lord;
40. [Ninsun,[38] the wise], who is versed in all knowledge, says to Gilgamesh:
41. "Thi[ne equal(?)] is the star of heaven
42. Which fell down to thee [as if it were the host of heav]en,
43. [Which thou didst try to lift but which] was too [hea]vy for thee,
44. [Which thou didst seek to move away but] couldst [not] remove,
45. Which [thou didst put] at my feet,
46. Which [I myself did put on a] par with thee,
47. (And) over which thou didst be[nd as (over) a woman].

Column vi

1. [He is a strong com]panion, one who helps a [friend] in need;
2. [He is the strong(est) on the steppe]; strength he [has];
3. (And) [his str]ength is as strong [as (that of) the host of heaven].
4. [That] thou didst be[nd] over him [as (over) a woman],
5. [Means that he will ne]ver forsake thee.
6. [This is the meani]ng of thy dream."
7. [Again Gilgamesh said] to his mother:
8. "[My mother, I] saw another dream.
9. [In Uruk, the enclosu]re, there lay an ax, and they were gathered about it;
10. [The la]nd [of Uruk] was standing about it,
11. [The land was gathe]red around it.
12. [The peop]le [pressed] toward it,
13. While I put it at thy feet,
14. [And] bent over it as (over) a woman,
15. [And thou thyself] didst put it on a par with me."

---

[38]The mother of Gilgamesh.

Tablet I

16. The wise, who is versed in all knowledge, says to her son;
17. [Ninsun, the w]ise, who is versed in all knowledge, says to Gilgamesh:
18. "[The ax] which thou didst see is a man.
19. That thou didst bend over him as (over) a woman,
20. [That I myself] did put him on a par with thee,
21. [Means that he] is a strong companion, one who helps a friend in need;
22. He is [the strong(est) on the steppe]; strength he has;
23. (And) his strength is as strong [as (that of) the host of heav]en."
24. [Gilgamesh opened his mouth] and said to his mother:
25. "[....] may (this) great [lot] fall to me;[39]
26. [....] that I may have [a companion(?)].
27. [....] I."
28. [While Gilgamesh revealed] his dreams,
29. [The courtesan] spoke to Enkidu,
30. [....] the two,
31. [Enkidu sitting] before her.
32. [Tablet I of "He who saw everything within the confi]nes(?) of the land."
33. (Colophon:) [....] who trusts [in] Ninlil
34. [....] Ashur.

Tablet II

The second tablet of the Assyrian version, which we have followed so far, is too fragmentary for connected translation, with the exception of a few passages. The text here given is that of the Old Babylonian version as recorded on the Pennsylvania Tablet.[40] The first part of this tablet corresponds to column v, lines 25 ff.,

---

[39]Lit.: may it fall to me [as] a great [lot] (cf. Schott and Landsberger in Zeitschrift für Assyriologie, XLII, 104).

[40]Published by Langdon, The Epic of Gilgamish (Philadelphia, 1917). For corrections see Morris Jastrow, Jr., and A. T. Clay, An Old Babylonian Version of the Gilgamesh Epic (New Haven, 1920), pp. 103-6; and Langdon in The Journal of the Royal Asiatic Society, 1929, pp. 343-46.

Tablet II

of Tablet I of the Assyrian version and thus repeats, with certain
variations, some of the lines already given here.

Column 1

1. Gilgamesh arose to reveal the dream,
2. Saying to his mother:
3. "My mother, last night
4. I felt happy and walked about
5. Among the heroes.
6. There appeared stars in the heavens.
7. [The h]ost of heaven fell down toward me.
8. I tried to lift it, but it was too heavy for me;
9. I tried to move it, but I could not move it.
10. The land of Uruk was gathered around it,
11. While the heroes kissed its feet.
12. I put my forehead (firmly) against (it),
13. And they assisted me.[41]
14. I lifted it up and carried it to thee."
15. The mother of Gilgamesh, who is versed in everything,
16. Says to Gilgamesh:
17. "Truly, O Gilgamesh, one like thee
18. Has been born on the steppe,
19. Whom the open country has reared.[42]
20. When thou seest him, thou wilt rejoice [as (over) a woman].
21. The heroes will kiss his feet;
22. Thou wilt embrace him ....
23. (And) wilt lead him to me."

---

[41]Ungnad in Zeitschrift für Assyriologie, XXXIV (1922), 17.

[42]The parallelism between these two lines and a comparison
with Tablet I, col. iv, 2, show unmistakably that shadû here refers
to the elevated region west of Babylonia and that this word must
therefore not be taken in the sense of "mountain" but "steppe,"
"field," or "open country" (cf. Hebrew שָׂדֶה). This meaning was recognized independently by Professor Poebel in an unprinted study on
Amurru and by me. I have since noticed that it had already been
suggested by P. Jensen, Assyrisch-babylonische Mythen und Epen
(Berlin, 1900), p. 385, Z. 30, for a certain passage in the Irra
Epic. In comparison to the low-lying land in the Tigro-Euphrates
Valley, the steppe west of Babylonia is rather high, so that the
designation shadû, which usually denotes a mountain or mountainous region, is not at all inappropriate.

Tablet II

24. He lay down and saw another [dream]
25. (And) said to his mother:
26. "My [mother], I saw another [dream].
27. [....] in the street
28. [Of Uru]k, the market place,
29. There lay an ax,
30. And they were gathered around it.
31. As for the ax itself, its form was different (from that of others).
32. I looked at it and I rejoiced,
33. Loving it and bending over it
34. As (over) a woman.
35. I took it and put it
36. At my side."
37. The mother of Gilgamesh, who is versed in everything,
38. [Says to Gilgamesh]:

(A small break)

Column ii

1. "Because I shall put him on a par with thee."
2. While Gilgamesh reveals the dreams,
3. Enki[du is si]tting before the courtesan.
4. [....] the two.
5. [Enkidu] forgot where he was born.
6. Sex dies et septem noctes
7. En[kidu]
8. Coibat cum mere[trice].
9. (Then) the co[urtesan] opened her [mouth]
10. And sa[id] to Enkidu:
11. "I look at thee, O Enkidu, (and) thou art like a god;
12. Why with the animals
13. Dost thou range at large over the steppe?
14. Come, I will lead thee
15. To [Uruk], the market place,
16. To the holy temple, the dwelling of Anu.
17. O Enkidu, arise, that I may lead thee
18. To Eanna, the dwelling of Anu,
19. Where [Gilgamesh] is, [mighty(?)] in deeds,

Tablet II

20. And ⌈. . . . .⌉.
21. Thou [wilt love him like] thyself.
22. Come, arise from the ground,
23. ⌈The bed(?)⌉ of the shepherd!"
24. He listened to her words (and) accepted her advice;
25. The counsel of the woman
26. He took to heart.[43]
27. She tore (her) garment in two;[44]
28. With one she clothed him,
29. With the other garm[ent]
30. She clothed herself.
31. She takes his hand
32. (And) leads him like a ⌈mother⌉
33. To the table[45] of the shepherds,
34. The place of the sheepfold.
35. The shepherds gathered around him.

(About four lines missing)

Column iii

1. The milk of the wild animals
2. He was accustomed to suck.
3. Bread they placed before him;
4. He felt embarrassed, looked
5. And stared.
6. Nothing does Enkidu know
7. Of eating bread,
8. (And) to drink strong drink
9. He has not been taught.
10. The courtesan opened her mouth,
11. Saying to Enkidu:
12. "Eat the bread, O Enkidu,
13. (It is) the staff of life;

---

[43]Lit.: Fell upon his heart.

[44]On this translation see the dictionaries under the various formations derived from the root shabâṭu.

[45]Jensen in Orientalistische Literaturzeitung, Vol. XXIV (1921), col. 269.

Tablet II

14. Drink the strong drink, (it is) the fixed custom of the land."
15. Enkidu ate bread
16. Until he was sated;
17. (Of) the strong drink he drank
18. Seven goblets.
19. His soul felt free (and) happy,
20. His heart rejoiced,
21. And his face shone.
22. He rubbed [....]
23. His hairy body;
24. He anointed himself with oil,
25. And he became like a human being.
26. He put on a garment,
27. (And now) he is like a man.
28. He took his weapon
29. To attack the lions,
30. (So that) the shepherds could rest at night.
31. He caught[46] the wolves
32. (And) captured the lions,
33. (So that) the great cattle bree[ders] could lie down;
34. Enkidu was their watchman.
35. A strong man,
36. A unique hero,
37. To .... he said.

(About five lines missing)

Column iv

(About eight lines missing)

9. He made merry.
10. He lifted up his eyes
11. And saw a man.
12. He says to the courtesan:
13. "Courtesan, bring the man.
14. Why has he come here?
15. I wish to know(?) his name."

---

[46]Cf. R. Campbell Thompson, The Epic of Gilgamish (Oxford, 1930), p. 76.

Tablet II

16. The courtesan called the man
17. That he might come to him and that he might see him.
18. "Sir, whither dost thou hasten?
19. What is (the purpose of) thy painful journey?"[47]
20. The man opened his mouth
21. And said to En[kidu]:
22. "To the family house[48] [....].
23. It is the lot of the people.
24-26. (Meaning uncertain)
27. To the king of Uruk, the market place,
28. Is open the ... of the people for the selection of the bride;
29. To Gilgamesh, the king of Uruk, the market place,
30. Is open the ... of the people
31. For the selection of the bride.
32. Coit cum uxoribus destinatis.
33. Is (venit) prior,
34. Maritus[49] posterior.
35. By the decree of the gods it was pronounced;
36. Since (the day) his umbilical cord was cut
37. It has been his portion."
38. At the words of the man
39. His face grew pale.
                    (About three lines missing)

Column v

                    (About six lines missing)
7. [Enkidu] walks [in front]
8. And the courtesan [be]hind him.
9. When he entered Uruk, the market place,
10. The populace gathered around him.
11. As he stood there in the street
12. Of Uruk, the market place,

---

[47]Schott in Orientalistische Literaturzeitung, Vol. XXXVI (1933), col. 519.

[48]The community house, where the men of the town met.

[49]Reading mutum(!). See Schott in Orientalistische Literaturzeitung, Vol. XXXVI, col. 521, n. 4. Ius primae noctis.

Tablet II

13. The people were gathered,
14. Saying about him:
15. "He looks like Gilgamesh ....
16. He is short(er) in stature,
17. (But) strong(er) in bo[ne].
18. [....] . . . .
19. [He is the strong(est) on the steppe; stren]gth he has.
20. The milk of the wild animals
21. He used to suck."
22. Ever in Uruk ....
23. The men rejoiced:
24. "A mighty one has arisen[50] (as a match)
25. For the hero whose appearance is (so) handsome;[51]
26. For Gilgamesh an equal
27. Like a god has arisen."
28. For Ishhara[52] the bed
29. Is made.
30. Gilgamesh [....],
31. At night [....].
32. As he approaches,
33. [Enkidu] sta[nds] in the street
34. To blo[ck the pa]ssage
35. To Gilgamesh
36. [....] with his strength.

(About three lines missing)

Column vi

(About five lines missing)

6. Gilgamesh [....]
7. On the steppe(?) [....]
8. Sprouts [....].
9. He arose and [went]

---

[50]Lit.: is set up.

[51]Lit.: right (cf. Ebeling in Archiv für Orientforschung, VIII [1932/33], 228).

[52]A goddess of love.

Tablet II

10. To him.
11. They met on the market place of the land;
12. Enkidu blocked the gate
13. With his foot,
14. Not permitting Gilgamesh to enter.
15. They grappled with each other,
16. Snorting(?) like bull(s);
17. They shattered the doorpost,[53]
18. That the wall shook.[54]
19. (Yea), Gilgamesh and Enkidu
20. Grappled with each other,
21. Snorting(?) like bull(s);
22. They shattered the doorpost,
23. That the wall shook.

A fragment of the Assyrian recension[55] has:

46. At the door of the family house Enkidu blocked (the entrance) with [his] feet,
47. Not permitting (them) to bring in Gilgamesh.
48. They grappled with each other in the doorway of the family house.
49. They fought together on the street, the market place(?) of the land;
50. They [shatt]ered(?) [the doorpost], that the wall shook.[56]

The Old Babylonian version continues:

24. Gilgamesh bent over,
25. With his foot on the ground;[57]
26. His fury abated,
27. And he turned away.[58]

---

[53]Cf. Schott in _Zeitschrift für Assyriologie_, XLII, 105-6.

[54]Cf. Ebeling in _Archiv für Orientforschung_, VIII, 228.

[55]Text in Thompson, _op. cit._, Pl. 9.

[56]Reading i-nu(!)-ush (cf. Ebeling in _Archiv für Orientforschung_, VIII, 227).

[57]This means that Gilgamesh won the wrestling match. Gilgamesh realizes what a valuable companion Enkidu could be to him and therefore forms a friendship with him (cf. Tablet III).

[58]_Lit._: he turned his breast.

Tablet II

28. After he has turned away,
29. Enkidu says to him,
30. To Gilgamesh:
31. "As one unique (among men) thy mother,
32. The wild cow[59] of the enclosures,
33. Ninsunna,
34. Did bear thee.
35. Thy head is exalted above (all other) men;
36. The kingship over the people
37. Enlil has decreed for thee."
38. The second tablet.
39. (Catch-line:) [Thy ...] surpasses.

Tablet III
A. The Old Babylonian Version

Of this tablet we again have two recensions, an Old Babylonian and an Assyrian. The Old Babylonian recension is inscribed on the Yale Tablet.[60] It continues the story of the Pennsylvania Tablet, which we have just considered, and belongs to the same edition of the epic.[61]

Column 1

The beginning of the column is destroyed. When the text becomes legible, Gilgamesh has already decided upon an expedition against Ḫuwawa or Ḫumbaba, who dwells in the cedar forest. Enkidu tries to dissuade him.

13. "[Why] dost thou desire
14. ⌈To do this thing⌉?
15. ⌈....⌉ very
16. ⌈....⌉ [thou de]sirest
17. ⌈To go down(?)⌉ [to the fo]rest.
18. A message ⌈....⌉."
19. They kissed one another
20. And formed a friendship.

---

[59] A poetical term for "the strong one" (cf. Poebel, op. cit., p. 125).

[60] Published by Jastrow and Clay, op. cit., Pls. 1-7.

[61] See ibid., pp. 17-18.

Tablet III

(Break)

Column ii

58-60. (Almost completely destroyed)
61. The mother of [Gilgamesh, who is versed in everything],
62. [Raised her hands] befo[re Shamash].
(Break)
72. The eyes [of Enkidu filled] with tea[rs];
73. He [felt ill] at heart
74. [And] sighed [bitterly].
75. [Yea, the eyes of En]kidu filled with tears;
76. [He felt ill] at heart
77. And sighed [bitterly].
78. [Gilgamesh tur]ned his face (toward him)
79. [And said] to Enkidu:
80. "[My friend, why] do thine eyes
81. [Fill with tea]rs?
82. (Why) dost thou [feel (so) ill at heart]
83. (And) sig[h (so) bitterly]?"
84. En[kidu opened his mouth]
85. And said to Gilgamesh:
86. "My friend, ...
87. Have bound(?) my sinews(?).
88. Mine arms have lost their power;
89. My strength has become weak."
90. Gilgamesh opened his mouth
91. And said to Enkidu:

Column iii

(Break)
96. "[In the forest dwells] terrible [Hu]wawa.
97. [Let us, me and thee, ki]ll [him],
98. [And let us des]troy [all the evil in the land]."
99-102. (Too fragmentary for translation)
103. Enkidu opened his mouth
104. And said to Gilgamesh:
105. "I learned (it), my friend,
106. When I was (still) ranging at large over the open country

Tablet III

with the game.

107. To (a distance of) ten thousand double-hours the forest ex-
tends(?)[62] in each (direction).

108. [Who is it that] would go down into its interior?

109. [Ḫuwa]wa—his roaring is (like that of) a flood-storm,

110. His mouth is fire,

111. His breath is death!

112. (So) why dost thou desire

113. To do this thing?

114. An irresistible onslaught is

115. The ... of Ḫuwawa."

116. Gilgamesh opened his mouth

117. And [sai]d to Enkidu:

118. "The mountain [of the ce]dar I will climb!"

119-26. (Almost completely destroyed)

127. Enkidu opened his mouth

128. And said t[o Gilgamesh]:

129. "How shall we go

130. To the [cedar] forest?

131. Its guardian, Gilgamesh, is a war[rior];

132. He is strong (and) never does he s[leep].

133-35. (Badly mutilated)

Column iv

136. To preserve [the cedar forest],

137. [Enlil has appointed him] as a sevenfold(?) terror."

A fragment belonging to the fifth column of the second tablet
of the Assyrian version[63] contains the following lines:

1. "To preserve the cedar [fore]st,

2. Enlil has appointed him as a terror to mortals.

3. Ḫumbaba—his roaring is (like that of) a flood-storm, his
mouth is fire, his breath is death!

---

[62]Cf. Langdon in *The Journal of the Royal Asiatic Society*,
1929, p. 346.

[63]Text in Thompson, *op. cit.*, Pl. 10.

Tablet III

4. At sixty double-hours he can hear the wild cows of his for-
    est;[64] who is it that would go down to his forest?

5. To preserve the cedar, Enlil has appointed him as a terror
    to mortals.

6. And on him who goes down to his forest weakness takes hold."

The Old Babylonian recension continues:

138. Gilgamesh opened his mouth
139. [And] said to [Enkidu]:
140. "Who, my friend, ...?
141. Only the gods d[well] forever with Shamash.
142. (But) as for mankind, their days are numbered.
143. Whatever they do is but wind!
144. Already here[65] thou art afraid of death.
145. What has become of thy heroic power?[66]
146. I will go before thee.
147. Thy mouth may (then) call to me: 'Approach! Be not afraid!'
148. If I fall, I will establish a name for myself!
149. 'Gilgamesh is fallen!' (they will say). '(In combat)
150. With terrible Ḫuwawa!'
151-56. (Badly mutilated)
157. [Thus call]ing to me thou hast afflicted my heart.
158. (But) [I will] put [my hand] (to it)
159. And [will cu]t down the cedar.
160. An everlasting [name] I will establish for myself!
161. [Orders(?)], my friend, to the armorer I will give(?);[67]
162. [Weapons] they shall cast in our presence."
163. [Orders(?)] to the armorers they gave (?).
164. The craftsmen sat down (and) held a conference.[68]

---

[64]Reading i-shim-mi-[e-ma a-na 60] bêru ri-mat ᶦˢkîshti.
Restored on the basis of an unpublished fragment (A 3444) in the
Oriental Institute of the University of Chicago, which has
i-shim-me-e-ma a-na 60 bêru ri-ma-at ᶦˢkîshti-shú.

[65]I.e., while we are still in Uruk (cf. J. Lewy in Revue
d'Assyriologie, XXXV [1938], 81-82).

[66]Cf. von Soden in Zeitschrift für Assyriologie, XL (1931),
200, n. 2.

[67]Cf. Thompson, op. cit., p. 77, n. 26.

[68]See F. Böhl in Archiv für Orientforschung, XI (1936/37),
200, n. 28.

Tablet III

165. Great weapons they cast.
166. Axes of three talents[69] each they cast.
167. Great swords they cast,
168. With blades of two talents each,
169. With the pommels(?) on the hilt(?) (weighing) thirty pounds each,
170. With golden sword [sheaths(?)] (weighing) thirty pounds each.
171. Gilgamesh and Enkidu were equipped with ten talents each.
172. In [Uru]k's [ga]te, with its seven bolts,
173. [....] ... the populace gathered.
174. [....] ... in the street of Uruk, the market place.
175. [....] ... Gilgamesh.
176. [The elders of Uruk], the market place,
177. [.... sa]t down before him,
178. [While Gilgamesh s]poke [thus]:
179. "[Hearken, O elders of Uruk, the m]arket place!
180. [. . . . .].

Column v

181. Him of whom they talk I, Gilgamesh, want to see.
182. Him with whose name the lands are filled,
183. Him I will vanquish in the cedar forest.
184. How strong the offspring of Uruk is,
185. That I will cause the land to hear!
186. I will put my hand (to it) and will cut down the cedar.
187. An everlasting name I will establish for myself!"
188. The elders of Uruk, the market place,
189. Replied to Gilgamesh:
190. "Thou art young, O Gilgamesh, and thy heart has carried thee away.
191. Thou dost not know what thou proposest to do.
192. We hear Ḫuwawa's appearance is different (from that of others).[70]
193. Who is there th[at can wit]hstand his weapons?

---

[69] One talent = sixty pounds.

[70] And therefore terrifying.

Tablet III

194. To (a distance of) ten thous[and double-hours] the forest
     extends(?) in each (direction).
195. Who is it w[ho would go] down into its interior?
196. As for Ḫuwawa, his roar is (like that of) a flood-storm.
197. His mouth is fire and his breath is death.
198. Why dost thou desire to do this thing?
199. An irresistible onslaught is the ... of Ḫuwawa."
200. When Gilgamesh heard the words of his counselors,
201. He looked at [his] friend and laughed.

The next few lines contained a speech of Gilgamesh directed
to his friend Enkidu. Unfortunately, almost every word of it has
been lost. When the text again becomes connected, the elders of
the city are addressing Gilgamesh.

212. "May thy (tutelary) god [protect] thee.
213. On the road (home) may he cause [thee to return in sa]fety.
214. To the quay of Uru[k may he cause thee to return]."
215. Gilgamesh prostrated himself [before Shamash]:
216. "The words which they speak [....].
217. I go, O Shamash; [to thee I raise my] hands.
218. May it then be well with [my] soul.
219. Bring me back to the quay of [Uruk].
220. Place [over me] (thy) protection."
221. Gilgamesh called [his friend]
222. [And consulted] his omen.

The omen appears to have been unfavorable; for, after a break,
the text continues:

Column vi

229. Tears are running down [the face] of Gilgamesh.
230. "[....] a road which I have never [traveled]."
231-35. (Almost completely destroyed)
236. [They brought(?)] his weapons.
237. [....] mighty [swor]ds,
238. [Bow] and quiver
239. They placed [into] (his) hands.
240. [He] took the axes,
241. [....] his quiver,

Tablet III

242. [The bow] of Anshan.[71]
243. [He put his sw]ord in his girdle.
244. [....] they marched.
245. [The people(?)] approach(?) Gilgamesh,
246. [Saying: "When] wilt thou return to the city?"
247. [The eld]ers bless him;
248. [For] the journey they counsel Gilgamesh:
249. "[Do not t]rust in thy strength, O Gilgamesh!
250. Let him lead the way and spare thyself;
251. [Let] Enkidu go before thee.
252. He has seen the [wa]y, has trodden the road
253. [To(?)] the entrance of the forest.
254. [....] Ḫuwawa.....
255. [He who goes b]efore will save the companion;
256. Let him lead the [way and spare thyself].
257. [May] Shamash [cause] thee [to gain] thy victory.
258. May he make thine eyes see what thy mouth has spoken.
259. May he open for thee the closed path.
260. May he open a road for thy treading;
261. May he open the mountain for thy foot.
262. May the night bring thee things over which thou wilt rejoice.
263. May Lugalbanda[72] stand by thee
264. In thy victory.
265. Gain thy victory as (over) a child.
266. In the river of Ḫuwawa, toward whom thou strivest,
267. Wash thy feet.
268. At eventide dig a well;
269. Let there always be pure water in thy waterskin;
270. Offer [co]ld water to Shamash.
271. Be thou [ever] mindful of Lugalbanda."
272. [Enkid]u opened his mouth and said to Gilgamesh:
273. "[....] ... set out on (thy) journey.
274. [Let not] thy heart be afraid; look at me.

---

[71]A district in southern Elam.

[72]The consort of Ninsun and the tutelary god of Gilgamesh (cf. A. Deimel, Pantheon Babylonicum [Rome, 1914], No. 1878).

Tablet III

275.   . . . .
276.   [The road whi.]ch Ḫuwawa is wont to travel.
277.   [....] command them[73] to return (home)."
        The next seven lines, in which Gilgamesh addressed the
elders, are too fragmentary for translation.
285.   [When they heard] this speech of his,
286.   They [set] the hero on (his) way:
287.   "Go, Gilgamesh, [....];
288.   May thy (tutelary) god walk [at thy side].
289.   May he let [thine eyes] see [what thy mouth has spoken]."
        The Old Babylonian version breaks off after three more badly
mutilated lines. The story is continued, however, in the Assyrian
version, which sets in after line 247, repeating some of the material which we have already gone over.

B.   The Assyrian Version
Column i

1.   [The elders opened their mouths and said to Gilgamesh]:
2.   "Gilgamesh, do not trust in the abundance of [thy] strength.
3.   Let thy ... be satisfied ....
4.   He who goes before safeguards the companion;
5.   He who knows the way protects his friend.
6.   Let Enkidu go before thee.
7.   He knows the way to the cedar forest.
8.   He has seen conflict and is experienced in warfare.
9.   Let Enkidu protect the friend, safeguard the companion.
10.   Let him bring his body[74] over the ditches.[75]
11.   In our assembly we have paid heed to thee, O king;
12.   In return, pay thou heed to us, O king!"
13.   Gilgamesh opened his mouth and spoke,
14.   Saying to Enkidu:
15.   "Come, my friend, let us go to (the temple) Egalmaḫ

---

[73]The elders.

[74]The body of the friend.

[75]Perhaps around the cedar forest. See Ungnad in Zeitschrift
für Assyriologie, XXXII (1918/19), 91, n. 1. The translation of
this line is quite uncertain.

Tablet III

16. Before Ninsun, the great queen!
17. Ninsun, the wise, who is versed in all knowledge,
18. Will recommend (well-)counseled steps for our feet."
19. They took each other by the hand,
20. Gilgamesh and Enkidu, as they went to Egalmaḫ
21. Before Ninsun, the great queen.
22. Gilgamesh set about and entered [....]:
23. "Ninsun, I will tell [thee ....],
24. A far journey, to the pla[ce of Ḫumbaba].
25. A b[attl]e which I do not kno[w I am about to face].
26. [A road] which [I do] not [know I am about to travel].
27. [Until] the da[y that I go and return],
28. [Until I reach the cedar forest],
29. [Until I slay fierce Ḫumbaba]
30. [And destroy from the land all the evil which Shamash abhors],
31. [Pray thou to Shamash for me]!"
    (The remainder of the break cannot be restored)

Column ii

1. [Ninsun e]ntered [her chamber].
2. [....] . . . .
3. [She put on a garment] as befitted her body;
4. [She put on an ornament] as befitted her breast;
5. [She put on a ...] and was covered with her tiara.
6. [....] ground ....
7. ..[....] she went up on the roof.
8. She went up to [....] Shamash (and) offered incense.[76]
9. She brought the offe[ring and] raised her hands before Shamash:
10. "Why didst thou give [my] son Gilgamesh (such) a restless heart (and) endow him (with it)?
11. And now thou hast touched him, and he goes
12. On a far journey, to the place of Ḫumbaba,
13. To face a battle which he does not know,
14. To travel a road which he does not know.
15. Until the day that he goes and returns,

---

[76]Cf. II Kings 23:12.

Tablet III

16. Until he reaches the cedar forest,
17. Until he kills fierce Humbaba
18. And destroys from the land all the evil which thou abhorrest,
19. The day that thou ....
20. .... may Aya, (thy) bride, remind thee (of it).
21. In[trust(?)] him to the watchmen of the night.

Here occurs a big gap. Virtually every word up to column iv, line 15, is destroyed.

Column iv

15. She[77] extinguished(?) the incense and .[....].
16. Enkidu she called and ⌈gave (him) information⌉:
17. "Strong Enkidu, (who) art not the offspring of my lap,
18. I have now adopted(?) thee,[78]
19. With the gifts(?) of Gilgamesh,
20. The priestesses, the hierodules, [and the vo]taries."
21. ... she placed around Enkidu's neck.

The rest of the column is too fragmentary for translation. The next column is almost completely destroyed. Also the beginning of column vi is gone. In the remaining lines of the tablet the elders of the city again address Gilgamesh.

Column vi

8. "Let [Enkidu] pr[otect the friend, safeguard the companion].
9. [Let him bring his body] over the ditches.
10. In our assembly [we have paid heed to thee, O king];
11. In return, p[ay thou heed to us, O king]!"
12. Enkidu opened his mouth [and spoke],
13. Saying [to Gilgamesh]:
14. "My friend, tu[rn ....]
15. A way not [....]."

(Remainder of the tablet broken away)

---

[77]Ninsun, the mother of Gilgamesh.

[78]See Schott in _Zeitschrift für Assyriologie_, XLII, 112.

Tablet IV

The first four columns of the Assyrian version are lost.
They undoubtedly contained a record of the journey to the cedar
forest. Part of such a record is found on the following fragment
from Uruk,[79] inscribed in Babylonian.

Column i

1. [After twenty] double-hours they ate[80] a morsel;
2. [After thi]rty (additional) double-hours they stopped for
   the night.
3. [Fifty double-hou]rs they walked all day.
4. [The stretch of a mo]nth and fifteen days [they covered(?)]
   in three days.
5. [Before Shamash] they dug [a well].[81]

(Break)

Column ii

1. After twenty double-hours they a[te a morsel];
2. After thirty (additional) double-hours they [stopped for
   the night].
3. Fifty double-hours they wa[lked all day].
4. The stretch of a month [and fifteen days they covered(?) in
   three days].

(Break)

Another fragment from Uruk[82] repeats the same words, with
the addition of the following lines, which in part have been restored from Tablet V.

14. Gilgamesh [ascended the mountain],
15. [He] poured out [his fine-meal ....]:
16. "[Mountain, bring] a dream with [a favorable] meaning."[83]

---

[79]Text in A. Falkenstein, Literarische Keilschrifttexte aus
Uruk (Berlin, 1931), No. 39.

[80]Lit.: they broke off.

[81]Cf. Tablet III:268-70 (Old Babylonian version).

[82]Text in Falkenstein, op. cit., No. 40.

[83]Lit.: word.

Tablet IV

Column v

When the Assyrian version again sets in, Gilgamesh and
Enkidu have arrived at the gate of the forest, which is guarded
by a watchman placed there by Ḫumbaba. At the sight of the
watchman Gilgamesh apparently loses his courage, for Enkidu calls
out to him:

39. "[Remember what] thou didst say [in] Uruk!
40. [Arise] and stand forth [that thou mayest kill him].
41. [.... Gil]gamesh, the offspring of Ur[uk ....]."
42. [Gilgamesh he]ard the word of [his] mouth and was full of
     confidence.
43. "[Hur]ry (now), step up to him [....].
44. [.... g]o down into the forest and [....].
45. [He is] wont to put on seven coats of mail(?) [....].[84]
46. [One he has just] put on, six of them are (still) doffed
     [....]."
47. Like a furious wild ox [....].
48. .... he withdrew and was full of [....].
49. The watchman of the woods calls out [....].
50. Ḫumbaba like ..[....].

Column vi

The beginning of this column is wanting. The missing portion
evidently related the story of the combat between the two heroes
and the watchman and Enkidu's unfortunate act of opening the enchanted gate with his bare hands.

23. [Enkidu] opened his [mouth] and sp[oke, saying to Gilgamesh]:
24. "[My friend, let us not] go down [into the forest].
25. [When] I opened [the gate, my hand] became paralyzed(?)."
26. [Gilgam]esh opened his mouth and spoke, saying [to Enkidu]:
27. "[....] my friend, like a weakling [....].
28. [.... we] have traversed, all(?) of them [....].
29. . . . .
30. [My friend], (who art) experienced in warfare, [skilful] in

---

[84]Apparently magical shirts or coats of mail, which make
the watchman invulnerable.

Tablet IV

battle,
31. [....] touch and thou wilt not be afraid of [death(?)].
32. [....] and remain(?) with me.[....].
33. [....] . . . . ,
34. So that the paralysis(?) of thy hand may depart and the
    weakness pass [....].
35. [Would] my friend want to remain(?) here? Let us go [down]
    (into the depths of the forest) together;
36. [Let] the combat [not diminish(?)] thy courage; forget
    death and [....].
37. [....] a man ready for action(?)[85] and circumspect.
38. [He who] goes [before] protects his person, may he (also)
    safeguard the companion.
39. [When] they fall, they have established a name for themselves."
40. [At the gr]een [mountain] they arrived together;
41. [Stilled into si]lence were their words, (and) they them-
    selves stood still.
42. (Catch-line:) They [stood still] and looked(?) at the
    forest.

Tablet V
Column 1

1. They stood still and looked(?) at the forest.
2. They beheld the height of the cedar.
3. They beheld the entrance to the forest.
4. Where Ḫumbaba was wont to walk there was a path;
5. Straight were the tracks and good was the passage.
6. They beheld the mountain of the cedar, the dwelling-place
   of the gods, the throne-dais of Irnini.[86]
7. The cedar uplifted its fulness before the mountain;
8. Fair was its shade (and) full of delight;
9. [Cov]ered was the brushwood (and) covered the [...].
    After a few more badly mutilated lines the description of the
wonders of the cedar forest unfortunately breaks off. The next
column is destroyed almost in its entirety. The sense does not

---

[85]Cf. Schott in Zeitschrift für Assyriologie, XLII, 117.

[86]A goddess, probably a form of Ishtar.

Tablet V

become connected until about the middle of the third column.

Column iii

32. "[The second dr]eam which I sa[w ....].[87]
33. [Within] (deep) mountain gorges [we were standing(?)].
34. [A mountain] fell [....].
35. [In comparison to it(?), we were] like a little 'fly of the canebrakes.'"
36. [He who] was born on the step[pe ....],
37. Enkidu, [said] to his friend, as he [interpreted the dream]:
38. "My [frie]nd, [thy] dream is favorable [....];
39. [The dr]eam is excellent [....].
40. My [frie]nd, the mountain which thou didst see [is Ḫumbaba].
41. [We] shall seize Ḫumbaba, we [shall kill him],
42. And [shall throw] his body on the plain.
43. .... morning ..[....]."

    A similar dream, if not simply a different version of the same dream, is recorded on the obverse of the Semitic recension from Boghazköy.[88] The beginning of the tablet is destroyed. When the text becomes intelligible we read:

5. They took each other's (hand and) went to retire for the night.
6. Sleep, the outpouring of the night, overcame [them].
7. At midnight the sleep [departed] from him.[89]
8. The dream he told to Enkidu, [his fri]end.
9. "If thou didst not wake me, what [has wakened me]?
10. Enkidu, my friend, I have seen a [second] dream.
11. If thou didst wake me, what [....]?
12. In addition to my first dream [I have seen] a second.
13. In my dream, my friend, a mountain [toppled];
14. It struck me, caught my feet [....].
15. The light became glaringly strong, a unique ma[n appeared].

---

[87]Gilgamesh is speaking.

[88]Text published by E. F. Weidner, Keilschrifturkunden aus Boghazköi, Heft IV (Berlin, 1922), No. 12 (cf. also ibid., Pl. 48, "Verbesserungen").

[89]From Gilgamesh.

Tablet V

16. His grace was (the most) beautiful in (all) the land.
17. He pulled me out from under the mountain.
18. He gave me water to drink, and my heart fel[t at ease].
19. On the ground he set [my] feet [....]."
20. Enkidu said to this god,[90] [speaking]
21. To Gilgamesh: "My friend, let us g[o down into the plain
     to take counsel together(?)]."

The interpretation of the dream is lost, for after a few
more fragmentary lines the obverse breaks off. The Assyrian
version goes on:

44. [After] twenty double-hours they broke [off a morsel];
45. After thirty (additional) double-hours they stopped [for
     the night];
46. Before Shamash they dug a well [....].
47. Gilgamesh ascended [the mountain].
48. He poured out his fine-meal [....].
49. "Mountain, bring a dream [for Enkidu].
50. Make for him [....]!"

Column iv

1. [The mountain] brought a dr[eam for Enkidu].
2. [He m]ade for him [....].
3. A cold shower [passe]d by, [....]..
4. [It caused] him to cower and [....]
5. [....] and like the grain of the mountains [....].
6. [Gi]lgamesh supports his chin on [his] knees.
7. [Sle]ep, such as is shed upon mankind, fell on him.
8. [In] the middle (of the night) he ended his sleep.
9. He arose and said to his friend:
10. "My friend, didst thou not call me? Why did I wake up?
11. Didst thou not touch me? Why am I frightened?
12. Did no god pass by? Why are my members benumbed (with fear)?
13. My friend, I saw a third dream;
14. And the dream which I saw was altogether frightful.
15. The heavens roared, the earth resounded;

---

[90]To Gilgamesh, who in this passage is expressly called a
god.

Tablet V

16. Daylight failed, darkness came;
17. Lightning [flash]ed, fire blazed;
18. [The clouds] thickened(?), raining death.
19. The brightness [vani]shed, the fire went out;
20. [And that which] fell down, turned to ashes.
21. [Let us go] down into the plain that we may take counsel
    together."
22. Enkidu [heard] his dream and interpreted it, saying to Gil-
    gamesh:

    The remainder of the Assyrian column is lost. The missing
portion probably related that Enkidu put a favorable interpretation
on the dream of his friend, whereupon both of them resolved to cut
down the cedar, for the Hittite recension has:

7. [Gilgamesh] took [the ax in his hand]
8. [And] cut down [the cedar].
9. [But when Ḫuwawa] heard the noise(?),
10. He became enraged (and said): "Who has come
11. [And disturbed the trees that] have grown up on my mountains,
12. And has cut down the cedar?"
13. [Then] the heavenly Shamash spoke to them
14. From heaven: "Approach,
15. Be not afraid [....]!"[91]

    After a few more fragmentary lines of uncertain meaning the
tablet unfortunately breaks off. What happened we do not know;
but apparently something did not turn out according to expec-
tations, for another Hittite fragment[92] continues:

6. His tears [gushed forth] in streams.
7. And Gilgamesh [said] to the heavenly Shamash:
8-9. (Badly damaged)
10. "I have [followed] the he[aven]ly Shamash,
11. And have pursued the road de[creed for me]."
12. The heavenly Shamash heard the prayer of Gilgamesh;
13. And mighty winds arise against Ḫuwawa:
14. The great wind, the north wind, [the south wind, the whirl-

---

[91]Translated by Friedrich in Zeitschrift für Assyriologie,
XXXIX, 9.

[92]Translated by Friedrich in ibid., pp. 11-13.

Tablet V

wind],
15. The storm wind, the chill wind, the tempe[stuous] wind,
16. The hot wind; eight winds arose against him
17. And beat against the eyes of [Huwawa].
18. He is unable to go forward,
19. He is unable to turn back.
20. So Huwawa gave up.
21. Then Huwawa said to Gilgamesh:
22. "Let me go, Gilgamesh; thou [shalt be] my [master],
23. And I will be thy servant. And [the trees]
24. That I have grown (on my mountains),
25. .... [....],
26. [I will] cut down and [build thee] houses."
27. But Enkidu [said] to [Gilgamesh]:
28-29. "Do not [hearken] to the w[ord] which Huwawa [has spoken];
30. Huwawa [must] not [remain alive]!"

Here the Hittite text again breaks off. Of the Assyrian
version a few more lines, belonging to columns v and vi, have
been preserved, but they are too badly damaged for translation.
All we can conclude from them is that Gilgamesh and Enkidu cut
off the head of Humbaba and that the expedition had a successful
issue. The two friends then returned to Uruk.

Tablet VI

1. He[93] washed his long hair[94] (and) polished his weapons.
2. The hair of his head he threw back over his shoulders.
3. He threw off his soiled (clothes and) put on his clean ones.
4. He clothed himself with asîtu-garments and fastened (them)
   with an aguhhu.
5. When Gilgamesh put on his tiara,
6. Great Ishtar lifted (her) eyes to the beauty of Gilgamesh.
7. "Come, Gilgamesh, be thou my consort.[95]

---

[93]Gilgamesh.

[94]Bruno Meissner, Beiträge zum assyrischen Wörterbuch, I
(Chicago, 1931), 52-53.

[95]A variant has: bridegroom (cf. Theo. Bauer in Orientalistische
Literaturzeitung, Vol. XXIV, col. 74).

Tablet VI

8. Grant me thy fruit as a gift.
9. Be thou my husband and I will be thy wife!
10. I will cause to be harnessed for thee a chariot of lapis
    lazuli and gold,
11. Whose wheels are gold and whose horns are ....
12. Storm-demons (for) great mules thou shalt hitch (to it).
13. Amid the fragrance of cedar thou shalt enter our house.
14. (And) when thou enterest our house,
15. Threshold (and) dais shall kiss thy feet.
16. Before thee shall bow down kings, rulers, (and) princes.
17. ⌜The yield(?)⌝ of mountain and plain they shall bring thee
    in tribute.
18. Thy goats shall bear triplets, thy sheep twins.
19. Thy burden-carrying donkey shall overtake the mule.
20. Thy chariot horses shall be famous for (their) running.
21. ⌜Thine ox⌝ in the yoke shall have no rival."
22. [Gilgamesh] opened his mouth and said,
23. [Addressing] great Ishtar:
24. ["But what must I give] thee, if I take thee in marriage?
25. [I must give (thee) oil] and clothing for (thy) body.
26. [I must give thee] bread and victuals.
27. [....] food fit for divinity.
28. [.... drin]k fit for royalty.
29-31. (Almost completely destroyed)
32. [What will be my advantage if] I take thee in marriage?
33. [Thou art but a ... which does not ...] in the cold(?);
34. A back door [which does not] keep out blast or windstorm;
35. A palace which crus[hes] the heroes (within it);
36. An elephant [that shakes off(?)] his carpet;
37. Pitch which [dirties] him who carries it;
38. A waterskin which [wets] him who carries it;
39. A limestone which [....] a stone rampart;
40. A jasper(?) [....] the enemy country;
41. A sandal which [causes] its wearer to t[rip(?)].
42. What lover [of thine is there whom thou dost love] forever?
43. What shepherd(?) of thine [is there] who can please [thee
    for all time]?
44. Come, and I will un[fold(?) thee the tale] of thy lovers.

Tablet VI

45. . . . .
46. For Tammuz, thy [youth]ful husband,[96]
47. Thou hast decreed wailing year after year.[97]
48. The variegated roller thou didst love.
49. (Yet) thou didst smite him and break his wing.
50. (Now) he stands[98] in the groves, crying 'Kappi!'[99]
51. Thou didst love the lion, perfect in strength.
52. (But) thou didst dig for him seven and yet seven pits.
53. Thou didst love the horse, magnificent in battle.
54. (Yet) thou hast decreed for him the whip, the spur, and the
     thong.[100]
55. To run seven double-hours thou hast decreed for him.
56. Thou hast decreed for him to trouble (the water before)
     drinking (it).
57. For his mother Silili thou hast decreed lamentation.
58. Thou didst love the shepherd of the herd,
59. [Who] without ceasing heaped up charcoals for thee
60. And [dai]ly sacrificed kids unto thee.
61. (Yet) [thou didst s]mite him and turn him into a wolf.
62. His own herd boys (now) chase him away,
63. And his dogs bite his shanks.

---

[96] Cf. Poebel, op. cit., p. 118, n. 6, and K. D. Macmillan in Beiträge zur Assyriologie, V (1906), 674-75. The text which Macmillan has published there obviously deals with the underworld. In line 24 occurs the phrase âl batûlim, "the city of the youth or young man," evidently a designation for the nether world. There can hardly be any doubt that the expression "the youth" refers to Tammuz (cf. the following note).

[97] These lines refer to the annual festival of wailing for Tammuz (cf. Ezek. 8:14), the god of vegetation, who was believed to descend to the underworld each autumn and to return with the advent of spring.

[98] Var.: sits, abides.

[99] The roller, so called because during the breeding season it performs loops and rolls in flight, after the manner of tumbler pigeons, utters a hoarse cry resembling the Babylonian expression kappi, meaning "my wing." Its cry and its occasionally irregular flight probably gave rise to the legend of the broken wing (cf. Thompson's translation of the Gilgamesh Epic, p. 33, n. 3).

[100] Meissner, op. cit., I, 44-45.

Tablet VI

64. Thou didst love Ishullanu, thy father's palm-gardener,
65. Who without ceasing brought thee date-bunches(?)
66. And daily provided thy table with plenty.
67. Thou didst cast (thine) eyes on him and didst go to him, (saying):
68. 'O Ishullanu of mine, come, let us enjoy thy vigor.
69. Put forth thy hand and touch our waist.'[101]
70. Ishullanu said to thee:
71. 'What dost thou ask of me?
72. Does my mother not bake? Have I not eaten,
73. That I should eat bread (that brings) evil(?) and curses?
74. (And) against the frost the bulrushes [afford sufficient] protection!'
75. When thou didst hear this [his speech],
76. Thou didst smite him (and) tran[sform him] into a mole(?).[102]
77. Thou didst cause him to dwell in the middle of ..[....].
78. He does not ascend the ..., he does not go down ....
79. And if thou wilt love me, thou wilt [treat me like] unto them."
80. When Ishtar [heard] this,
81. Ishtar burst into a rage and [ascended] to heaven.
82. Ishtar went before Anu, [her father];
83. She we[nt] before Antum, her mother, [and said]:
84. "My father, Gilgamesh has cursed me.
85. Gilgamesh has enumerated mine evil deeds(?),
86. Mine evil deeds(?) and my cur[ses]."[103]
87. Anu opened his mouth and said,
88. Speaking to great Ishtar:
89. "Thou thyself didst invite the ...[....];
90. And so Gilgamesh enumerated thine evil deeds(?),
91. Thine evil deeds(?) and [thy] cur[ses]."
92. Ishtar opened her mouth and said,
93. Speaking to [Anu, her father]:

---

[101]Jensen in Orientalistische Literaturzeitung, Vol. XXXII (1929), cols. 649-50.

[102]Schott in Zeitschrift für Assyriologie, XLII, 121-22.

[103]The misfortunes which she has brought on her former lovers.

Tablet VI

94. "My father, create for me the bull of heaven [that he may destroy Gilgamesh]!

95. Fill Gil[gamesh with ....].

96. (But) if [thou wilt not create] for me the bull of [heaven],

97. I will sm[ash the door of the underworld and break the bolt];

98. I will let [the door stand wide open(?)];

99. I will cause [the dead to rise that they may eat as the living],[104]

100. [So that the dead will be] more [numerous than the living]!"[105]

101. A[nu opened his mouth and said],

102. Speaking [to gre]at Ish[tar]:

103. "[If I do what] thou desirest of [me],

104. [There will be] seven years of (empty) st[raw].

105. Hast [thou] gathered [(enough) grain for the people]?

106. Hast [thou] grown (enough) fodder [for the cattle]?"

107. [Ishtar opened her mouth] and said,

108. [Speaking to A]nu, her father:

109. "I have heaped up [grain for the people],

110. I have grown [fodder for the cattle].

111. [If there will be seven] years of (empty) straw,

112. [I have] gathered [(enough) grain for the people],

113. [And I have grown (enough)] fodder [for the cattle]."

The next eight lines are extremely fragmentary. It is clear, however, that Anu finally acceded to Ishtar's demand, for the epic continues:

122. [The bull of heaven] descended [....].

123. With his [first] snort [he killed a hundred men].[106]

124-25. Two hundred men [.... three hundred] men.

126. With [his] second snort [he killed a hundred ....] in addition(?),

[104]And so consume the nourishment which would otherwise have been offered the gods.

[105]For the restoration of lines 97-100 see "Ishtar's Descent to the Underworld," obv. 17-20 (translated in the second chapter of this volume).

[106]On lines 123-28 see Schott in Zeitschrift für Assyriologie, XLII, 123.

Tablet VI

127. Two hundred men [.... in addition(?) ....] three hundred
     men
128. [....] in addition(?).
129. With [his] third snort [.... h]e attacked(?) Enkidu.
130. (But) Enkidu .... his onslaught.
131. Enkidu leaped and sei[zed] the bull of heaven by [his] horns.
132. The bull of heaven foamed[107] at the mouth.
133. With the thick of his tail [....].
134. Enkidu opened his mouth an[d said],
135. Speaking [to Gilgamesh]:
136. "My friend, we boasted [....]."
137-44. (Too fragmentary for translation)
145. And [betw]een the na[pe] (and) his [horn]s [....].
146. . . . .
147. Enkidu chased (him) and [....] the bull of heaven.
148. [He sei]zed him by [the thick of] his [ta]il.
149-51. (Badly damaged)
152. Between the nape (and) the horns [he thrust] his sword
     [....].
153. When they had killed the bull of heaven, they to[re out his]
     heart
154. (And) placed (it) before Shamash.
155. They stepped back and prostrated themselves before Shamash.
156. The two brothers sat down.
157. Ishtar went up on the wall of Uruk, the enclosure;
158. She ascended to the (rampart's) crest(?) and uttered a
     curse:
159. "Woe unto Gilgamesh, who has besmirched me (and) has killed
     the bull of heaven!"
160. When Enkidu heard this speech of Ishtar,
161. He tore out the right thigh of the bull of heaven and tossed
     (it) before her, (saying):
162. "If only I could get hold of thee,
163. I would do unto thee as unto him;
164. (Or) I would tie his entrails to thy side!"
165. Ishtar assembled the girl-devotees,
166. The prostitutes, and the courtesans;

---

[107]Lit.: threw foam.

Tablet VI

167. Over the right thigh of the bull of heaven she set up a lamentation.
168. But Gilgamesh called the craftsmen, the armorers,
169. All of them.
170. The artisans admired the size of the horns.
171. Thirty pounds each was their content of lapis lazuli.
172. Two inches[108] was their thickness.[109]
173. Six gur[110] of oil, the capacity of the two,
174. He presented as ointment to his (tutelary) god, Lugalbanda.
175. He brought (them) into the room of his rulership(?) and hung (them) up (therein).
176. In the Euphrates they washed their hands.
177. They took each other's (hand) and went away.
178. They rode through the street of Uruk.
179. The people[111] of Uruk were gathered to see [them].
180. Gilgamesh says (these) words
181. To the maids(?) of U[ruk(?)]:
182. "Who is the (most) glorious among heroes?
183. Who is the (most) eminent among men?"
184. "Gilgamesh is the (most) glorious among heroes!
185. [Gilgamesh is the (most) emine]nt among men!"
186-88. (Too badly damaged for translation)
189. Gilgamesh celebrated a joyful feast in his palace.
190. The heroes lay down, resting on (their) night couches.
191. Also Enkidu lay down, and saw a dream.
192. Enkidu arose, to reveal the dream,
193. Saying to his friend:
194. "My friend, why did the great gods take counsel together?"

---

[108]Var.: two pounds each.

[109]Cf. Ebeling in Archiv für Orientforschung, VIII, 230.

[110]In the older period, to which the Gilgamesh Epic dates back, one Babylonian gur was equal to about sixty-five gallons.

[111]Var: the heroes.

Tablet VI
(Colophon:)

195. Tablet VI of "He who saw everything," of the series of
      Gilgamesh.
196. Written down according to its original and collated.

Tablet VII
Column 1

With the exception of the first line, preserved as the
catch-line on the preceding tablet (line 194), the beginning of
the seventh tablet of the Assyrian version is lost. Fortunately,
however, it can be supplied from the Hittite recension.[112]

1. [....] .... Then came the day.
2. [And] Enkidu said to Gilgamesh:
3. "[My friend, hear] what a drea[m I had] last night.
4. Anu, Enlil, Ea, and the heavenly Shamash [took counsel to-
    gether].
5. And Anu said to Enlil:
6. 'Because they have killed the bull of heaven and have killed
    Ḫuwa[wa],
7. [That one of the two shall die],' said Anu,
8. 'Who stripped the mountains of the cedar!'
9. But Enlil said: 'Enkidu shall die;
10. Gilgamesh shall not die!'
11. Now the heavenly Shamash replied to Enlil, the hero:
12. 'Have they not killed the bull of heaven and Ḫuwawa at my
    command?[113]
13. And now the innocent Enkidu shall die?'
14. But Enlil was enraged

---

[112] Translated by Friedrich in Zeitschrift für Assyriologie,
XXXIX, 17-19.

[113] The text has: "at thy command." But this is probably a
scribal error. For in our epic it is stated that it was Shamash
who abhorred the evil wrought by Ḫumbaba and who induced Gilgamesh
to proceed against this ogre (cf. the Assyrian version, Tablet III,
col. 11, 9-18). Moreover, since it was Enlil who appointed Ḫumbaba
to guard the cedar forest, it is not very likely that he would have
ordered Ḫumbaba's death (see Schott, op. cit., p. 45, n. 1).

Tablet VII

15. At the heavenly Shamash (and said):
16. 'Because daily thou descendest to them as though thou wert one of their own(?)!'"
17. E[nkidu] lay (ill) before Gilgamesh.
18. And as his tears gushed forth in streams,
19. (Gilgamesh said to him): "My brother, my dear brother, why do they acquit me instead of thee?"
20. Moreover (he said): "Shall I sit down by the spirit of the dead,
21. At the door(?) of the spirit of the dead?
22. And [shall I] never (again) [see] my dear brother with mine eyes?"

The remainder of the Hittite text is wanting. As Enkidu is lying on his sickbed, knowing that the end is near, he evidently reviews his life and feels that it would have been far better if he had remained on the steppe and had never been introduced to civilization, for what has it brought him? In his distress he curses the gate that lamed his hand, he curses the hunter who brought the courtesan to him, and then he curses the courtesan herself for having lured him to Uruk. The Assyrian version, after a break, relates these episodes as follows.

36. Enki[du ....] lifted up [his eyes].[114]
37. With the gate he speaks as if [it were human],
38. (Although) the gate of the forest is irra[tional]
39. (And) has no understanding[115] [....]:
40. "At (a distance of) twenty double-hours I admired[116] thy timber [....].
41. Till I sighted the towering cedar [....].
42. There was nothing strange about thy timber [....].
43. Seventy-two cubits was thy height, twenty-four cubits thy breadth [....].

---

[114] Thompson, op. cit., Pls. 14-15, places this fragment at the beginning of the fourth tablet of the Assyrian version. On the present arrangement see Schott in Zeitschrift für Assyriologie, XLII, 113 ff.

[115] Cf. Jensen, op. cit., p. 460.

[116] Ibid.

Tablet VII

44. Thy ..., thy ..., and thy ... [....].
45. Thy craftsman(?) made thee in Nippur [....].
46. O gate, had I known that this was [thy purpose],
47. And that [thy] beauty [would bring on] this (disaster),
48. I would have lifted an ax (and) [shattered thee all]![117]
49. I would have constructed a reed frame [out of thee]!"

Gap of about fifty lines. Enkidu now calls upon Shamash to curse the hunter.

Column iii

1. "[....] his possession(s)[118] destroy, his power decrease.
2. [May] his [wa]y [be unacceptable] before thee.
3. May [the game which he tries to trap] escape from him.
4. [.... may] the hunter [not obt]ain the desire[119] of his heart."
5. [His heart] prompted him to curse (also) [the courte]san, the prostitute.
6. "[Co]me, O prostitute, thy de[stin]y I will decree,
7. [A des]tiny that shall not end for all eternity.
8. [I will] curse thee with a mighty curse.
9. [....] may its curses rise up early[120] against thee.
10-18. (Too fragmentary for translation)
19. [....] the street shall be thy dwelling-place.
20. [The shade of the wall shall be] thine abode.
21. [....] thy feet.
22. [May the drunken and the thirsty (alike) smite] thy cheek."[121]
23-32. (Too fragmentary for translation)
33. When Shamash heard [the word]s of his mouth,

---

[117]In the last three lines I follow the interpretation of W. E. Leonard, Gilgamesh, Epic of Old Babylonia (New York, 1934), p. 3

[118]Reading ni-mil-shu.

[119]Lit.: the fulness.

[120]Reading bar-pish (cf. Landsberger in Archiv für Orientforschung, III [1926], 166).

[121]With lines 6-22 cf. "Ishtar's Descent to the Underworld," rev. 23-28.

Tablet VII

34. He forthwith called him [from] heaven:
35. "Why, O Enkidu, dost thou curse the courtesan, the
    prostitute,
36. Who taught thee to eat bread fit for divinity,
37. To drink wine fit for royalty,
38. Who clothed thee with a magnificent garment,
39. And who gave thee splendid Gilgamesh for thy companion?
40. And now, my friend, Gilgamesh, thine own brother,[122]
41. [Lets] thee rest on a magnificent couch;
42. He lets thee rest [on] a couch of honor.[123]
43. [He lets] thee sit on a seat of ease, the seat at (his)
    left,
44. [So that the prin]ces of the earth kiss thy feet.
45. Over thee [he will cause] the people of Uruk [to wee]p
    (and) to lament.
46. [The thriving] people he will burden with service for thee.
47. [And he himself], after thou (art buried), will cause [his]
    body to wear long hair.
48. [He will clothe himself] with the skin of a lion and will
    roam over the d[esert]."
49. [When] Enkidu [heard] the words of valiant Shamash,
50. [....] his angry heart grew quiet.
    About two lines wanting. Enkidu relents and turns the curse
    into a blessing.

Column iv

1. . . . .
2. "[Kings, prin]ces, and grandees shall love [thee].
3. [.... s]mite his thigh.
4. [.... shall] shake the hair of his head.
5. [.... the ....].... shall unloose his girdle for thee.
6. [....] basalt(?), lapis lazuli, and gold.
7. [....].....
8. [For thee ....].. his storehouses are filled.[124]

---

[122]Schott in _Zeitschrift für Assyriologie_, XLII, 124.

[123]Cf. _ibid._, pp. 125 ff.

[124]_Lit._: heaped up.

Tablet VII

9. [Before] the gods [the priest] shall lead thee.

10. [On account of thee(?)] the wife, the mother of seven,
    shall be forsaken."

11. [.... Enki]du, whose body is sick.

12. [....] he sleeps alone.

13. [....] during the night [he pours out] his heart to his
    friend.

14. "[My friend], I saw a dream this night.

15. The heavens [roared], the earth resounded,

16. [....] I was standing(?) by myself.

17. [.... appeared], somber was his face.

18. His face was like [that of Zû(?)].

19. [....] his talons were (like) the talons of an eagle.

20. [....] he overpowered(?) me.

21. [....]... he leaps.

22. [....] submerged me.

(Break)

31. [....].. he transformed me,

32. [That] mine arms [were covered with feathers] like a bird.

33. He looks at me (and) leads[125] me to the house of darkness,
    to the dwelling of Irkalla;[126]

34. To the house from which he who enters never goes forth;

35. On the road whose path does not lead back;

36. To the house whose occupants are bereft of light;

37. Where dust is their food and clay their sustenance;

38. (Where) they are clad like birds, with garments of wings;

39. (Where) they see no light and dwell in darkness.[127]

40. In the h[ouse of dus]t, which I entered,

41. I loo[ked at the kings(?)], and (behold!) the crowns had
    been deposited.[128]

---

[125]Cf. von Soden in _Orientalistische Literaturzeitung_, Vol.
XXXVIII (1935), col. 146.

[126]The queen of the underworld.

[127]With lines 33-39 cf. "Ishtar's Descent to the Underworld,"
obv. 4-10.

[128]Thureau-Dangin in _Revue d'Assyriologie_, XVII (1920), 108:93,
translates _kamâsu_ with "cacher, mettre en réserve, garder."

Tablet VII

42. ..[....] those who (used to wear) crowns, who from the days
     of old had ruled the land,
43. [The representatives(?)] of Anu and Enlil, (it was) they
     who served the fried meat,
44. Who served the ⌈baked goods⌉, who served cold water from
     the skins.
45. In the house of dust, which I entered,
46. Dwell high priest and acolyte;
47. There dwell incantation priest and ecstatic;
48. There dwell the attendants of the lavers of the great gods;
49. There dwells Etana,[129] there dwells Sumuqan;
50. [There also dwells] Ereshkigal, the queen of the underworld.
51. [Bêlit]-ṣêri, the scribe of the underworld, kneels before
     her.
52. [She holds a tablet(?)] and reads before her.
53. [She lifted] her head (and) saw me.
54. [....] and she took that ⌈man⌉[130] away."

      Here follows a gap of about fifty-five lines. The following
fragment contains a speech by Gilgamesh, presumably addressed to
his mother.

5. "[My] friend saw a dream with ominous [meaning ....].[131]
6. The day on which he saw the dream was ended [....].
7. Enkidu lay stricken, one day [....],
8. Which Enkidu on his couch [....].
9. A third day and a fourth day [....];
10. A fifth, a sixth, a seventh, an eighth, a ninth, [and a
    tenth day].
11. Enkidu's illness [grew worse and worse].
12. An eleventh and a twelfth day [....].
13. Enkidu [lay] upon [his] couch [....].
14. He called Gilgamesh [....]:
15. '[My] friend, [....] has cursed me.

---

[129]A king of Kish, who was carried to heaven by an eagle.

[130]Enkidu means himself.

[131]Thompson, op. cit., Pls. 15-16, assigns this fragment to
Tablet IV. On the present arrangement see Schott in Zeitschrift
für Assyriologie, XLII, 113 ff.

Tablet VII

16. [I shall not die] like one who [falls] in [battle].
17. I was afraid of the battle and [....].
18. My friend, he who [falls] in bat[tle is blessed(?)],[132]
19. (But) I, [I shall die in disgrace(?)].'"

                    (Break)

Tablet VIII
Column i

1. [As soon as] the first shimmer of[133] [morning beamed forth],
2. Gilga[mesh opened his mouth and said to] his [friend]:
3. "O En[kidu, ... like(?)] a gazelle;
4. And it was thou [whom ....];
5. It was thou whom the [....] reared.
6. And [....] the pasture.
7. Moun[tains we ascended(?) and went down(?) to] the cedar forest."

In the next fourteen lines, too fragmentary for translation, Gilgamesh apparently continues the recital of the valiant deeds which the two heroes performed together. After that the text breaks off. Gilgamesh is steeped in sorrow at the death of his friend and turns to the elders of the city with these plaintive words:

Column ii

1. "Hearken unto me, O elders, [and give ear] unto me!
2. It is for Enk[idu], my [friend], that I weep,
3. Crying bitterly like unto a wailing woman.
4. The hatchet at my side, [the bo]w in my hand,
5. The dagger in my belt, [the shield] that was before me,
6. My festal attire, my [only(?)] joy!
7. An evil [foe(?)] arose and [robbed(?)] me.

---

[132]Cf. Tablet XII:148-49.

[133]Lit.: [As soon as] something of. The expression "the first shimmer of morning" has been taken over from Leonard, op. cit., p. 39.

Tablet VIII

8. [My friend], my [younger broth]er(?),[134] who chased the
   wild ass[135] of the open country (and) the panther of the
   steppe;

9. E[nkidu], my friend, my younger brother(?), who chased
   the wild ass of the open country (and) the panther of the
   steppe.

10. We who [conquered] all (difficulties), who ascended [the
    mountains];

11. Who seized and [killed] the bull of heaven;

12. Who overthrew Ḫubaba,[136] that [dwelt] in the [cedar]
    forest—!

13. Now what sleep is this that has taken hold of [thee]?

14. Thou hast become dark and canst not hear [me]."

15. But he does not lift [his eyes].

16. He touched his heart, but it did not beat.

17. Then he veiled (his) friend like a bride [....].

18. He lifted [his voice] like a lion,

19. Like a lioness robbed of [her] whelps

20. He went back and forth before [his friend],

21. Pulling out (his hair) and throwing (it) away [....],[137]

22. Taking off and throwing down (his) beautiful (clothes)
    [....].

23. [As soon as] the first shimmer of [morning] beamed forth,
    Gil[gamesh ....].

(Break)

Column iii

1. "On a couch [of honor I let thee recline].

2. I let thee sit [on a seat of ease, the seat at my left],

3. So that the princes of the earth [kissed thy feet].

4. ˙Over thee I will cause the people [of Uruk] to weep [and to

---

[134]See Jensen, op. cit., pp. 464-65.

[135]Cf. Meissner in Mitteilungen der altorientalischen
Gesellschaft, XI, Heft 1/2 (1937), 11-12.

[136]Sic!

[137]Cf. Jer. 7:29; 16:6; 48:37.

Tablet VIII

lament].

5. The thriving people [I will burden with service for thee].
6. And I myself, after thou (art buried), [will cause my body to wear long hair].
7. I will clothe myself with the skin of a l[ion and will roam over the desert]."
8. As soon as the first shimmer of morning be[amed forth, Gilgamesh ....].
9. He loosened his girdle [....].

From here to column v, line 42, hardly anything has been preserved. The missing portion probably dealt with the burial of Enkidu.

Column v

42. [....] judge of the Anunna[ki ....].
43. When [Gilga]mesh heard this,
44. He conceived [in his heart] an image(?) of the river(?).
45. As soon as the first shimmer of morning beamed forth, Gilgamesh fashioned [....].
46. He brought out a large table of elammaqu-wood.
47. A bowl of carnelian(?) he filled with honey.
48. A bowl of lapis lazuli he filled with butter.
49. [....] he adorned and exposed to the sun.

With the exception of about four signs, column vi has been completely destroyed.

Tablet IX
Column 1

1. Gilgamesh for Enkidu, his friend,
2. Weeps bitterly and roams over the desert.
3. "When I die, shall I not be like unto Enkidu?
4. Sorrow has entered my heart.
5. I am afraid of death and roam over the desert.
6. To Utnapishtim,[138] the son of Ubara-Tutu,
7. I have (therefore) taken the road and shall speedily go there.

---

[138]The Babylonian Noah.

Tablet IX

8. When (on previous occasions) I arrived at mountain passes by night,
9. (And) saw lions and was afraid,
10. I lifted my head to Sin[139] (and) prayed;
11. To the ⌈light(?)⌉ of the gods my prayers ascended.
12. [Also now, O Sin], preserve me!"
13. [During the night he] lay down and awoke from a dream:
14. [....] they were rejoicing in life.
15. He took [his] hatchet in his hand.
16. He drew [the sword] from his belt.
17. Like an ar[row(?)] he fell among them.
18. He smote [....] and broke (them) to pieces.
19-28. (Too fragmentary for translation)

(Remainder broken away. Gilgamesh arrives at a mountain range.)

Column ii

1. The name of the mountain is Mâshu.[140]
2. As he arri[ves] at the mountain of Mâshu,
3. Which every day keeps watch over the rising [and setting of the sun],
4. Whose peak(s) r[each] (as high as) the "banks of heaven,"
5. (And) whose breast reaches down to the underworld,
6. The scorpion-people keep watch at its gate,
7. Those whose radiance is terrifying and whose look is death,
8. Whose frightful splendor overwhelms mountains,
9. Who at the rising and setting of the sun keep watch over the sun.
10. When Gilgamesh saw them,
11. His face became gloomy with fear and dismay.
12. (But) he collected his thoughts and bowed down before them.
13. The scorpion-man calls to his wife:
14. "He who has come to us, his body is the flesh of gods!"
15. The wife of the scorpion-man answers him:

---

[139]The moon-god.

[140]If this name is Babylonian, it can be translated "Twins," which would fit quite well into the context (cf. col. iv, 40-41).

Tablet IX

16. "Two-(thirds) of him is god, one-third of him is man."
17. The sco[rpion-m]an calls the man,
18. Speaking (these) words [to the offspri]ng of the gods:
19. "[Why hast thou traveled such] a long journey?
20. [Why hast thou come all the way] to me,
21. [Crossing seas]¹⁴¹ whose crossings are difficult?
22. [The purpose of] thy [comi]ng I should like to learn."
                    (Remainder broken away)

Column iii

1-2. (Destroyed)
3.   "[For the sake of] Utnapishtim, my father, [have I come],
4.   Who entered into the assembly of [the gods ....].
5.   Concerning life and death [I would ask him]."
6.   The scorpion-man opened his mouth [and said],
7.   Speaking to [Gilgamesh]:
8.   "There has not (yet) been anyone, Gilgamesh, [who has been able to do that].
9.   No one has (yet) [traveled] the paths of the mountains.
10. At twelve double-hours the heart [....].
11. Dense is the darkness and [there is] no [light].
12. To the rising of the sun [....].
13. To the setting of the sun [....].
14. To the setting of [the sun ....]."
15-20. (Too badly damaged)
                    (Remainder broken away)

Column iv

                    (Top broken off)
33. "[Though it be] in sorrow [and pain],
34. In cold and [heat],
35. In sighing [and weeping, I will go]!
36. [Open] now [the gate of the mountains]."
37. The scorpion-man [opened his mouth and said]
38. To Gilgamesh [....]:
39. "Go, Gilga[mesh, ...].

---

¹⁴¹Cf. Tablet X (Assyrian version), col. v, 27.

Tablet IX

40. The mountains of Mâshu [I permit thee to cross];
41. The mountains (and) mounta[in ranges thou mayest traverse].
42. Safely may [thy feet carry thee back].
43. The gate of the mountain(s) [is open to thee]."
44. [When] Gilga[mesh heard this],
45. [He followed(?)] the word of [the scorpion-man].
46. Along the road of the sun [he went(?)].
47. One double-hour [he traveled];
48. Dense is the dark[ness and there is no light];
49. Neither [what lies ahead of him nor what lies behind him]
    does it per[mit him to see].[142]
50. Two double-hours [he traveled].

Column v

(Top broken off)

23. Four [double-hours he traveled];
24. Dense [is the darkness and there is no light];
25. Neither [what lies ahead of him nor what lies behind him]
    does it per[mit him to see].
26. Five double-hours [he traveled];
27. Dense is the da[rkness and there is no light];
28. Neither [what lies ahead of him nor what lies behind him]
    does it permit [him to see].
29. [Six double-hours he traveled];
30. Dense is the darkness a[nd there is no light];
31. Neither [what lies ahead of him nor what lies behind him]
    does it permit [him to see].
32. After he has traveled seven double-hours [....];
33. Dense is the darkness and [there is] no [light];
34. Neither what lies [ahe]ad of him nor what lies behind [him]
    does it permit him [to see].
35. Eight double-hours [he traveled, and] he cries out(?);
36. Dense is the dar[kness and] there is [no] light;
37. Neither what lies [ahead] of him nor what lies behind him
    does it per[mit him to see].

---

[142]Lit.: It does not per[mit him to see its front nor his rear].

Tablet IX

38. Nine double-[hours he traveled, and he feels(?)] the north wind.
39. [....] his face.
40. [(But) dense is the darkness and there is no] light;
41. [Neither what lies ahea]d of him nor what lies behind him [does it permit him to see].
42. [After] he [has trave]led [ten double-hours],
43. [....] is close.
44. [....] of the double-hour.
45. [After he has traveled eleven double-hours he co]mes out before sun(rise).
46. [After he has traveled twelve double-hours], it is light.
47. Be[fore him stand] shrubs of (precious) [stone]s; as he sees (them) he draws nigh.
48. The carnelian bears its fruit;
49. Vines hang from it, good to look at.
50. The lapis lazuli bears ...;
51. Also fruit it bears, pleasant to behold.[143]

Column vi
(Top broken away)

24-36. These lines are too fragmentary for translation. Enough is left, however, to show that they continue the description of the marvelous garden of precious stones.
37. Sid[uri, the barmaid], who dwells by the edge of the sea.
(Colophon:)
38. Ta[blet IX] of "He who saw everything," of the series of Gi[lgamesh].
39. Palace of Ashurbanipal,
40. King of the world, king of Assyria.

---

[143]Cf. V. Christian in Wiener Zeitschrift für die Kunde des Morgenlandes, XL (1933), 148. With the description of this garden, compare the story of Abu Muhammed the Lazy (E. W. Lane, The Arabian Nights' Entertainments [New York, 1927], esp. p. 485).

Tablet X
A. The Old Babylonian Version[144]
Column i

(Top broken away)

1. " . . . .
2. With their skins ⌜he clothes himself⌝ (and) eats (their) flesh.
3. .... Gilgamesh, which has never been,
4. ⌜As long as(?)⌝ my gale[145] drives the water."
5. Shamash felt distressed, he went to him,
6. (And) said to Gilgamesh:
7. "Gilgamesh, whither runnest thou?
8. The life which thou seekest thou wilt not find."
9. Gilgamesh said to him, to valiant Shamash:
10. "After walking (and) running over the steppe,[146]
11. Shall I rest my head in the midst of the earth
12. That I may sleep all the years?
13. Let mine eyes see the sun that I may be sated with light.
14. (Banished) afar is the darkness, if the light is sufficient(?).
15. May he who has died the death see the light of the sun."[147]

Column ii

(The top is broken away. Gilgamesh is addressing Siduri, the barmaid.)

1. "He who went with me through all hard[ships],
2. Enkidu, whom I loved (so) dearly,
3. Who went with me through all hardships,
4. He has gone to the (common) lot of mankind.
5. Day and night I have wept over him.

---

[144]The Meissner Fragment. Text published by Meissner in Mitteilungen der vorderasiatischen Gesellschaft, VII (1902), Heft 1, 14-15.

[145]Perhaps the gale of Siduri, the divine barmaid.

[146]Cf. Schott in Zeitschrift für Assyriologie, XLII, 132.

[147]The translation of the last two lines is quite uncertain.

Tablet X

6. For burial I did not want to give him up, (thinking):
7. 'My friend will rise after all[148] at my lamentation!'
8. Seven days and seven nights,
9. Until the worm fell upon his face.
10. Since he is gone, I find no life.
11. I have roamed about like a hunter in the midst of the steppe.
12. (And) now, O barmaid, that I see thy face,
13. May I not see death, which I dread!"
14. The barmaid said to him, to Gilgamesh:

Column iii

1. "Gilgamesh, whither runnest thou?
2. The life which thou seekest thou wilt not find;
3. (For) when the gods created mankind,
4. They allotted death to mankind,
5. (But) life they retained in their keeping.
6. Thou, O Gilgamesh, let thy belly be full;
7. Day and night be thou merry;
8. Make every day (a day of) rejoicing.
9. Day and night do thou dance and play.
10. Let thy raiment be clean,
11. Thy head be washed, (and) thyself be bathed in water.
12. Cherish the little one holding thy hand,
13. (And) let the wife rejoice in thy bosom.
14. This is the lot of [mankind ....]."

(Remainder broken away)

Column iv

1. In his wrath he destroys them.[149]
2. He returns and steps up to him.[150]
3. His eyes behold Sursunabu.

---

[148]On this translation of man see Ungnad in Zeitschrift für Assyriologie, XXXI (1917/18), 266-67.

[149]The stone images(?) (cf. the Assyrian version, Tablet X, col. ii, 29, and iii, 38).

[150]To Sursunabu, the boatman of Utnapishtim. In the Assyrian recension the boatman is called Urshanabi.

Tablet X

4. Sursunabu says to him, to Gilgamesh:
5. "Tell me, what is thy name?
6. I am Sursunabu, belonging to Utanapishtim[151] the Distant."
7. Gilgamesh said to him, to Sursunabu:
8. "Gilgamesh is my name,
9. Who have come from Uruk, the house of Anu,[152]
10. Who have traversed[153] the mountains,
11. A long journey, (from) the rising of the sun.
12. Now that I see thy face, Sursunabu,
13. Show me ⌈Utanapishtim⌉ the Distant."
14. Sursunabu [said] to him, to Gilgamesh:

(Remainder lost)

B. The Assyrian Version
Column i

1. Siduri, the barm[aid, who dwells by the edge of the sea],
2. (Who) dwells [....],
3. For her they made a jug, for her they made a golden mashing-vat.[154]
4. She is covered with a veil and [....].
5. Gilgamesh comes along and [....].
6. He is clad in pelts, [....].
7. He has the flesh of gods in [his body],
8. (But) there is woe in [his heart].
9. [His] face [is like] unto (that of) one who has made a far journey.
10. The barmaid looks [out] into the distance;
11. She says to her heart (and) [speaks] (these) words,

---

[151] The text has ú-ta-na-ish-tim, which is probably a scribal error for ú-ta-na-pi-ish-tim (cf. Poebel, op. cit., p. 86). This name occurs again in line 13, where the text is damaged. There, I believe, we can read ú-ta-na-p[i-ish-ti]m just as well as ú-ta-na-i[sh-ti]m.

[152] Cf. Schott in Zeitschrift für Assyriologie, XLII, 134-35.

[153] Thus von Soden, according to Landsberger in Zeitschrift für Assyriologie, XLII, 135, n. 1.

[154] This line has been completed on the basis of the Hittite version (cf. Friedrich in Zeitschrift für Assyriologie, XXXIX, 22).

Tablet X

12. [As she takes counsel] with herself:
13. "Surely, this (man) is a murder[er]!
14. Whither is he bound ..[....]?"
15. When the barmaid saw him, she barred [her door],
16. She barred her gate, barring it [with a crossbar].
17. But he, Gilgamesh, heard [the sound of her shutting(?)].
18. He lifted his chin and pla[ced(?) ....].
19. Gilgamesh [said] to her, [the barmaid]:
20. "Barmaid, what didst thou see [that thou hast barred thy door],
21. That thou hast barred thy gate, [barring it with a crossba]r?
22. I shall smash [thy] door [and bre]ak [thy gate]!"

The remainder of the column is broken away. But the greater part of it can be restored from fragment Sp. 299[155] and from the succeeding columns of this tablet.

1. [Gilgamesh said to her, to the barmaid]:
2. "[I am Gilgamesh; I seized and killed the bull which came down out of heaven];
3. [I killed the watchman of the forest];
4. [I overthrew Humbaba, who dwelt in] the ce[dar forest];
5. [In the mountain passes(?) I kil]led the lions."
6. [The barmaid sa]id [to him], to Gilgamesh:
7. "[If thou art Gilgamesh], who didst kill the watchman (of the forest);
8. [(If) thou didst overthrow Humb]aba, who dwelt in the cedar forest,
9. Kill the lions in the mountain [passes(?)],
10. [Seize and] kill the bull which came down out of heaven,
11. [Why are (thy) chee]ks (so) [emaciated], (and why) is thy face downcast?
12. [(Why) is thy heart (so) sad], (and why) are thy features (so) [distor]ted?
13. [(Why) is there woe] in thy heart,
14. (And why is) thy face like [unto (that of) one who has made a far journey]?

---

[155]Published by Thompson, op. cit., Pl. 42. On the present position of this fragment see Schott in Zeitschrift für Assyriologie, XLII, 132-33.

Tablet X

15. [(Why) ....] is thy countenance burned [with cold and heat]?
16. [(And why) ....] dost thou roam over the steppe?"
17. [Gilgamesh said to her, to the barmaid]:
18. "[Barmaid, should not my cheeks be emaciated (and) my face
     be downcast]?
19. [Should not my heart be sad (and) my features be distorted]?
20. [Should there not be woe in my heart]?
21. [Should my face not be like unto (that of) one who has made
     a far journey]?
22. [Should my countenance not be burned with cold and heat]?
23. [And should .... I not roam over the steppe]?
24. [My friend, my younger brother(?), who chased the wild ass
     of the open country (and) the panther of the st.. pe],
25. [Enkidu, my friend, my younger brother(?), who chased the
     wild ass of the open country (and) the panther of the steppe]!
26. [We who conquered all difficulties and ascended the mountains],

Column ii

1. [Who seized and killed the bull of heaven],
2. [Who overthrew Ḫumbaba, that dwelt in the cedar forest]!
3. [My friend, whom I loved (so) dearly, who went with me
    through all hardships];
4. [Enkidu, my friend, whom I loved (so) dearly, who went with
    me through all hardships],
5. [Him the fate of mankind has overtaken]!
6. [Six days and seven nights I wept over him],
7. [Until the worm fell upon his face].
8. [I became afraid of death, so that I now roam over the
    steppe]. The matter of my friend [rests heavy upon me],
9. [Hence far and wide I roam over the ste]ppe; the matter of
    Enkidu, [my friend, rests heavy upon me],
10. [Hence far and wide] I roam over [the steppe].
11. [How can I be sile]nt? How can I be quiet?
12. [My friend, whom I loved, has turn]ed to clay; Enkidu, my
    friend, whom I loved, has tu[rned to clay].
13. [And I], shall I [not like unto him] lie down
14. [And not rise] forever?"
15. [Gilgamesh furthermore] said to her, to the barmaid:

Tablet X

16. "[Now], barmaid, which is the way to Utnapi[shtim]?
17. [What are] the directions?   Give me, oh, give me the directions![156]
18. If it is possible, (even) the sea will I cross!
19. (But) if it is not possible, I will roam over the steppe."
20. The barmaid said to him, to Gilgamesh:
21. "Gilgamesh, there never has been a crossing;
22. And whoever from the days of old has come thus far has not been able to cross the sea.
23. Valiant Shamash does cross the sea, (but) who besides Shamash crosses (it)?
24. Difficult is the place of crossing (and) very difficult its passage;
25. And deep are the waters of death, which bar its approaches.
26. Where, Gilgamesh, wilt thou cross the sea?
27. (And) when thou arrivest at the waters of death, what wilt thou do?
28. Gilgamesh, there is Urshanabi, the boatman of Utnapishtim.
29. With him are the stone images(?);[157] in the woods he picks ...
30. [Hi]m let thy face behold.
31. [If it is possi]ble, cross over with him; if it is not possible, turn back (home)."
32. When [Gilgam]esh heard this,
33. [He took (his) hat]chet in hi[s hand];
34. [He drew the dagger from his belt], slipped into (the woods), and went down to them.[158]
35. [Like an arrow(?) he f]ell among them.
36-50. (Too fragmentary for translation)

---

[156]Lit.:   [What is] its mark?   Give me, oh, give me its mark!

[157]Lit.:   those of stones.   The Hittite version has: "two images of stone."   These images may perhaps have been idols of an apotropaic character enabling Urshanabi to cross the waters of death (cf. Friedrich in Zeitschrift für Assyriologie, XXXIX, 26 and 58-60).

[158]To the stone images(?).

Tablet X
Column iii

1. Urshanabi said to him, to Gi[lgamesh]:
2. "Why are thy cheeks (so) emaciated, (and why) [is thy face]
    dow[ncast]?
3. (Why) is thy heart (so) sad, [and (why) are thy features
    (so) distorted]?
4. (Why) is there woe in [thy heart]?
5. (Why) [is thy face like unto] (that of) one who has made a
    far journey?
6. (Why) [is thy countenance bur]ned with cold and heat?
7. (And why) [....] dost thou [roam over the steppe]?"
8. [Gilgamesh] said [to him], to [Urshanabi]:
9. "[Urshanabi, should not my ch]eeks [be emaciated (and) my
    face be downcast]?
10. [Should not] my [hea]rt [be sad] (and) [my features] be
    distorted?
11. [Should there not be] woe in [my heart]?
12. [Should my] fa[ce not be like unto (that of) one who has
    made a far journey]?
13. [Should my countenance] not be bu[rned with cold and heat]?
14. [(And) should .... I not roam over the steppe]?
15. [My friend, my younger brother(?), who chased the wild ass
    of the open country (and) the panther of the steppe],
16. [Enkidu, my friend, my younger brother(?), who chased the
    wild ass of the open country (and) the panther of the
    steppe]!
17. [We who conquered all (difficulties) and ascended the
    mountains],
18. [Who seized and killed the bull of heaven],
19. [Who overthrew Ḫumbaba, that dwelt in the cedar forest]!
20. My friend, [whom I loved (so) dearly, who went with me
    through all hardships],
21. Enk[idu, my friend, whom I loved (so) dearly, who went with
    me through all hardships],
22. [Him the fate of mankind] has overtaken!
23. Six days [and seven nights I wept over him],
24. Until [the worm fell upon his face].
25. I became frighte[ned .... and became afraid of death, so
    that I now roam over the steppe].

Tablet X

26. The matt[er of my friend rests heavy upon me],
27. Hence far and wide[159] I [roam over the steppe; the matter of Enkidu, my friend, rests heavy upon me],
28. [Hence] far and wide [I roam over the steppe].
29. How can I be sil[ent? How can I be quiet]?
30. My friend, whom I loved, has tur[ned to clay].
31. (And) I, shall I not like unto him lie [down and not rise forever]?"
32. Gilgamesh (furthermore) said to him, to [Urshanabi]:
33. "Now, Urshanabi, which [is the road to Utnapishtim]?
34. What are the directions? Give me, oh, give [me the directions]!
35. If it is possible, (even) the sea will I cross; (but) if it is not possible, [I will roam over the steppe]."
36. Urshanabi said to him, to [Gilgamesh]:
37. "Thy hands, O Gilgamesh, have prevented [thy crossing the sea];
38. (For) thou hast destroyed the stone images(?) ....
39. The stone images(?) are destroyed ....
40. Take the hatchet in [thy hand], O Gilgamesh.
41. Go down to the forest and [cut one hundred and twenty] punting-poles, each sixty cubits (in length).
42. Put bitumen[160] and plates(?)[161] (on them and) bring [them to me]."
43. When Gilgamesh [heard] this,
44. He took the hatchet in his hand, he d[rew the sword from his belt],
45. He went down to the forest and [cut one hundred and twenty] punting-poles, each sixty cubits (in length).
46. He put bitumen and plates(?) (on them) and brought (them) [to him].

---

[159] Lit.: [a lo]ng ro[ad].

[160] To judge from modern practice in Babylonia, this expression probably refers to the knobs of bitumen at the upper end of the punting-pole (cf. Thompson, op. cit., p. 85).

[161] The term here employed probably refers to some kind of plate or socket at the lower end of a punting-pole (cf. ibid., and G. Meier in Orientalistische Literaturzeitung, Vol. XLIII [1940], col. 307).

Tablet X

47. Gilgamesh and Urshanabi (then) boarded [the ship].
48. They launched the ship on the billows and [glided along].
49. On the third day their voyage was the same as (an ordinary one of) a month and fifteen days.
50. Thus Urshanabi arrived at the waters of [death].

Column iv

1. Urshanabi [said] to him, [to Gilgamesh]:
2. "Press on, Gilgamesh! [Take a pole (for thrusting) ....].
3. Let not thy hand touch the waters of death [....].
4. Gilgamesh, take thou a second, a third, and a fourth pole;
5. Gilgamesh, take thou a fifth, a sixth, and a seventh pole;
6. Gilgamesh, take thou an eighth, a ninth, and a tenth pole;
7. Gilgamesh, take thou an eleventh, (and) a twelfth pole!"
8. With one hundred and twenty (thrusts) Gilgamesh had used up the poles.[162]
9. He ungirded his loins ..[....].
10. Gilgamesh pulled off [his] clothes [....].
11. With his hands he raised the mast(?).
12. Utnapishtim looks into the distance;
13. He says to his heart (and) [speaks] (these) words,
14. [As he takes counsel] with himself:
15. "Why are [the stone images(?)] of the ship destroyed?
16. And (why) does one who is not its master ride [upon it]?
17. The man who is coming there is none of mine[163] ..[....].
18. I look, but not [....].
19. I look, but not [....].
20. I look, but [....]."

The remainder of the column is broken away. Gilgamesh meets Utnapishtim and is asked the same questions that were addressed to him by the barmaid and the boatman. Gilgamesh answers Utnapish-

---

[162]Each pole was good for only one thrust; for after one thrust each pole used was wet almost to its full length and could no longer be employed with both hands, lest they "touch the waters of death," wherefore it had to be thrown away (cf. Thompson, op. cit., p. 85).

[163]See von Soden in Zeitschrift für Assyriologie, XL, 194 n.

Tablet X

tim in exactly the same words.

> [Gilgamesh said to him, to Utnapishtim]:
> "[Utnapishtim, should not my cheeks be emaciated (and) my face be downcast]?

Column v

1. [Should not my heart be sad] (and) my fea[tures be distorted]?
2. [Should there not be woe in] my [he]art?
3. [Should] my [face] not be like [unto (that of) one who has made a far journey]?
4. [Should] my countenance [not be burned with heat and cold]?
5. [(And) should .... I not] roam over the steppe?
6. [My friend, my younger brother(?), who chased the wild ass of the open country] (and) the panther of the steppe,
7. [Enkidu, my friend, my younger brother(?)], who chased the wild ass of the open country (and) the panther of the steppe!
8. [We who conquered all (difficulties) and ascended] the mountains,
9. [Who captured and] killed [the bull of] heaven,
10. [Who overthrew Ḫumbaba, that] dwelt in the cedar forest!
11. [My friend, who kil]led [with me] the lions,
12. [My friend, who went with me through] all hardships,
13. [Enkidu, my friend, who] killed [with me] the lions,
14. [Him the fate of mankind has overtaken! Six days and seven nights] I wept over him,
15. For burial [I did not want to give him up],
16. [Until the worm fell upon] his [face].
17. [I became frightened .... and] became afra[id of] death, [so that I now roam over the s]teppe.
18. [The matter of my friend rests] heavy upon me, so that far and wide [I roam over the ste]ppe;
19. [The matter of Enkidu], my friend, rests heavy upon me, so that far and wide [I roam over the steppe].
20. [How] can I be silent? How can I be quiet?
21. [My friend, wh]om I loved, has turned to clay; Enkidu, [my] friend, [whom I loved, has turned to clay].
22. [(And) I], shall I not like unto him lie down and not rise

Tablet X

forever?"

23. Gilgamesh (furthermore) said to him, to Utnapi[shtim]:
24. "That [no]w I might come and see Utnapishtim, whom they call 'the Distant,'
25. [I] went roaming around over all the lands,
26. I crossed many difficult mountains,
27. I crossed all the seas;
28. Of sweet sleep my face has not had its fill;
29. [I] have wearied myself with walking around (and) have filled my joints with woe.
30. Not (yet) had I come [to the ho]use of the barmaid when my clothing was worn out.
31. [I kille]d bear, hyena, lion, panther, tiger, stag, ibex, wild game, and the creatures of the steppe;
32. Their [flesh] I ate (and) their pelts I pu[t on(?)].
33. [....] let them bar her gate, with pitch and bitu[men ....]."
34-35. (Too fragmentary for translation)
36. [Utnapishtim] said to him, to [Gilgamesh]:
37-50. (Too fragmentary for translation)

Column vi

(Top broken away)

26. "Do we build a house (to stand) forever? Do we seal (a document to be in force) forever?
27. Do brothers divide (their inheritance to last) forever?
28. Does hatred remain in [the land] forever?
29. Does the river raise (and) ca[rry] the flood forever?
30. . . . .
31. Does its face see the face of the sun (forever)?
32. From the days of old there is no [permanence].
33. The sleeping(?) and the dead, how alike [they are]!
34. Do they not (both) draw the picture of death?
35. .... [....]
36. The Anunnaki, the great gods, ga[ther together];
37. Mammetum, the creatress of destiny, de[crees] with them the destinies.
38. Life and death they allot;
39. The days of death they do not reveal."

Tablet X

40. Gilgamesh said to him, to Utnapishtim the Distant:
                    (Colophon:)
41. Tablet X of "He who saw everything," of the series of
    Gilgamesh.
42. Palace of Ashurbanipal, king of the world, king of Assyria.

Tablet XI

1. Gilgamesh said to him, to Utnapishtim the Distant:
2. "I look upon thee, Utnapishtim,
3. Thine appearance is not different; thou art like unto me.
4. Yea, thou art not different; thou art like unto me.
5. My heart had pictured thee as one perfect for the doing of
   battle;[164]
6. [But] thou liest (idly) on (thy) side, (or) on thy back.
7. [Tell me], how didst thou enter into the company of the
   gods and obtain life (everlasting)?"
8. Utnapishtim said to him, to Gilgamesh:
9. "Gilgamesh, I will reveal unto thee a hidden thing,
10. Namely, a secret of the gods will I tell thee.
11. Shurippak[165]—a city which thou knowest,
12. [And which] is situated [on the bank of] the river Euphrates—
13. That city was (already) old, and the gods were in its midst.
14. (Now) their heart prompted the great gods [to] bring a deluge.
15. [There was(?)] Anu, their father;
16. Warlike Enlil, their counselor;
17. Ninurta, their representative;
18. Ennugi, their vizier;
19. Ninigiku, (that is,) Ea, also sat with them.
20. Their speech he repeated to a reed hut:[166]
21. 'Reed hut, reed hut! Wall, wall!

---

[164]This translation was suggested to me by Dr. Jacobsen.
With the above interpretation of the permansive of the pi'el
stem may be compared von Soden in Zeitschrift für Assyriologie,
XLIII, p. 266, lines 22 ff.

[165]Usually called Shuruppak.

[166]Probably the dwelling of Utnapishtim. Some good photographs
of reed houses have recently been published by John van Ess in The
National Geographic Magazine, LXXXII (1942), 410-11.

Tablet XI

22. Reed hut, hearken! Wall, consider!
23. Man of Shurippak,[167] son of Ubara-Tutu!
24. Tear down (thy) house, build a ship!
25. Abandon (thy) possessions, seek (to save) life!
26. Disregard (thy) goods, and save (thy) life!
27. [Cause to] go up into the ship the seed of all living creatures.
28. The ship which thou shalt build,
29. Its measurements shall be (accurately) measured;
30. Its width and its length shall be equal.
31. Cover it [li]ke the subterranean waters.'
32. When I understood this, I said to Ea, my lord:
33. '[Behold], my lord, what thou hast thus commanded,
34. [I] will honor (and) carry out.
35. [But what] shall I answer the city, the people, and the elders?'
36. Ea opened his mouth and said,
37. Speaking to me, his servant:
38. 'Thus shalt thou say to them:
39. [I have le]arned that Enlil hates me,
40. That I may no (longer) dwell in yo[ur ci]ty,
41. Nor turn my face to the land of Enlil.
42. [I will therefore g]o down to the apsû and dwell with Ea, my [lor]d.[168]
43. [On] you he will (then) rain down plenty;
44. [.... of b]irds(?), ... of fishes.
45. [....] harvest-wealth.
46. [In the evening the leader] of the storm(?)[169]

---

[167]This expression, as shown by the following lines, refers to Utnapishtim.

[168]The apsû, the place where Ea had his dwelling, was the subterranean sweet-water ocean, from which, e.g., the water of the rivers and marshes was thought to spring forth. But here, in view of all the things Utnapishtim takes along, the reference probably is to the marshy area at the northern shores of the Persian Gulf.

[169]Cf. Thompson, op. cit., p. 86, note on line 46.

Tablet XI

47. Will cause a wheat-rain to rain down upon you.'[170]
48. As soon as [the first shimmer of mor]ning beamed forth,
49. The land was gathered [about me].
50-53 (Too fragmentary for translation)
54. The child [brou]ght pitch,
55. (While) the strong brought [whatever else] was needful.
56. On the fifth day [I] laid its framework.
57. One ikû[171] was its floor space,[172] one hundred and twenty cubits each was the height of its walls;
58. One hundred and twenty cubits measured each side of its deck.[173]
59. I 'laid the shape' of the outside (and) fashioned it.[174]
60. Six (lower) decks I built into it,
61. (Thus) dividing (it) into seven (stories).
62. Its ground plan I divided into nine (sections).[175]
63. I drove water-stoppers into it.[176]

---

[170]Here the original obviously has a play on words, the purpose of which is to deceive the inhabitants of Shurippak to the last moment (see Carl Frank in Zeitschrift für Assyriologie, XXXVI [1925], 218). This line can also be translated: "He will cause a destructive rain (lit.: a rain of misfortune) to rain down upon you." This evidently is the real meaning of the passage. But Ea knew that the people of Shurippak would interpret these words differently.

[171]About 3,600 square meters, or approximately an acre (see A. J. Sachs in the Bulletin of the American Schools of Oriental Research, No. 96 [December, 1944], pp. 29-39).

[172]See Schott in Zeitschrift für Assyriologie, XLII, 137.

[173]Placing the Babylonian cubit at about half a meter (see the article by Sachs referred to above), the deck had a surface of approximately 3,600 square meters, or one ikû. Utnapishtim's boat was an exact cube.

[174]The ship. Utnapishtim now attached the planking to the framework.

[175]Each of the seven stories was divided into nine sections, or compartments.

[176]This line probably means that he drove wedge-shaped pieces of wood between the seams to help make the boat watertight. Thus Paul Haupt in Beiträge zur Assyriologie, X, Heft 2 (1927), 6, and Armas Salonen, Die Wasserfahrzeuge in Babylonien (Helsinki, 1939), pp. 100-101.

Tablet XI

64. I provided punting-poles and stored up a supply.[177]
65. Six shar[178] of pitch I poured into the furnace,
66. (And) three shar of asphalt [I poured] into it.
67. Three shar of oil the basket-carriers brought:[179]
68. Besides a shar of oil which the saturation(?) (of the water-stoppers) consumed,[180]
69. Two shar of oil [which] the boatman stowed away.
70. Bullocks I slaughtered for [the people];
71. Sheep I killed every day.
72. Must, red wine, oil, and white wine,[181]
73. [I gave] the workmen [to drink] as if it were river water,
74. (So that) they made a feast as on New Year's Day.
75. I [....] ointment I put my hands.
76. [....].. the ship was completed.
77. Difficult was [the ....].
78. .... above and below.
79. [....].. its two-thirds.
80. [Whatever I had I] loaded aboard her.

---

[177]Or: what was needful (cf. line 55).

[178]Var.: three shar. One shar is 3,600. The measure is not given in these lines. Perhaps we have to supply sûtu; one sûtu was equal to a little over two gallons. Three shar would then correspond to about 24,000 gallons (cf. Schott, op. cit., p. 67, n. 11).

[179]If the translation "basket-carriers" is correct, we may perhaps assume that the baskets were coated with asphalt, or some such substance (so Haupt in Beiträge zur Assyriologie, X, Heft 2, 18). But I am rather inclined to believe that the oil was contained in vessels carried in some kind of slings. Thus in Egypt large pottery amphorae filled with wine were transported in netted pot-slings carried on a pole (for a beautiful and easily accessible illustration see the National Geographic Magazine, LXXX [1941], 495). The same mode of transportation is depicted on a plaque discovered by the Oriental Institute among the ruins of Opis, in Babylonia (a good picture of this plaque is found in J. H. Breasted, Ancient Times [Boston, etc., 1935], p. 155). Attention may be drawn also to the manner in which a demijohn is inclosed and carried. Salonen's view (op. cit., p. 15, n. 2), that sussullu denotes a kind of ladle, has been refuted by Meier in Orientalistische Literaturzeitung, Vol. XLIII, col. 306.

[180]See Salonen, op. cit., pp. 149-50.

[181]Cf. Poebel in Zeitschrift für Assyriologie, XXXIX, 146 ff.

Tablet XI

81. Whatever I had of silver I loaded aboard her;
82. Whatever I [had] of gold I loaded aboard her;
83. Whatever I had of the seed of all living creatures [I loaded] aboard her.
84. After I had caused all my family and relations to go up into the ship,
85. I caused the game of the field, the beasts of the field, (and) all the craftsmen to go (into it).
86. Shamash set for me a definite time:
87. 'When the leader of the sto[rm(?)] causes a destructive rain to rain down in the evening,
88. Enter the ship and close thy door.'[182]
89. That definite time arrived:
90. In the evening the leader of the sto[rm(?)] caused a destructive rain to rain down.
91. I viewed the appearance of the weather;
92. The weather was frightful to behold.
93. I entered the ship and closed my door.
94. For the navigation(?)[183] of the ship to the boatman Puzur-Amurri
95. I intrusted the mighty structure with its goods.
96. As soon as the first shimmer of morning beamed forth,
97. A black cloud came up from out the horizon.
98. Adad[184] thunders within it,
99. While Shullat and Ḫanish go before,
100. Coming as heralds over hill and plain;
101. Irragal[185] pulls out the masts;
102. Ninurta[186] comes along (and) causes the dikes to give way;

---

[182]Var.: the ship.

[183]Thus Ebeling in Archiv für Orientforschung, VIII, 231, and Friedrich Delitzsch, Assyrisches Handwörterbuch (Leipzig, 1896), p. 519. The translation "for the calking of the ship," while obviously correct elsewhere (cf. Salonen, op. cit., p. 152), does not fit into the present context.

[184]The god of storm and rain.

[185]Another name for Nergal, the god of the underworld.

[186]God of war and lord of the wells and irrigation works (Knut Tallqvist, Akkadische Götterepitheta [Helsinki, 1938], pp. 424-26).

Tablet XI

103. The Anunnaki[187] raised (their) torches,
104. Lighting up the land with their brightness;[188]
105. The raging of Adad reached unto heaven
106. (And) turned into darkness all that was light.
107. [....] the land he broke(?) like a po[t(?)].
108. (For) one day the tem[pest blew].
109. Fast it blew and [....].
110. Like a battle [it ca]me over the p[eople].
111. No man could see his fellow.
112. The people could not be recognized from heaven.
113. (Even) the gods were terror-stricken at the deluge.
114. They fled (and) ascended to the heaven of Anu;[189]
115. The gods cowered like dogs (and) crouched in distress(?).
116. Ishtar cried out like a woman in travail;
117. The lovely-voiced Lady of the g[ods][190] lamented:
118. 'In truth, the olden time has turned to clay,
119. Because I commanded evil in the assembly of the gods!
120. How could I command (such) evil in the assembly of the gods!
121. (How) could I command war to destroy my people,
122. (For) it is I who bring forth[191] (these) my people!
123. Like the spawn of fish they (now) fill the sea!'
124. The Anunnaki-gods wept with her;
125. The gods sat bowed (and) weeping.
126. Covered were their lips .....
127. Six days and [six] nights
128. The wind blew, the downpour, the tempest, (and) the flo[od]
      overwhelmed the land.
129. When the seventh day arrived, the tempest, the flood,
130. Which had fought like an army, subsided in (its) onslaught.

---

[187] The judges in the underworld.

[188] These two lines perhaps refer to sheet lightning on the horizon; forked lightning, which is accompanied by thunder peals, is attributed to Adad (Jensen, op. cit., p. 496, and Ebeling in Reallexikon der Assyriologie, I [Berlin and Leipzig, 1932], 24).

[189] The sky-god.

[190] Bêlit-i[lê].

[191] Lit.: give birth to.

Tablet XI

131. The sea grew quiet, the storm abated, the flood ceased.
135. I opened a window, and light fell upon my face.[192]
132. I looked upon the sea,[193] (all) was silence,
133. And all mankind had turned to clay;
134. The .... was as level as a (flat) roof.
136. I bowed, sat down, and wept,
137. My tears running down over my face.
138. I looked in (all) directions for the boundaries of the sea.
139. At (a distance of) twelve[194] (double-hours) there emerged a stretch of land.
140. On Mount Niṣir[195] the ship landed.
141. Mount Niṣir held the ship fast and did not let (it) move.
142. One day, a second day Mount Nisir held the ship fast and did not let (it) move.
143. A third day, a fourth day Mount Niṣir held the ship fast and did not let (it) move.
144. A fifth day, a sixth day Mount Niṣir held the ship fast and did not let (it) move.[196]
145. When the seventh day arrived,
146. I sent forth a dove and let (her) go.
147. The dove went away and came back to me;
148. There was no resting-place, and so she returned.
149. (Then) I sent forth a swallow and let (her) go.
150. The swallow went away and came back to me;
151. There was no resting-place, and so she returned.
152. (Then) I sent forth a raven and let (her) go.
153. The raven went away, and when she saw that the waters had abated,

---

[192] On the transposition of this line see Schott in Zeitschrift für Assyriologie, XLII, 139-40.

[193] Var.: at the weather.

[194] Var.: fourteen.

[195] This name could also be read Nimush.

[196] In place of the words "held the ship fast and did not let (it) move," in lines 142-44, the original has the sign of reduplication or repetition, which means that the statement is to be completed on the basis of the preceding line. In this instance, the sign of reduplication could be rendered with "etc."

Tablet XI

154. She ate, she flew about,[197] she cawed, (and) did not return.
155. (Then) I sent forth (everything) to the four winds and offered a sacrifice.
156. I poured out a libation on the peak of the mountain.
157. Seven and (yet) seven kettles I set up.
158. Under them I heaped up (sweet) cane, cedar, and myrtle.
159. The gods smelled the savor,
160. The gods smelled the sweet savor.
161. The gods gathered like flies over the sacrificer.
162. As soon as[198] the great goddess[199] arrived,
163. She lifted up the great jewels which Anu had made according to her wish:
164. 'O ye gods here present, as surely as I shall not forget the lapis lazuli on my neck,
165. I shall remember these days and shall not forget (them) ever!
166. Let the gods come near to the offering;
167. (But) Enlil shall not come near to the offering,
168. Because without reflection he brought on the deluge
169. And consigned my people to destruction!'
170. As soon as Enlil arrived
171. And saw the ship, Enlil was wroth;
172. He was filled with anger against the gods, the Igigi:[200]
173. 'Has any of the mortals escaped? No man was to live through the destruction!'
174. Ninurta opened his mouth and said, speaking to warrior Enl[il]:
175. 'Who can do things without[201] Ea?
176. For Ea alone understands every matter.'
177. Ea opened his mouth and said, speaking to warrior Enlil:
178. 'O warrior, thou wisest among the gods!

---

[197]Cf. von Soden in Orientalistische Literaturzeitung, Vol. XXXVIII, col. 146.

[198]Cf. Jensen, op. cit., pp. 398 and 502.

[199]I.e., Ishtar.

[200]The gods of heaven.

[201]Cf. E. S. Rimalt in Wiener Zeitschrift für die Kunde des Morgenlandes, XXXIX (1932), 114-15.

Tablet XI

179. How, O how couldst thou without reflection bring on (this)
     deluge?
180. On the sinner lay his sin; on the transgressor lay his
     transgression!
181. Let loose, that he shall not be cut off; pull tight, that
     he may not ge[t (too) loose] [202]
182. Instead of thy sending a deluge, would that a lion had come
     and diminished mankind!
183. (Or) instead of thy sending a deluge, would that a wolf had
     come and dim[inished] mankind!
184. (Or) instead of thy sending a deluge, would that a famine
     had occurred and [destroyed] the land!
185. (Or) instead of thy sending a deluge, would that Irra[203]
     had come and smitten mankind!
186. (Moreover,) it was not I who revealed the secret of the
     great gods;
187. (But) to Atraḫasis[204] I showed a dream, and so he learned
     the secret of the gods.
188. And now take counsel concerning him.
189. Then Enlil went up into the ship.
190. He took my hand and caused me to go aboard.
191. He caused my wife to go aboard (and) to kneel down at my side.
192. Standing between us, he touched our foreheads and blessed us:
193. 'Hitherto Utnapishtim has been but a man;
194. But now Utnapishtim and his wife shall be like unto us gods.
195. In the distance, at the mouth of the rivers, Utnapishtim
     shall dwell!'
196. So they took me and caused me to dwell in the distance, at
     the mouth of the rivers.
197. But now as for thee, who will assemble the gods unto thee,
198. That thou mayest find the life which thou seekest?
199. Come, do not sleep for six days and seven nights."

---

[202] I.e., punish man, lest he get too wild; but do not be too
severe, lest he perish (cf. Ebeling in Archiv für Orientforschung,
VIII, 231).

[203] The god of pestilence.

[204] This name—in reality a descriptive epithet meaning "the
exceedingly wise"—is another designation for Utnapishtim.

Tablet XI

200. (But) as he sits (there) on his hams,
201. Sleep like a rainstorm blows upon him.
202. Utnapishtim says to her, to his wife:
203. "Look at the strong man who wants life (everlasting).
204. Sleep like a rainstorm blows upon him."
205. His wife says to him, to Utnapishtim the Distant:
206. "Touch him that the man may awake,
207. That he may return in peace on the road by which he came,
208. That through the gate through which he came he may return to his land."
209. Utnapishtim says to her, to his wife:
210. "Deceitful is mankind, he will try to deceive thee.[205]
211. Pray, (therefore,) bake loaves of bread for him (and) place (them) at his head.
212. And the days that he has slept mark on the wall!"
213. She baked loaves of bread for him (and) placed (them) at his head;
214. And the days that he slept she noted on the wall.
215. His first loaf of bread was all dried out;
216. The second was ....; the third was (still) moist; the fourth was white, his ....;
217. The fifth was moldy; the sixth had (just) been baked;
218. The seventh—suddenly he[206] touched him, and the man awoke.
219. Gilgamesh said to him, to Utnapishtim the Distant:
220. "Hardly did sleep spread over me,
221. When quickly thou didst touch me and rouse me."
222. Utnapishtim [said to him], to Gilgamesh:
223. "[.... Gilga]mesh, count thy loaves of bread!
224. [The days which thou didst sleep] may they be known to thee.
225. Thy [first] loaf of bread [is(already) all dried out];
226. [The second is ....]; the third is (still) moist; the fourth is white, thy ....;
227. [The fifth is mol]dy; the sixth has (just) been baked;
228. [The seventh—s]uddenly thou didst wake."

---

[205]I.e., he will deny that he slept (so Landsberger in *Zeitschrift für Assyriologie*, XLII, 141, n. 1.).

[206]Utnapishtim.

Tablet XI

229. [Gilg]amesh said to him, to Utnapishtim the Distant:
230. "[Oh, what] shall I do, Utnapishtim, (or) where shall I go,
231. As the robber[207] has (already) taken hold of my [member]s?
232. Death is dwelling [in] my bedchamber;
233. And wherever [I] set [my feet] there is death!"
234. Utnapishtim [said to him,] to Urshanabi, the boatman:
235. "Urshanabi, [may] the qua[y not re]joice in thee, may the place of crossing hate thee!
236. Him who walks about on its shore banish from its shore.
237. The man before whose face thou didst walk, whose body is covered with long hair,
238. The grace of whose members pelts have distorted,
239. Take him, Urshanabi, and bring him to the place of washing;
240. Let him wash his long hair (clean) as snow in water.
241. Let him throw off his pelts and let the sea carry (them) away, that his fair body may be seen.
242. Let the band around his head be replaced with a new one.
243. Let him be clad with a garment, as clothing for his nakedness.
244. Until he gets to his city,[208]
245. Until he finishes his journey,
246. May (his) garment not show (any sign of) age, but may it (still) be quite new."
247. Urshanabi took him and brought him to the place of washing.
248. He washed his long hair (clean) as snow in [water].
249. He threw off his pelts, that the sea might carry (them) away,
250. (And that) his fair body appeared.
251. He rep[laced the band around] his head with a new one.
252. He clothed him with a garment, as clothing for his nakedness.
253. Until he [would come to his city],
254. Until he would finish his journey,
255. [(His) garment should not show (any sign of) age but] should (still) be quite new.
256. Gilgamesh and Urshanabi boarded the ship;
257. They launched the ship [on the billows] (and) glided along.

---

[207]I.e., death?

[208]Var.: to his land.

Tablet XI

258. His wife said to him, to Utnapishtim the Distant:
259. "Gilgamesh has come hither, he has become weary, he has exerted himself,
260. What wilt thou give (him wherewith) he may return to his land?"
261. Then he, Gilgamesh, took a pole
262. And brought the ship near to the shore.[209]
263. Utnapishtim [said] to him, [to] Gilgamesh:
264. "Gilgamesh, thou hast come hither, thou hast become weary, thou hast exerted thyself;
265. What shall I give thee (wherewith) thou mayest return to thy land?
266. Gilgamesh, I will reveal (unto thee) a hidden thing,
267. Namely, a [secret of the gods will I] tell thee:
268. There is a plant like a thorn ⌈....⌉.
269. Like a rose(?) its thorn(s) will pr[ick thy hands].
270. If thy hands will obtain that plant, [thou wilt find new life]."
271. When Gilgamesh heard that, he opened [....].
272. He tied heavy stones [to his feet];
273. They pulled him down into the deep, [and he saw the plant].
274. He took the plant, (though) it pr[icked his hands].
275. He cut the heavy stones [from his feet],
276. (And) the .... threw him to its shore.
277. Gilgamesh said to him, to Urshanabi, the boatman:
278. "Urshanabi, this plant is a wondrous(?) plant,
279. Whereby a man may obtain his former strength(?).[210]
280. I will take it to Uruk, the enclosure, I will give (it) to eat ⌈....⌉ may cut off the plant(?).
281. Its name is 'The old man becomes young as the man (in his prime).'

---

[209]Gilgamesh was no doubt called back by Utnapishtim.

[210]Cf. Schott in _Zeitschrift für Assyriologie_, XLII, 142.

Tablet XI

282. <u>I myself will eat (it) that I may return to my youth.</u>"[211]
283. After twenty double-hours they broke off a morsel.
284. After thirty (additional) double-hours they stopped for the night.
285. Gilgamesh saw a pool with cold water;
286. He <u>descended into it and bathed in the water.</u>
287. <u>A serpent perceived the fragrance of the plant;</u>
288. It came up [from the water] and snatched the plant,
289. Sloughing (its) skin on its return.[212]
290. Then Gilgamesh sat down (and) wept,
291. His tears flowing over his cheeks.
292. [....] of Urshanabi, the boatman:
293. "[For] whom, Urshanabi, have my hands become weary?
294. For whom is the blood of my heart being spent?
295. For myself I have not obtained any boon.
296. For the 'earth-lion'[213] have I obtained the boon.
297. Now at (a distance of) twenty[214] double-hours (such a) one(?) snatches it away (from me)!
298. When I opened the .....
299. I have found something that [has been s]et for a sign unto me; I will withdraw
300. And will leave the ship at the shore."[215] After twenty [double-hours] they broke off a morsel.

---

[211] The purpose of this plant was to grant rejuvenated life; and it was to be eaten after a person had reached old age. For this reason Gilgamesh does not eat the plant at once but decides to wait until after his return to Uruk, until he has become an "old man" (cf. Christian in <u>Wiener Zeitschrift für die Kunde des Morgenlandes</u>, XL, 149).

[212] Cf. W. F. Albright in <u>Revue d'Assyriologie</u>, XVI (1919), 189-90. By eating this magic plant, the serpent gained the power to shed its old skin and thereby to renew its life (cf. J. Morgenstern in <u>Zeitschrift für Assyriologie</u>, XXIX [1914/15], 284 ff.).

[213] Apparently the serpent (cf. lines 287 ff. and Jensen in <u>Orientalistische Literaturzeitung</u>, Vol. XXXII, col. 650).

[214] We should expect "fifty" (cf. lines 283-84).

[215] In the loss of the plant Gilgamesh sees a sign that he should leave the ship behind and proceed by land. The boatman goes along, for, according to line 235, he apparently has been banished from the shores of the blessed for bringing Gilgamesh there.

Tablet XI

301. After thirty (additional) double-hours they stopped for
     the night. When they arrived in Uruk, the enclosure,
302. Gilgamesh said to him, to Urshanabi, the boatman:
303. "Urshanabi, climb upon the wall of Uruk (and) walk about;
304. Inspect the foundation terrace and examine the brickwork,
     if its brickwork be not of burnt bricks,
305. And (if) the seven wise men did not lay its foundation!
306. One shar is city, one shar orchards, one shar prairie;
     (then there is) the uncultivated land(?) of the temple of
     Ishtar.
307. Three shar and the uncultivated land(?) comprise[216] Uruk."
308. O that today I had left[217] the pukku in the house of the
     carpenter!

(Colophon:)

309. Tablet XI of "He who saw everthing," [of the series of]
     Gilgamesh.
310. Written down according to its original and collated.
311. Palace of Ashurbanipal, king of the world, king of Assyria.

Tablet XII

This tablet, of which the first twelve lines are almost completely broken away, contains the Semitic version of the second
part of a Sumerian story dealing with some additional feats performed by Gilgamesh and his friend Enkidu.[218] Since the Sumerian
legend contains the key to the understanding of our tablet, we
shall give a brief résumé of the contents of the Sumerian narrative
up to the point where the Gilgamesh Epic sets in.

The Sumerian legend, like numerous other accounts from the
Tigro-Euphrates Valley, takes us back to the time of creation.
After heaven and earth had been separated and mankind had been

---

[216]Reading tam-ḫu (thus Ebeling in Archiv für Orientforschung,
VIII, 232).

[217]Adhering to the old reading, viz., e-⌈zib⌉.

[218]The first part of the Sumerian composition has been published by Kramer, Gilgamesh and the Ḫulupou-Tree (Chicago, 1938),
and C. J. Gadd in Revue d'Assyriologie, XXX (1933), 127 ff.; cf.
also Kramer, Sumerian Mythology (Philadelphia, 1944), pp. 30 ff.,
and the same author's article in the Journal of the American
Oriental Society, LXIV, esp. 19-23.

Tablet XII

brought into being; after Anu and Enlil had taken control of heaven
and earth, respectively; after Ereshkigal had been presented with
the underworld and Enki had set sail for the underworld—at that
time a tree, probably a willow tree, which had been planted on the
bank of the Euphrates, was uprooted by the south wind and carried
off by the Euphrates. Inanna,[219] the queen of heaven, walking a-
long the river, seized the floating tree and took it to her "holy
garden" in Uruk. There she tended it with loving care, hoping that
some day she could have a bed and a chair made of its wood.

However, when the tree had grown large and strong, Inanna
found herself unable to utilize its wood; for in the meantime a
serpent had made his nest at the root of the tree, the Zû-bird[220]
had placed his young in its crown, and in the middle the demoness
Lilith[221] had built her house. When Gilgamesh heard of Inanna's
plight, he rushed to her aid and slew the serpent with his ax.
Thereupon the Zû-bird, terror-stricken, took his young and fled
to the mountains, while Lilith destroyed her house and escaped to
the desert. Then Gilgamesh and the men of Uruk, who had accompanied him, cut down the tree and gave it to Inanna for her bed and
her chair. Of the base of the tree Inanna made an object called
pukku and of its crown she made a related object called mikkû and
gave them to Gilgamesh.[222]

On a certain day, these objects, to the great distress of Gilgamesh, fell into the underworld. Gilgamesh, endeavoring to recover them, "put forth his hand, but he could not reach them; he
put forth his foot, but he could not reach them." Gilgamesh sat
down and wept, as he lamented: "O my pukku! O my mikkû!" After
two more lines, whose meaning is not quite certain as yet, the
Semitic version set in, as we know from the catch-line on Tablet
XI:308, and continued the story, beginning in the midst of Gilgamesh's lamentation.

_____

[219]I.e., Ishtar.

[220]The divine storm-bird.

[221]Cf. Isa. 34:14.

[222]Landsberger would translate these objects with "drum" and
"drumstick," respectively (see R. Ranoszek in Zeitschrift der
deutschen Morgenländischen Gesellschaft, LXXXVIII [1934], 210).

Tablet XII

1. "O that today[223] I had left the _pukku_ in the house of the carpenter!

2. O that I had left it with the wife of the carpenter, who was to me like the mother who bore me!

3. O that I had left it with the daughter of the carpenter, who was to me (like) my younger sister![224]

4. Now, who will bring the _pukku_ up from the underworld?

5. (And) who will bring the _mikkû_ up from the underworld?"

6. Enkidu, his servant, said to him, [to Gilgamesh]:

7. "My lord, why dost thou weep? Why does thy heart feel ill?

8. Today I will bring up the _pukku_ from the underworld,

9. I will bring up the _mikkû_ from the underworld!"[225]

10. Gilgamesh said to him, to Enkidu:

11. "If today thou wilt go down into the underworld,

12. A word I will speak to thee, follow my word;

13. Instruction I will offer thee, follow mine instruction:[226]

14. [Do not] be clothed with clean raiment,

15. (Or) they[227] will cry out(?) against thee as if thou wert a stranger;

16. Do not be anointed with the precious oil from the ointment-box,

17. (Or) at its fragrance they will gather about thee;

18. Do not hurl a spear(?) in the underworld,

19. (Or) they who have been struck down by the spear(?) will surround thee;

20. Do not take a staff in thy hands,

---

[223]The Sumerian text has: on that day. With the Assyrian translation, compare lines 56-58.

[224]Had Gilgamesh left his _pukku_ and his _mikkû_ in the house of the carpenter, they would have been safe and would not have fallen into the underworld. The translation of the first three lines is somewhat tentative.

[225]Cf. Kramer in the Journal of the American Oriental Society, LXIV, 20-22.

[226]Cf. Kramer in the Bulletin of the American Schools of Oriental Research, No. 79 (October, 1940), p. 25. The preceding line and the first half of this line are found only in the Sumerian text.

[227]The dead.

Tablet XII

21. (Or) the spirits will tremble before thee;
22. Do not put sandals on thy feet;
23. Do not make a sound in the underworld;
24. Thy wife whom thou lovest do not kiss,
25. Thy wife whom thou hatest do not strike,
26. Thy son whom thou lovest do not kiss,
27. Thy son whom thou hatest do not strike,
28. (Or) the wailing of the underworld will seize thee."
29. She who rests,
    She who rests,
    The mother of Ninazu,[228]
    She who rests,
30. Her holy shoulders
    Are not covered with raiment,
31. Her bosom, like ....-bowls,
    Is not clothed with linen.[229]
32. En[kidu] paid no heed to the word of his lord.[230]
33. [He was c]lothed [with clean raiment],
34. (And) as if he were a stra[nger they cried out(?) against] him;
35. [He was an]ointed with the [precious] oil from the ointment-box,
36. (And) at [its] fragrance [they ga]thered about him;
37A. [He hurled] a spear(?) i[n the underworld],
38. (And) those who [had been struck down] by the spear(?) [surrou]nded him;
39. [He took] a staff in [his] hand,
37B. (And) the spirits trembled (before him);
40. [He put] sandals on [his feet];

---

[228]Ninazu was one of the husbands of Ereshkigal, the queen of the underworld.

[229]The words "with linen" are based on the Sumerian version (see Kramer in the Journal of the American Oriental Society, LXIV, p. 21, n. 105). On the basis of the context and the Sumerian recension, I tentatively take the verb shadâdu in the sense of the German anziehen ("to clothe"), rather than ziehen ("to pull or draw"). This short poem, occurring twice on our tablet, perhaps served to change the scene.

[230]See Kramer, ibid., p. 23, n. 115.

Tablet XII

41. [He made] a sound [in the underworld];
42. His wife [whom he loved he kissed],
43. [His] wife whom he ha[ted he struck],
44. [His son wh]om he loved [he kissed],
45. [His] son whom he hated he str[uck],
46. (And) the wa[ili]ng of the underworld seized him.
47. She who rests,
    [She who re]sts,
    The mother of Ninazu,
    She who res[ts],
48. [Her] holy shoulders
    Are not covered with raiment,
49. Her bosom, like ....-bowls,
    Is not clothed with linen.
50. To come up from the underworld [she[231] did not allow(?)
    E]nkidu.
51. Nam[tar[232] did not sei]ze him, disease did not seize him, the
    underworld [seized h]im.
52. The unsparing dep[uty of Nergal][233] did not seize him, the
    underworld [seized h]im.
53. On [the battle]field of men he did not fall, the underworld
    [seized h]im.
54. ..[....] my [lord], the son of Ninsun,[234] weeps for his ser-
    vant Enkidu.
55. To E[kur, the ho]use of Enlil, he went all alone:
56. "Father [Enli]l, on the day that my _pukku_ fell into the
    underworld
57. And my _mikkû_ fell into the underworld,
58. Enkidu, whom [I sent] to bring [them] up, [the underworld
    seized].

---

[231] The mother of Ninazu?

[232] A god of death and pestilence and the minister of Ereshkigal.

[233] Nergal was the lord of the underworld.

[234] "The son of Ninsun" refers, of course, to Gilgamesh.

Tablet XII

59. Namtar did not seize him, disease did not seize him, the underworld has seized him.[235]
60. The unsparing deputy of Nergal did not seize him, the underworld has seized him.
61. On the battlefield of men he did not fall, the underworld has seized him."[236]
62. Father Enlil did not answer him a word. [To Ekishshirgal, the house of Sin], he went [all alone]:
63. "Father Sin, on the day that my pukku fell into the underworld
64. And my mikkû fell [into the underworld],
65. Enkidu, whom [I sent] to bring [them] up, the underworld seized.
66. Namtar did not seize him, disease [did] not [seize] him, the underworld has seized him.
67. The unsp[aring] deputy of Nergal [did not seize him, the underworld has seized him].
68. On [the battle]field [of men] he did not fall, [the underworld has seized him]."
69. [Father Sin did not answer him a word. To Eabzu, the house of Ea], he went [all alone]:[237]
70. "Father Ea, on the day that my pukku fell into the underworld
71. And my mikkû fell into the underworld,
72. Enkidu, whom I sent to bring them up, the underworld seized.

---

[235]With lines 59-68, compare the Assyrian fragment published by Weidner in Archiv für Orientforschung, X (1935/36), 363 ff.

[236]Gilgamesh probably wants to say: "Since Enkidu did not enter the underworld in the ordinary way, i.e., via death, but instead descended to it as a living person and as my deputy, to get my pukku and my mikkû, he ought to be released" (cf. Jensen, op. cit., p. 526).

[237]The Sumerian text has: "To Eridu he went." From here on the translation is in part based on the Sumerian fragments published by Langdon, Historical and Religious Texts from the Temple Library of Nippur (Munich, 1914), No. 35, and Hugo Radau in the Hilprecht Anniversary Volume (Leipzig, etc., 1909), No. 11. In the translation of this Sumerian material I enjoyed the help of Dr. Jacobsen. The translation was made before the appearance of Kramer's Sumerian Mythology.

Tablet XII

73. Na[mt]ar did not seize him, disease did not seize him, the underworld has seized him.

74. The unsparing deputy of Nergal [did] not [seize him], the underworld has seized him.

75. On the battlefield of men he did not fall, the underworld has seized him."

76. [When] father Ea [heard this],

77. [He said] to [Nergal], the warlike h[ero]:

78. "N[ergal], thou warlike hero, [thou son of Bêlit-ilê(?)],[238]

79. Open now[239] a hole in the underworld,

80. That the ·spirit of E[nkidu] may issue forth from the underworld,

81. [That he may declare the ways of the underworld] to [his] brother."

82. Nerg[al], the warlike hero, [hearkened to Ea].

83. He immediately opened a hole in the underworld,

84. So that the spirit of Enkidu issued forth from the underworld like a wind.

85. They embraced and kissed one another.[240]

86. They took counsel together, as they conversed together.

87. "Tell me, my friend; tell me, my friend;

88. Tell me the way(s) of the underworld, which thou hast seen."

89. "I will not tell thee, my friend; I will not tell thee.

90. (But) if I must tell thee the way(s) of the underworld, which I have seen,

91. Sit down (and) weep."

92. "[....] I will sit down and weep."

93. "[My body(?) ....] which thou didst touch, while thy heart rejoiced,

94. Vermin are devouring (it) as though it were an old [gar]ment.

95. [My body(?) .... which thou didst] touch, while thy heart

---

[238]The Sumerian version has: "Father Enki (i.e., Ea) stood by him in this matter, saying to Utu (i.e., Shamash), the warlike hero, the son born of Ningal."

[239]The Sumerian text has i-bi-[sh]è for the Babylonian lûman.

[240]Cf. Ebeling in Archiv für Orientforschung, VIII, 232. The Sumerian version has: "They embrace, they kiss."

Tablet XII

rejoiced,

96. [....] is full of dust."[241]

97. He cried "[Woe!]" and threw himself down in the dust;

98. [Gilgamesh] cried "[Woe!]" and threw himself down in the dust, (saying):

99. "He who had no son, hast thou seen (him)?"[242] "I have seen (him)."

100-101. (Almost completely destroyed)[243]

102. "[He who had] one [son], hast thou seen (him)?" "I have seen (him).

103. He lies prostrate at [the foot] of the wall (and) weeps bitterly [ov]er (it)."

104. "He who had two sons, hast thou seen (him)?" "I have seen (him).

105. He dwells in a brick-structure (and) eats bread."

106. "He who had three sons, hast thou seen (him)?" "I have seen (him).

107. He drinks water out of the waterskins of the deep."

108. "He who had four sons, hast thou seen (him)?" "I have seen (him).

109. Like [....].. his heart rejoices."

110. "He who had five sons, hast thou seen (him)?" "I have seen (him).

111. Like (that of) a good scribe, his arm is bared,[244]

112. (And) [....] straightway he enters the palace."

113. "He who had six sons, hast thou seen (him)?" "I have seen (him).

---

[241] What appeared to Gilgamesh was a living but incorporeal or ethereal image of Enkidu's body (cf. line 84), which lay in the bosom of the earth and was being devoured even as the two friends communed together.

[242] See Radau, op. cit., No. 11:19.

[243] With the following fifteen lines, compare the Assyrian fragment published by Weidner in Archiv für Orientforschung, X, 363 ff.

[244] Piecing together the literary remnants on the two aforementioned Sumerian fragments published by Langdon and Radau, the Sumerian version of this line runs thus: dub-sar-sag₄-ga-gim da-ni [ig] bí-in-kíd. The Babylonian text is, accordingly, to be read as follows: [ki-ma ṭupsharri] dam-qí id-su ni-ta-at.

Tablet XII

114. [. . . . .]."
115. "He who had seven sons [hast thou seen (him)?"   "I have seen (him)].
116. . . . ."
117. "[He who ...., hast thou seen (him)?"   "I have seen (him)].
118. Like a beautiful standard [....]."

(Break)

144. "He who ⌈fell(?)⌉ from the mast, hast thou seen (him)?"
["I have seen (him)].
145. Straightway to [....] at the pulling out of the bollards."
146. "He who died the death of ..[.., hast thou] seen (him)?"
["I have seen (him)].
147. He is at rest upon a night-couch and drinks pure water."
148. "He who was slain in battle, hast thou seen (him)?"   "I have
[seen (him)].
149. His father and his mother support his head, and his wife
weeps[245] over him."
150. "He whose body lies (unburied) on the steppe, hast thou
seen (him)?"   "I have seen (him).
151. His spirit does not rest in the underworld."
152. "He whose spirit has none to take care of him,[246] hast thou
seen (him)?"   "I have seen (him).
153. What was left over in the pot (and) the pieces of bread that
were thrown into the street he eats."
154. Tablet XII of "He who saw everything."[247]

---

[245] The restoration of this word can be considered certain on
the basis of the Sumerian text.

[246] Who has none among the living to make food and drink offerings to him.

[247] Var.: Tablet XII of the series of Gilgamesh.   Completed.

CHAPTER II

RELATED MATERIAL

A Sumerian Deluge Version from Nippur[1]

Of the various episodes in the Gilgamesh Epic, the one which
enjoyed perhaps the most popular favor among the Babylonians and
Assyrians, and which certainly is the most important from the viewpoint of the Old Testament scholar, is the story of the great flood
and of Utnapishtim's enviable attainment of blessed immortality.
This episode originally formed an independent account and has come
down to us in a number of different recensions. The oldest of them
undoubtedly is the Sumerian version inscribed on a tablet excavated
at Nippur. While the tablet itself dates only to about the time of
Hammurabi, the story it relates is unquestionably older.

This tablet contains six columns of writing, three on the obverse and three on the reverse. The upper part, representing about
two-thirds of the original, has unfortunately been broken off, so
that large gaps occur in the text. The preserved portions of the
first two columns contain a brief account of the creation and of
the founding of five prediluvian cities of Babylonia. The remainder of the composition deals with the story of the deluge, to which
the first two episodes are probably introductory. In the preserved
portion of the third column the gods have already decided to send
a deluge. But not all are ready to carry into execution what has
been decreed in the assembly. Nintu, the goddess of birth and here
probably identical with the "holy Innanna," laments over the impending destruction of mankind, while Enki, the god of wisdom and
the friend of man, is trying to devise ways and means of saving at
least one of the human race, his favorite Ziusudra. The text
follows.

---

[1] Inscription published by A. Poebel, Historical and Grammatical Texts (Philadelphia, 1914), Pl. I; translated by the same author in his volume Historical Texts (Philadelphia, 1914), pp. 18 ff.;
and translated again by L. W. King, Legends of Babylon and Egypt
in Relation to Hebrew Tradition (London, 1918), pp. 63 ff.

Column iii

At that time Nintu[2] [cried out] like a [woman in travail];
Holy Innanna lamented for her people.
Enki[3] [took] counsel in his own heart.
Anu Enlil,[4] Enki, and Ninḫursag[5] [....].
The gods of heaven and earth [call]ed upon the name of Anu Enlil.
At that time Ziusudra[6] was king, the administrator of the temple
  provisions of [...].
He made a very great .[...].
He prostrates himself in humility, [....] in reverence.
Daily (and) perseveringly he stands in attendance [at the shrine].
A dream, such as had not been (before), comes forth [....].
He conjures by the name of heaven and earth [....].

The dream mentioned at the end of these lines is evidently
related to the warning which Ziusudra receives in the next column,
where the purpose of the gods is revealed to him in direct speech.

Column iv

For [....] the gods a wal[l(?) ....].
Ziusudra, standing at its(?) side, heard [a voice]:
"Stand at the wall at my left and [listen].
I will speak a word to thee at the wall; [follow my] word,
[And give] ear (to) mine instruction.[7]
By our hand a rainflood .[...] will be [sent];
To destroy the seed of mankind, [to ....],
Is the decision, the word, of the assembly [of the gods].
The commands of Anu En[lil ....].

---

[2]Commonly known as Ninḫursag.

[3]Another name for Ea.

[4]In this text Enlil is consistently referred to as "Anu
Enlil." This title indicates that Enlil has received the supreme
power and functions of Anu, the highest god of the Sumerian pantheon, and that he thus exercises not only his own authority but
also that of Anu (cf. Poebel, Historical Texts, pp. 36-37).

[5]A goddess of birth and rulership.

[6]On this reading see Thorkild Jacobsen, The Sumerian King List
(Chicago, 1939), pp. 76, n. 34, and 217 (K 11624).

[7]Cf. S. N. Kramer in the Bulletin of the American Schools of
Oriental Research, No. 79 (October, 1940), p. 26.

Their rule (and) dominion [....]."

The missing portion of this column, about three-fourths of the text, undoubtedly dealt with the construction of Ziusudra's boat, for the opening lines of the next column already treat of the deluge itself.

Column v

All the mighty windstorms blew together;
At the same time the rainflood swept over the ....[8]
When for seven days (and) seven nights
The rainflood had swept over the land
(And) the windstorms had driven the giant boat about on the mighty waters,
The sun-god came forth, shedding light over heaven and earth.
Ziusudra opened an opening of the giant boat
(And) let the light of the hero, the sun-god, enter the interior(?) of the giant boat.
Ziusudra, the king,
Prostrates himself before the sun-god;
The king kills an ox (and) offers an abundant sacrifice of sheep.

The remainder of the column, now broken away, probably contained an account of the arrival of the other gods. The final column of the tablet opens with a passage of rather uncertain meaning. Where the text again becomes intelligible Ziusudra prostrates himself before Enlil, who had been chiefly responsible for bringing on the deluge, and, as in the Gilgamesh Epic, Enlil is appeased and bestows divinity and immortality upon the hero of the flood. Ziusudra is then taken to a distant land, the land of Dilmun, on the shores of the Persian Gulf, where henceforth he enjoys the immortal life of the gods.

Column vi

The first five lines of this column are quite obscure. Then the text continues:
Ziusudra, the king,
Prostrates himself before Anu Enlil.
Life like (that of) a god he gives to him,

---

[8]Cf. Jacobsen, op. cit., p. 59.

An eternal soul like (that of) a god he creates for him.
At that time Ziusudra, the king,
(Called) the name of the ... "Preserver of the Seed of Mankind."
In a ... land, the land of Dilmun,[9] the place where the sun rises,
they caused him to dwell.

What the remainder of the column, about three-fourths of the
text, may have contained cannot be determined with certainty. However, we can offer a reasonable conjecture. For the left edge of
the tablet contains a line which, though badly damaged, may perhaps
indicate that the present deluge version, like so many Babylonian
creation stories, was used as part of the introduction to an incantation in order to increase the efficacy of the spell, by re-
citing some of the mighty deeds of the gods. Should this prove
to be correct, it would, of course, mean that the missing portion
of this column was inscribed with some magic formula.[10]

This is the only Sumerian deluge version known at present.
Thirty years ago, the late Stephen Langdon of Oxford published a
Sumerian myth which he claimed treated of paradise, the flood, and
the fall of man. It has since been shown, however, that his interpretation of the text was erroneous and that the story recorded on
that tablet has no bearing whatever on the account of the deluge.[11]

A Semitic Deluge Fragment from Nippur[12]

In addition to the Sumerian tablet which we have just considered, the mounds of Nippur have yielded also a fragment of a
deluge version composed in Old Babylonian. With the exception of
the ends of three overlapping lines preserved on the right edge of

---

[9]On this reading of the name see Kramer in the Bulletin of the
American Schools of Oriental Research, No. 96 (December, 1944),
pp. 18-19.

[10]Cf. King, op. cit., pp. 50-51.

[11]See Kramer in the Bulletin of the American Schools of Oriental Research ("Supplementary Studies," No. 1 [1945]).

[12]Text published and translated by H. V. Hilprecht, The Baby-
lonian Expedition of the University of Pennsylvania, Series D, Vol.
V, Fasc. 1 (Philadelphia, 1910); and translated again by A. T. Clay,
A Hebrew Deluge Story in Cuneiform (New Haven, 1922), pp. 81-82;
Erich Ebeling in Hugo Gressmann, Altorientalische Texte zum Alten
Testament (Berlin and Leipzig, 1926), p. 199; and others.

the tablet, the text of the obverse is completely destroyed; and
of the reverse only a few badly mutilated lines have been preserved. Nevertheless, enough of it remains to justify its publication in these pages. The beginning of the reverse is unfortunately broken off. The remainder, together with a few minor
restorations, reads as follows.

"[....] I will loosen.

[....] will seize all the people together.

[....] before the flood comes forth.

[....] as many as there are, I will cause overthrow, destruction,
annihilation(?).

[....] build a great ship.

[....] total ... shall be its structure.

The same [ship] shall be a giant boat, and its name shall be
'Preserver of Life.'[13]

[....] cover (it) with a strong cover.

[Into the ship] which thou shalt make,

[Thou shalt bring] beasts of the field (and) fowl of the heavens."

(Remainder broken away)

The Atrahasis Epic[14]

Of this great epic, which, according to the colophon on fragment No. II, consisted of at least three large tablets with a total
of 1,245 lines, only four deplorably small pieces are known to us.
Fragments I and II come from Babylonia and date back to the time

---

[13]Cf. Poebel, Historical Texts, p. 61, n. 3.

[14]Text of fragment No. I published by Clay, op. cit., Pls.
I-II, with photographs on Pls. V-VI; of No. II by A. Boissier in
Revue d'Assyriologie, XXVIII (1931), 92-95, with photographs facing
p. 91; of No. III by Friedrich Delitzsch, Assyrische Lesestücke
(Leipzig, 1885), p. 101, and Sir H. C. Rawlinson, The Cuneiform
Inscriptions of Western Asia, Vol. IV (London, 1891), Additions,
p. 9; and of No. IV by King in Cuneiform Texts from Babylonian
Tablets, etc., in the British Museum, Vol. XV (London, 1902), Pl.
49, and K. D. Macmillan in Beiträge zur Assyriologie, V (1906),
688.   Translations by P. Jensen, Assyrisch-babylonische Mythen und
Epen (Berlin, 1900), pp. 255 ff. and 275-91; R. W. Rogers, Cuneiform Parallels to the Old Testament (New York and Cincinnati, 1926),
pp. 103-7 and 114-21; Clay, op. cit., pp. 58-69; D. D. Luckenbill
in the American Journal of Semitic Languages and Literatures, XXXIX
(1922/23), 155-59; Ebeling in Gressmann, op. cit., pp. 200-206;
Ebeling, Tod und Leben nach den Vorstellungen der Babylonier (Berlin
and Leipzig, 1931), pp. 176-77; Boissier in Revue d'Assyriologie,
XXVIII, 95-96; and others.

•

of King Ammizaduga (First Babylonian Dynasty), while the other two pieces, belonging to the Assyrian recension of the epic, were found among the ruins of King Ashurbanipal's (668-ca. 633 B.C.) library in Nineveh. The fragments at our disposal deal with the story of the deluge, which, according to this version, was preceded by severe plagues which Enlil, the chief of the gods, sent in a vain effort to make people discontinue their noisy gatherings and was followed by the creation of fourteen human beings for the speedy repopulation of the earth. The epic may perhaps owe its origin to the thought expressed by Ea on Tablet XI:177-85 of the Gilgamesh Epic, viz., that Enlil, instead of sending a deluge, should have afflicted mankind with plagues and the like to correct their evil ways; some later mythographer, or group of mythographers, may have taken up Ea's idea and developed it. As we can see from fragment No. IV, the epic was used as a birth incantation to facilitate delivery.

Fragment No. I
Column i

1. [. . . .]
2. The land became great,[15] the peop[le mu]ltiplied;
3. The land became sated(?) like cattle.
4. The god[16] became disturbed [by] their gatherings.
5. [The go]d heard their noise
6. (And) said to the great gods:
7. "Great has become the noise of mankind;
8. With their tumult they make sleep impossible.[17]
9. [Let] the fig tree [be c]ut off for the people;
10. [In] their [belli]es let vegetables be wanting.
11. Ab[ove] let Adad[18] make scarce his [rain],

---

[15]Lit.: wide.

[16]The god par excellence, meaning Enlil in this case (cf. fragment No. IV, col. iii).

[17]Reading ⌈ú⌉-za-am-ma shi-it-ta (see Sidney Smith in Revue d'Assyriologie, XXII [1925], 67-68).

[18]The god of storm and rain.

12. [Below]^{19} let the springs not flow.
13. [Let the floods not rise] from the source.
14. Let the wind blow
15. . . . .
16. Let the clouds hold back(?)
17. [That rain from heaven] pour not forth.
18. [Let] the field [dimi]nish its products,
19. [Let it turn] the breast of Nisaba."^{20}

From here up to line 387 almost everything is destroyed.
Column ii, lines 70-72, can probably be rendered as follows: "In
the morning let him cause a heavy rain to [pour down]; let it continue during the night [....].^{21} Let him cause it to rain .[...]."

Column vii

(Beginning broken away)

387. Enki [opened] his mouth
388. [And] said to E[nlil]:
389. "Why hast thou commanded [....]?
390. I will stretch out my hand to the pe[ople(?) ....].
391. The flood which thou dost order [....]."

(Remainder too badly damaged for translation)

Column viii

(Beginning destroyed)

438. Atrahasis^{22} opened his mouth
439. And said to his lord.

(Colophon:)

440. 37 (lines on this column).
441. Tablet II (of the series): "When God Man."

---

^{19}The copy has ḫi-pí ish-[shu], "a new break," which means
that at this point the scribe found a new break on the tablet from
which he was copying. On the basis of fragment No. IV, as well as
from the context, the missing word can easily be supplied.

^{20}Nisaba was a goddess of grain. The meaning of this line is:
"The field shall not permit grain to grow up."

^{21}Cf. W. F. Albright in the American Journal of Semitic Languages and Literatures, XL (1923/24), 135.

^{22}Later forms of this name are Atrahasis and Atarhasis.

442. Its total:[23] 439 (lines).

443. By the hand of Ellit-Aya, the assistant scribe.

444. The month of Shabâṭu, the twenty-eighth day.

445. The year when Ammizaduga, the king,

446. Rebuilt

447. Dûr-Ammizaduga,

448. At the mouth of the Euphrates.[24]

Fragment No. II
Column i

(Beginning wanting)

1. [Atramḫasis] opened his mouth

2. And [said] to his lord:

3. "[Of the dream], make known unto me its meaning!

4. [....] make known that I may provide(?) for its ...."

5. [Ea] opened his mouth

6. And said to his servant:

7. ". . . . .

8. The message which I am about to give thee,

9. Guard thou (it).

10. Wall, listen to me!

11. Reed hut, guard all my words![25]

12. Destroy (thy) house, build a ship.

13. Disregard (thy) goods,

14. And save (thy) life!

15. The ship which thou shalt build."

From here to the colophon on column viii virtually everything is destroyed. On column ii the word kupru, "pitch," and the first four letters of the name Atramḫasis are still preserved.

Column viii

(Beginning lost)

1. [....] 390 (lines on the tablet) [....].

---

[23]The total of the tablet, not counting the lines of the colophon.

[24]I.e., the eleventh year of Ammizaduga's reign.

[25]Reading zi-ik-ri(!)-ia, as suggested by Dr. F. W. Geers. The text has zi-ik-zi-ia.

2.   Total: 1,245 (lines) [....]
3.   Of three tablets.
4.   By the hand of Ellit-Aya, the assistant scribe.
5.   The month of Iyyar, [the ... day].
6.   The year when Ammiza[duga, the king],
7.   [His] image [....].[26]

Fragment No. III

(Beginning broken away)

1.   "................
2.   [....] like the vault(?) [....].
3.   [....] strong above and b[elow].
4.   [....] close [....].
5.   [....] at the appointed time, of which I will inform th[ee],
6.   Enter [the ship] and shut the door of the ship.
7.   [Bring in]to it thy grain, thy goods and chattels;
8.   Th[y wife], thy family, thy relations, and the craftsmen.
9.   [Game] of the field (and) beasts of the field, as many as eat herbs,
10. [I will s]end unto thee, and they shall guard thy door."[27]
11. [Atr]aḥasis opened his mouth and said,
12. [Spea]king to Ea, [his] lord:
13. "[Ne]ver have I built a ship [....].
14. Draw a de[sign of it on the gr]ound,
15. That I may look upon the [desi]gn and [build] the ship.
16. [....] on the ground d[raw(?) ....].
17. [Then I will carry out(?)] what thou has commanded [me to do]."

(Remainder broken away)

---

[26]Since almost all of the date formula is destroyed, it is impossible to say whether it refers to the fifth, the ninth, the twelfth, the fifteenth, or the seventeenth year of Ammizaduga's reign, as the term alam, "image," occurs in the date formulas of all these years (see Reallexikon der Assyriologie, II, 189-91). In view of the fact that this text was written by the same scribe who copied fragment No. I, the twelfth year seems to be the most likely.

[27]This undoubtedly means that the animals shall remain indoors, in the ship.

Fragment No. IV

Column i

(Beginning broken away)

25. [When the second ye]ar [arrived ....].
26. [When the thi]rd year [arrived],
27. The people changed in their [....].
28. When the fourth year ar[rived, ...] their ... were in straits.
29. Their wide [...] became narrow.
30. The people [wan]dered about in the streets downcast.[28]
31. When the fifth year arrived, the daughter looks for the entrance of the mother;[29]
32. (But) the mother does not open h[er] door to the daughter.
33. The daughter lo[oks] upon the balances of the mother;
34. [The mother] looks upon the balances of the daughter.[30]
35. When the sixth year arrived, they prepared [the daughter] for a meal,
36. For food they prepared the child. Full were the [....].
37. One house [devoured] the other.
38. Like unto the ghost(s) of the dead[31] their faces [were covered].[32]
39. The people [lived] with bated [breath].
40. They took a message [....].[33]

(Remainder almost completely destroyed)

---

[28] Reading qa-da-nísh.

[29] Evidently forsaken by her husband because of the famine, the daughter returns to the home of her mother.

[30] All disinterestedness has ceased; everyone expects full weight and measure from the other, even the mother from the daughter, and vice versa.

[31] Reading she-dim me-te. Reading and translation uncertain.

[32] Cf. col. ii, 51, and the Gilgamesh Epic, Tablet VIII, col. ii, 17.

[33] After six years of punishment the people became quiet and were granted rest and prosperity, but after a certain period they again disturbed the peace of Enlil (cf. col. iii) and were afflicted anew.

Column ii

(Beginning wanting)

29. Above [Adad made scarce his rain];
30. Bel[ow] (the fountains) were stopped, [so that the flood did not rise at the source].
31. The fie[ld dimi]nished [its products],
32. [It turned the breast of] Nisaba. [During the nights the fields became white];
33. [The wide-open plain b]rought forth sa[lt;[34] her bosom[35] revolted],
34. [So that no plant came for]th, [no] grai[n sprouted].
35. [Disease was let loose upon the people].
36. [The womb was closed, so that it could not bring forth a child].
37. [. . . . .].
38. [When the second year arrived, ...] the supply.
39. [When the third year] arrived,
40. [The people] changed [in their ....].
41. [When the fourth year arrived, ...] their [...] were in straits.
42. [Their wide ...] became narrow.
43. [The people wandered about] in the streets [downcast].
44. [When the fifth year arrived], the daughter looks for [the entrance of] the mother;
45. (But) [the mother does not op]en her door [to the daughter].
46. [The daughter] looks upon [the balances of the mother];
47. The mother looks upon [the balances of the daughter].
48. [When the sixth year arrived, they prepared] the daughter for a meal,
49. [For food] they prepared [the child].
50. [Full were the ....]. One [house] devoured the other.
51. [Like unto the ghosts of the dead their faces] were covered.
52. [The people] lived [with bated] breath.
53. [The wise] man Atrahasis

---

[34] On this translation of idranu see Smith in Revue d'Assyriologie, XXII, 63-64. Under the influence of the drought, the ground became covered with salt.

[35] The bosom of Nisaba, whence the fields of grain derived their nourishment.

54. Turns his thoughts[36] [to Ea, his lord];
55. [He speaks] with his god.
56. [His lord, E]a, speaks with him.[37]
57. [....] the gate of his god.
58. By the river he places his bed.[38]
59. [....] the rain(?) ....

Column iii

(Beginning broken off)

1. . . . .
2. [Because of] their noise he[39] is distur[bed];
3. [Because of] their tumult he cannot catch any [sleep].[40]
4. [Enl]il held a meeting.
5. [He sa]id to the gods, his sons:
6. "Great is the noise of mankind.
7. [Because of their] noise I am disturbed;
8. [Because of th]eir [tu]mult I cannot catch any sleep.[41]
9. [....] let there be malaria.
10. [Instantaneous]ly the pestilence shall put an end to their noise!
11. [Like] a storm let it blow upon them,
12. [Sick]ness, headache, malaria, disease!"
13. [....] there was malaria.
14. [Instan]taneously the pestilence put an end to their noise.

---

[36]Lit.: His ear is opened.

[37]After the clay of the tablet was nearly dry, the scribe wrote la-shú ("there is or was nothing") on the blank space between ìt-tì-shú ("with him") and i-ta-mu ("he speaks") to indicate, for some reason, that the original from which he had copied had an uninscribed space between these two expressions. In the parallel passage, col. iii, 20, this remark is not found.

[38]Apparently for the purpose of securing rain by means of enchantment, for which he undoubtedly had the blessing of Ea, his lord. Atraḫasis evidently was successful in his efforts; but, since the people became as hilarious and tumultuous as before, they were punished again.

[39]Enlil.

[40]Lit.: [Sleep] does not catch him. Reading i-ṣa-ba-su [shi-tu] (so Smith in Revue d'Assyriologie, XXII, 67).

[41]Lit.: Sleep does not catch me.

15. [Like] a storm it blew upon them,
16. [Sic]kness, headache, malaria, disease.
17. [The wi]se man Atarḫasis
18. Turns his thoughts [to] Ea, his [lord].
19. [He s]peaks with his god;
20. [His lord], Ea, speaks with him.
21. Atarḫasis opened his mouth, saying
22. To Ea, his lord:
23. "Lord, mankind groans.
24. Your [anger(?)] consumes the land.
25. O Lord Ea, mankind groans.
26. [The anger(?)] of the gods consumes the land.
27. [....] ye have created us.
28. [Let] sickness, headache, malaria, (and) disease [be cut] off."
29. [Ea opened his mouth and] said to Atarḫasis, as he addressed him:
30. "[...]. in the land.
31. [....] pray to your goddess."
32-36. (Destroyed)[42]
37. [Enlil] held a meeting (and) said to the gods, his sons:
38. "[...]. do not place them.
39. [The people] have not become fewer, (but) are more numerous than before.
40. [Because of] their noise I am disturbed;
41. [Because of] their tumult I cannot catch any sleep.
42. Let the fig tree [be cut] off for the people.
43. [In] their bellies let vegetables be wanting.
44. Above let Adad make scarce his rain;
45. Below [let (the fountains) be] stopped, so that the flood cannot rise at the source.
46. [Let] the field diminish its products;
47. [Let] it turn the breast of Nisaba. During the nights let the fields become white;
48. Let the wide-open plain bring forth salt.

---

[42] As indicated by what follows, Atraḫasis again effected a cessation of the plague; but, since men again incurred the displeasure of Enlil, they were punished for the fourth time.

49. Let her bosom[43] revolt, that no plant may come forth, no grain may sprout.

50. Let disease be let loose upon the people.

51. Let [the womb] be closed, that it bring forth no child."

52. They cu[t off] the fig tree for the people.

53. In their bellies vegetables became wanting.

54. Above Adad made scarce his rain;

55. Below (the fountains) were stopped, so that the flood could not rise at the source.

56. The field diminished its products;

57. It turned the breast of Nisaba. During the nights the fields became white;

58. The wide-open plain brought forth salt; her bosom revolted,

59. So that no plant came forth, no grain sprouted;

60. Disease was let loose upon the people.

61. The womb was closed, so that it could not bring forth a child.

Column iv

(Beginning destroyed)

8. [....] they kis^r d her feet,

9. [Saying: "The creatress of mankind] we call thee.

10. [The lady] of all the gods be thy name!"

11. [They went] to the house of destiny,

12. [Nin]igiku, (that is,) Ea, (and) wise Mama.

13. [Fourteen w]ombs were gathered together,

14. To tread upon the clay before her.

15. [....] said Ea, as he repeatedly recited the incantation.

16. Ea caused her to recite [the incanta]tion as he sat before her.

17. [Mama recited] the incantation. After she had recited[44] her incantation,

18. [.... she] threw upon her clay.

19. [Fourteen pie]ces she pinched off; seven pieces she laid on the right.

20. Seven pieces she laid on the left; between them she placed a brick.

_____

[43]The bosom of Nisaba.

[44]Var.: completed.

21. [...]. opened its navel.
22. [.... she] then called the wise women(?),
23. [Seven a]nd seven wombs; seven created men,
24. [Seven] created women.
25. The womb(s), the creatresses of destiny,
26. They complete them, (yea), them(?);[45]
27. Them(?) they complete before her.
28. The forms of the people Mami forms.
29. In the house of the bearing one the woman in travail shall let the brick lie for seven days.
30. .... from the temple of Mah, the wise Mami.
31. They that are angry(?) let them rejoice in the house of the woman in travail.
32. As the bearing one gives birth,
33. May the mother of the child give birth by herself.[46]

(Remainder broken away)

The Deluge Account of Berossus

The latest known Babylonian deluge version is that of Berossus, a priest of Marduk at Babylon. It is taken from the history of Babylonia which he compiled from native documents and published in Greek about 275 B.C. His writings have perished, but extracts from his history have survived to our day. Of his account of the flood we have two excerpts, both of which are, in turn, based upon an excerpt made by Alexander Polyhistor (last century B.C.). The first and more important of the two reads as follows:[47]

After the death of Ardatēs,[48] his son Xisuthros reigned for 64,800 years; under him a great deluge took place; the story has

[45]The people(?) (cf. line 28).

[46]I.e., may the delivery be so easy that no assistance is required.

[47]Text in Eusebi chronicorum libri duo, ed. Alfred Schoene, Vol. I (Berlin, 1875), cols. 20-24. Translated by A. M. Harmon in Clay, op. cit., pp. 82-83; Rogers, op. cit., pp. 109-12; Ebeling in Gressmann, op. cit., pp. 200-201; and others.

[48]On column 10 of the work from which we have taken the present story, Eusebius calls this king Ōtiartēs (Ὠτιάρτης), which is a corruption of Ōpartēs (Ὠπάρτης), corresponding to the Babylonian Ubara-Tutu. Both Ardatēs and Ōpartēs may go back to a form Ōpardatēs, or the like (cf. Jacobsen, op. cit., p. 75, n. 32).

been recorded as follows: Kronos[49] appeared to him in (his) sleep and revealed (to him) that on the fifteenth of the month Daisios[50] mankind would be destroyed by a deluge. He therefore commanded (him) to set down in writing the beginning, middle, and end of all things, to bury (these writings) in Sippar,[51] the city of the sun(-god); to build a boat, and to go aboard it with his relatives and close friends; to store up in it food and drink, to put into it also living creatures, winged and four-footed, and, when all was made ready, to set sail. If asked whither he was sailing, he should say: "To the gods, in order to pray that it may be well with mankind!" He obeyed and built a boat, five stadia[52] in length and two stadia in width; all these orders he carried out and embarked with (his) wife and children and his close friends.

After the deluge had occurred, Xisuthros let go some birds as soon as it ceased; but as they found no food nor a place to alight, they returned to the ship. After certain days Xisuthros again let the birds go; these again returned to the ship, but with their feet stained with mud. But, when they were let go for the third time, they did not again return to the ship. Xisuthros concluded that land had appeared; and, unstopping a part of the seams of the ship and perceiving that the ship had grounded upon a certain mountain, he disembarked with (his) wife, (his) daughter, and the pilot; and after he had prostrated himself to the ground, had built an altar, and had sacrificed to the gods, he disappeared with those who had disembarked from the ship. Those who had remained on the ship disembarked when Xisuthros and his companions did not return, and sought him, calling (him) by name; but Xisuthros himself never appeared to them; however, a voice came from the air, commanding them to be god-fearing, as was proper; for because of his piety he had gone to dwell with the gods, and his wife and (his) daughter and the pilot had received a share in the same honor. (The voice)

---

[49]Corresponding to the Babylonian Ea.

[50]Corresponding roughly to the month of May.

[51]A town in northern Babylonia. The text has Sispara throughout.

[52]The Armenian version has "fifteen stadia." This is probably a scribal error, which may be due to the preceding date "on the fifteenth of the month Daisios" (so Paul Haupt in Beiträge zur Assyriologie, X, Heft 2 [1927], 26).

told them also that they should go back to Babylon and, as had been
decreed unto them by fate, that they should recover the writings
at Sippar and pass (them) on to men; also that the land where they
were belonged to Armenia.

When they had heard these things, they sacrificed to the gods
and went on foot[53] to Babylon. But of this ship that grounded in
Armenia some part still remains in the mountains of the Gordyaeans
in Armenia, and some get pitch from the ship by scraping (it) off,
and use it for amulets. These, then, went to Babylon, dug up the
writings at Sippar, founded many cities, erected temples, and rebuilt Babylon.

The second excerpt, which Abydenus (probably second century
A.D.) made on the basis of Polyhistor's epitome,[54] runs thus:

After him reigned others, (among them) also Sisithros,[55] to
whom Kronos foretold that on the fifteenth of Daisios there would
occur copious rains; (wherefore) he commanded (him) to hide all
available writings in Sippar, the city of the sun(-god). As soon
as Sisithros had carried out these commands, he sailed for Armenia,
and immediately the rainstorms sent by the god came upon him.[56]
The third day, after the rain had subsided, he sent forth (some)
of the birds to determine whether they could see land emerging somewhere from the water; but (the birds,) greeted by an unbounded sea
(and) at a loss where they should alight, returned to Sisithros,
and others after them (did likewise). But when upon the third trial
he succeeded—for they returned with their feet full of mud—the
gods removed him from the ken of man. But the vessel in Armenia

---

[53]Thus the Armenian version. The Greek has "by a roundabout
way" (πέριξ).

[54]See P. Schnabel, Berossos und die babylonisch-hellenistische
Literatur (Leipzig and Berlin, 1923), pp. 164 ff. Text in Eusebi
chronicorum libri duo, ed. Schoene, Vol. I, cols. 32-34. Translated by H. Usener, Die Sintfluthsagen (Bonn, 1899), p. 15, and
B. Bonkamp, Die Bibel im Lichte der Keilschriftforschung (Reckling-
hausen, 1939), pp. 131-32.

[55]Identical with Xisuthros. A few lines preceding our text,
Abydenus calls him Sisuthros.

[56]Lit.: and immediately the things from the god came upon him.
The god referred to evidently is the chief god of the pantheon, and
not Kronos (i.e., not Ea).

furnished the inhabitants with wooden amulets to ward off evil.

Ishtar's Descent to the Underworld

The myth treating of Ishtar's descent to the realm of the dead
has been transmitted to us both in Sumerian and in Semitic Babylonian. The Sumerian version is inscribed on tablets excavated at Nippur and dating from about 2000 B.C. Since the meaning of numerous
lines in the Sumerian recension is still rather uncertain and since
much of the text is repetition, we shall not publish a translation
of the Sumerian account in these pages but shall, instead, give the
reader a summary of the more salient points.[57] In brief outline,
the Sumerian story runs as follows.

For unspecified reasons, Ishtar, called Inanna on the Sumerian
tablets, forsakes heaven and earth and her seven favorite temples
in Babylonia in order to descend to the underworld. She provides
herself with all the appropriate divine decrees, dresses herself
in her queenly robes, puts on her crown or tiara, bedecks herself
with costly jewels, and is ready to enter the abode of the dead.
But fearing that her older sister and bitter enemy, Ereshkigal, the
queen of the underworld, will put her to death, Ishtar instructs
her vizier, Ninshuburra, that if after three days and three nights
she has not returned to the upper world, he is to go to the temple
Ekur in Nippur and, with tearful eyes, to plead with the great god
Enlil to restore Ishtar to life and to rescue her from the realm
of death. If Enlil refuses to come to her aid, he is to go to Ur
and to repeat his plea before Nanna, the great Sumerian moon-god.
And if Nanna refuses, he is to go to Eridu and present the same
petition to Enki, the lord of wisdom. "He knows the food of life"
and "he knows the water of life." He will surely restore Ishtar
to life.

Having taken these precautionary measures, Ishtar goes down
into the underworld. As she comes near Ereshkigal's palace of
lapis lazuli, she calls out: "Open the house, gatekeeper, open
the house! Open the house, Neti, open the house! I, all alone,
would enter!" The gatekeeper then inquires as to her identity and

---

[57]For the most recent transliteration, translation, and discussion of the Sumerian version see Kramer's study in the Proceed-
ings of the American Philosophical Society, LXXXV, No. 3 (1942),
295-314 (cf. also his Sumerian Mythology [Philadelphia, 1944],
pp. 83-96).

the reason for her coming. Ishtar answers him that she is the
Queen of Heaven and, giving a fictitious reason, tells him that
she has come to witness the funeral rites of Ereshkigal's husband,
Gugalanna, who has met with a violent death. The gatekeeper reports her presence to Ereshkigal and, upon instructions from his
mistress, leads her through the seven gates of the lower world.
But each time she passes through a gate, a part of her apparel is
taken away, in spite of her protests. After having passed through

the seventh and final gate she is brought stark naked before Ereshkigal, the queen of the underworld, and "the Anunnaki, the seven
judges" of the underworld. The Anunnaki fasten their "eyes upon
her, the eyes of death," and Ishtar dies.

After three days and three nights have passed without Ishtar's
return, Ninshuburra, in conformity with his instructions, approaches
the various gods mentioned by Ishtar with the request to restore his
mistress to life. Enlil and Nanna, as Ishtar had suspected, turn
a deaf ear to his plea. But Enki, distressed at what has happened,

comes to the rescue of Ishtar. He creates two beings called kurgarra and galatur, respectively. To the former he intrusts "the
food of life" and to the latter "the water of life," with instructions to descend to the nether world and to sprinkle this life-
giving food and water upon the dead body of Ishtar. These instructions they carry out, and Ishtar is restored to life. Ishtar then
ascends to the earth, accompanied by a host of demons, with whom
she wanders from one city to another.[58] Here the preserved portion
of the Sumerian version breaks off.

The Semitic account of Ishtar's descent to the abode of the
dead has come down to us in two recensions, the Nineveh and the
Ashur recensions.[59] The tablets of the Ninevite version were found

---

[58]Albright, in the Bulletin of the American Schools of Oriental
Research, No. 79, p. 21, n. 3, in comparing Ishtar's resurrection
with that of Christ, attaches great significance to the three-day
period mentioned in this text. But the Sumerian myth relates merely
that after three days and three nights Ninshuburra began to make the
rounds of the gods and does not indicate in any way when Ishtar actually rose from the dead. This point should not be overlooked.

[59]Text published by King in Cuneiform Texts ...., Vol. XV,
Pls. 45-48, and Ebeling in Keilschrifttexte aus Assur religiösen
Inhalts (Leipzig, 1919-23), No. 1 and p. 321. Translated by Jensen,
op. cit., pp. 80-91; S. Geller in Orientalistische Literaturzeitung,
Vol. XX (1917), cols. 41 ff.; Rogers, op. cit., pp. 121-31; Ebeling
in Gressmann, op. cit., pp. 206-10; and others.

among the ruins of Ashurbanipal's library and date from about the
middle of the seventh century B.C., while the tablet from Ashur
may be considerably older. The Semitic story of Ishtar's descent,
differing quite substantially from the Sumerian account, reads as
follows:

(Obverse)

1. To the land of no return, the land of [Ereshkigal(?)],[60]
2. Ishtar, the daughter of Sin, [turned] her attention;
3. Yea, the daughter of Sin turned [her] attention
4. To the dark house, the dwelling of Irkal[la];[61]
5. To the house from which he who enters never goes forth;
6. To the road whose path does not lead back;
7. To the house in which he who enters is bereft of li[ght];
8. Where dust is their food (and) clay their sustenance;[62]
9. (Where) they see no light (and) dwell in darkness;
10. (Where) they are clad like birds with garments of wings;
11. (Where) over door (and) bolt dust has spread.[63]
12. When Ishtar arrived at the door of the land of no return,[64]
13. She said (these) words to the doorkeeper:
14. "O doorkeeper, open the door!
15. Open the door that I may enter!
16. If thou wilt not open the door that I may enter,
17. I will smash the door (and) break the bolt;
18. I will smash the doorpost and remove the doors.
19. I will cause the dead to rise that they may eat as the living,

---

[60]Ereshkigal was the queen of the underworld.

[61]Irkalla = Ereshkigal. As indicated by the last part of this
epic, the purpose of Ishtar's descent to the nether world was to
bring back her brother, Tammuz, the dead god of vegetation. But
she was imprisoned by Ereshkigal and became herself one of the dead.

[62]If they cannot get anything else (cf. lines 31-36).

[63]The Assyrian recension adds: "[....] silence is poured out."

[64]The gate of the city in the land of no return.

20. So that the living will be more numerous than the dead."[65]
21. The doorkeeper opened his mouth and said,
22. Speaking to great Ishtar:[66]
23. "Hold on, my lady, do not tear it[67] down!
24. I will go (and) announce thy name to Queen E[reshk]igal."
25. The doorkeeper entered and said [to] Eresh[kigal]:
26. "This is it: Thy sister Ishtar ⌈is standing⌉ at [the door],
27. She who holds the great festivals, who stirs up the sub-
     terranean waters before Ea, the k[ing]."
28. When Ereshkigal heard this,
29. Her face turned yellow like unto a cut-down tamarisk;
30. Her lips turned black like unto broken-down kunînu(-reeds).
31. "What has prompted her heart (to come) to me? What has
     turned her thoughts to me?[68]
32. This is it: I am to drink water with the Anunnaki![69]
33. Instead of bread I am to eat clay; instead of beer I am to
     drink turbid water!
34. I am to weep over the men who had to leave (their) wives be-
     hind!
35. I am to weep over the maidens who were torn from the laps of
     their lovers!

---

[65]Thus the Ashur version. Ishtar threatens to restore the
dead to life and to return them to the earth, so that they may
again eat and drink as before. The number of the living would thus
be increased while the number of the dead would be correspondingly
decreased (Geller in Orientalistische Literaturzeitung, Vol. XX,
col. 48). Should the underworld be emptied of its dead, the offerings for the spirits in the lower region would cease, and Ereshkigal
and her court would have to starve. The Ninevite recension has:
"That the dead (i.e., those who have been released from the underworld) may be more numerous than the living!"

[66]Var.: to Lady Ishtar.

[67]The door.

[68]Cf. Geller in Orientalistische Literaturzeitung, Vol. XX,
col. 67, Z. 32.

[69]The administrators of justice in the underworld.

36. I am to weep over the tender infant who was snatched away before its time![70]

37. Go, doorkeeper, open the door for her;

38. Treat her in accordance with the ancient laws!"

39. The doorkeeper went (and) opened the door for her.

40. "Enter, my lady, that the underworld may greet thee with jubilation;

41. That the palace of the land of no return may rejoice before thee!"

42. The first door he made her enter, he loosened(?) the great crown on her head (and) took (it) off.

43. "Why, O doorkeeper, hast thou taken the great crown from my head?"

44. "Enter, my lady, thus are the laws of the Lady of the Underworld."[71]

45. The second door he made her enter, he loosened(?) the pendants on her ears (and) took (them) off.

46. "Why, O doorkeeper, hast thou taken the pendants from mine ears?"

47. "Enter, my lady, thus are the laws of the Lady of the Underworld."

48. The third door he made her enter, he loosened(?) the chains around her neck (and) took (them) off.

49. "Why, O doorkeeper, hast thou taken the chains from around my neck?"

50. "Enter, my lady, thus are the laws of the Lady of the Underworld."

51. The fourth door he made her enter, he loosened(?) the ornaments on her bosom (and) took (them) off.

52. "Why, O doorkeeper, hast thou taken the ornaments from my bosom?"

---

[70]Ereshkigal evidently fears that Ishtar has come to release the dead from the underworld. Should the dead be set free and be enabled to return to the land of the living, such action would result in the discontinuation of the offerings for the nether world and would mean that Ereshkigal and her court would have to eat clay instead of bread and drink turbid water instead of beer. This would indeed be sufficient reason why she should weep over the loss of the dead. That sort of thing Ereshkigal is determined to prevent.

[71]d bêlit irsitim^{tim}.

53. "Enter, my lady, thus are the laws of the Lady of the Underworld."

54. The fifth door he made her enter, he loosened(?) the girdle[72] with the birthstones on her hips (and) took (it) off.

55. "Why, O doorkeeper, hast thou taken the girdle with the birthstones from my hips?"

56. "Enter, my lady, thus are the laws of the Lady of the Underworld."

57. The sixth door he made her enter, he loosened(?) the bracelets on her hands and feet (and) took (them) off.

58. "Why, O doorkeeper, hast thou taken the bracelets from my hands and feet?"

59. "Enter, my lady, thus are the laws of the Lady of the Underworld."

60. The seventh door he made her enter, he loosened(?) the breechcloth on her body (and) took (it) off.

61. "Why, O doorkeeper, hast thou taken the breechcloth from my body?"

62. "Enter, my lady, thus are the laws of the Lady of the Underworld."

63. As soon as Ishtar had descended to the land of no return,[73]

64. Ereshkigal saw her and became enraged in her presence.

65. (And) Ishtar, without a moment's reflection, rushed at her!

66. Ereshkigal opened her mouth and said,

67. Addressing (these) words to Namtar, her vizier:

68. "Go, Namtar, lock [her] up [in] my [palace]!

69. Let loose against her sixty ma[ladies, against] Ishtar:

70. Malady of the eyes [against] her [eyes];

71. Malady of the sides ag[ainst] her [sides];

72. Malady of the feet ag[ainst] her [feet];

73. Malady of the inwards ag[ainst her inwards];

74. Malady of the head ag[ainst her head],

75. Against her altogether, again[st her whole body]!"

76. After Lady Ishtar [has descended to the land of no return],

77. Taurus non (iam) salit in vaccam, [asinus non (iam) implet

---

[72] An amulet worn to facilitate delivery.

[73] This line refers to the innermost part of the land of no return.

asinam],
78. [Vir non (iam) gravidat] puellam in via;
79. The man lay (alone) [in his chamber, the maiden lay on her side].
80. [.... l]ay [....].[74]

(Reverse)

1. The countenance of Papsukkal, the vizier of the great gods, was fallen, his face [darkened].
2. He was clad in a mournihg garment (and) wore long hair.
3. Papsukkal[75] went before Sin, his father, and we[pt],
4. [His] tears flowing before Ea, the king:
5. "Ishtar has descended to the underworld, (but) she has not come up (again).
6. Ever since Ishtar has descended to the land of no return,
7. Taurus non (iam) salit in vaccam, asinus non (iam) implet[76] asinam,
8. Vir non (iam) gravidat puellam in via;
9. The man lies (alone) in his chamber,
10. The maiden lies on her side."
11. Then Ea, the king, conceived an image in his wise heart,
12. And created Aṣûshunamir,[77] a eunuch.
13. "Come, Aṣûshunamir, set thy face toward the gate of the land of no return!
14. The seven doors of the land of no return shall be opened before thee.[78]
15. Ereshkigal shall see thee and rejoice before thee.
16. When her heart has become quiet, and her mind is glad,
17. Let her swear by the great gods.
18. (Then) lift up thy head (and) turn thy attention to the ḫalziqqu-waterskin, (saying):

---

[74]Ishtar was the goddess of love; during her absence in the realm of the dead all propagation ceased.

[75]So the Ashur tablet. The Ninevite text has: Shamash.

[76]On this translation of ú-shá-ra see B. Landsberger in Zeitschrift für Assyriologie, XLI (1933), 228.

[77]Instead of Aṣûshunamir, the Ashur version consistently has Aṣnamer.

[78]Var.: unto thee.

19. 'O Lady, let them give me the ḫalziqqu-waterskin, that I
     may drink water therefrom!'"[79]

20. When Ereshkigal heard this,

21. She smote her lap[80] and bit her finger:

22. "Thou hast expressed a desire which must not be desired!

23. Come, Aṣûshunamir, I will curse thee with a mighty curse!
     (The Ashur version has: "Come, Aṣnamer, I will decree for
thee a destiny that shall not be forgotten! A destiny will I
decree for thee that shall not be forgotten throughout eternity!")

24. The food in the gutters(?) of the city shall be thy food,

25. The sewers(?) of the city shall be thy drinking-place!

26. The shade of the wall shall be thy dwelling-place,

27. The threshold shall be thy habitation!

28. The drunken and the thirsty (alike) shall smite thy cheek!"

29. Ereshkigal opened her mouth and said,

30. Addressing (these) words to Namtar, her vizier:

31. "Go, Namtar, knock at Egalgina.[81]

32. Bedeck the thresholds with ṭaeritu-stone.[82]

33. Bring forth the Anunnaki and let (them) be seated upon golden
     throne(s).

34. Sprinkle Ishtar with the water of life and take her away
     from my presence."

35. Namtar went (and) knocked at Egalgina.

36. He bedecked the thresholds with ṭaeritu-stone.[82]

37. He brought forth the Anunnaki and let (them) be seated upon
     golden throne(s).

---

[79]It would seem that Aṣûshunamir, whose name signifies "His
going forth is brilliant," was sent to the nether world to enchant
Ereshkigal with his beauty and thus to win her favor. Thereupon
he was to make Ereshkigal swear that she would grant him anything
he desired of her. Having accomplished this, he was to ask for the
ḫalziqqu-waterskin, which obviously contained "the water of life."
Once in possession of this water, Aṣûshunamir apparently was to
free Ishtar by sprinkling some of this water upon her (cf. lines
34 and 38 and the Sumerian version). Because of her oath, Ereshkigal was forced to comply, in the final analysis, with Aṣûshunamir'
request aiming at the release of Ishtar; but this release she granted
through Namtar, her vizier, and not by letting Aṣûshunamir sprinkle
Ishtar with the water of life.

[80]Var.: thigh.

[81]The palace of justice and the dwelling of the Anunnaki.

[82]Var.: of ṭaeritu-stone.

38. He sprinkled Ishtar with the water of life and took her
away from her presence.

(The Ashur version adds: "[....] 'Go, Namtar, [ta]ke [Ishtar]
away. [But i]f she does not pa[y thee] her ransom price, [br]ing
her back here.'[83] Namtar took her away and [....].")

39. He caused her to go out through the first door and returned
to her the breechcloth of her body.

40. He caused her to go out through the second door and returned
to her the bracelets of her hands and feet.

41. He caused her to go out through the third door and returned
to her the girdle with the birthstones for her hips.

42. He caused her to go out through the fourth door and returned
to her the ornaments of her bosom.

43. He caused her to go out through the fifth door and returned
to her the chains from around her neck.

44. He caused her to go out through the sixth door and returned
to her the pendants from her ears.

45. He caused her to go out through the seventh door and returned
to her the great crown from her head.

46. "If she does not pay thee her ransom price," (Ereshkigal had
said,) "bring [her] back here.[84]

47. As for Tammuz, [her] youthful husband,[85]

48. Wash (him) with pure water (and) anoint (him) with precious
oil.

49. Clothe him with a red garment (and) let him play upon the
flute of lapis lazuli [....].

50. Let the courtesans put his mind[86] at ease(?)."[87]

---

[83] In the Ninevite recension this line follows after line 45.

[84] That Ishtar paid her ransom price and was released is clear
from lines 39-45. In the Sumerian version it is expressly stated
that Ishtar ascended from the nether world.

[85] See the note on Tablet VI:46 of the Gilgamesh Epic.

[86] The Ashur text has [ka-bít-ti]-i-shu. The corresponding
expression in the Ninevite recension ought therefore probably to
be read kab-ta-a[s-su].

[87] Tammuz, as the personification of vegetation, which dies
in the burning summer heat and rises to new life with the arrival
of spring, was believed to descend to the underworld with the dying
of vegetation and to rise again with the coming of spring. He, too,
is now released and joyfully ascends to the upper world.

51. [When] Belili[88] pu[t on] her jewelry[89] for him,
52. And [her] lap was filled with "eye[ston]es,"[90]
53. She heard the (joyful) noise of her brother; Belili smote
     (her breast and) [dropped(?)] her jewelry,
54. The "eyestones" which had filled [her lap]:
55. "My only brother, bring no woe upon me!
56. On the day that Tammuz greets me with jubilation(?), that
     with him the flute of lapis lazuli (and) the ring[91] of
     carnelian greet me with jubilation(?),
57. (And) that with him (even) the wailing-men and the wailing-
     women greet me with jubilation(?),
58. Let the dead come up and smell the incense!"[92]
                        (Colophon:)
59. Palace of Ashurbanipal, king of the world, king of Assyria,
60. Whom Nabû a[nd Tashmêtum have given a wide understanding].

---

[88]In O. Schroeder, Keilschrifttexte aus Assur verschiedenen
Inhalts (Leipzig, 1920), No. 50, col. iv, 5, Belili is equated with
the goddess Sigzaginna, who in Cuneiform Texts ...., Vol. XXIV
(London, 1908), Pl. 6:16, is equated with Bêlit-ilê. And this god-
dess, according to ibid., Pls. 1:23 and 29; 20:15 and 20, and the
Gilgamesh Epic, Tablet XI:116-17, is, in turn, identical with Ishtar.
It would therefore seem that in line 51 Belili is merely another
name for Ishtar. This would yield very good sense.

[89]Lit.: her treasure.

[90]Precious stones of some kind.

[91]A tambourine inlaid with carnelian?

[92]The meaning of the last part of this story is still uncertain. Perhaps we may assume that the Babylonians and Assyrians
conceived the situation to have been as follows: While Ishtar arrayed herself in costly attire, she heard the joyful noise of the
returning Tammuz and his company. The arrival of her brother filled
Ishtar with such excitement that she feared some ill might come to
her, or she may have feared that some ill might befall him, Tammuz
thus becoming in either case the unintentional cause of her distress.
And when she saw how everything round about her broke forth in jubilation at the return of Tammuz, her brother, she expressed the wish
that also the shades of the nether world might come up and likewise
participate in this glorious celebration (cf. M. Witzel in
Orientalia, I [new ser., 1932], 83 ff.).

Nergal and Ereshkigal[93]

This myth has survived to us on two fragments uncovered in 1887 at Tell El-Amarna, a village in Upper Egypt, where it, together with the Adapa legend, served as a Babylonian school text. Of these pieces, fragment No. I is in the British Museum, while fragment No. II is in the Berlin Museum. Both belong to the same tablet and date from the fourteenth century B.C. The myth relates how Nergal, the god of disease and death, with the help of fourteen plague demons, overpowered Ereshkigal, the queen of the underworld, and subsequently became her husband and the king of the underworld.

Fragment No. I
(Obverse)

1. When the gods prepared a feast,
2. They sent a messenger
3. To their sister Ereshkigal, (saying):
4. "Even if we should descend to thee,
5. Thou wouldest not ascend to us.[94]
6. (Therefore) send hither that someone may get thy meal."
7. So [Ere]shkigal sent Namtâru, her vizier.
8. N[amt]âru ascended [to] high heaven
9. (And) ente[red the place where] the gods [were si]tting.
10. [They arose and greeted] Namtâru,
11. The messenger of their great [sister].

The next few lines are almost completely destroyed. However, from the subsequent passages the thread of the narrative can be restored as follows. When Namtâru, or Namtar, entered the assembly of the gods, all arose and greeted the messenger and representative of the queen of the underworld, but Nergal remained seated. This insult on the part of Nergal, Namtâru reported to his mistress, who naturally interpreted it as an insult to her and therefore sent Namtâru back to the gods demanding that Nergal be delivered up

---

[93] Text of fragment No. I published by C. Bezold and E. A. Wallis Budge, The Tell El-Amarna Tablets in the British Museum (London, 1892), No. 82; and of fragment No. II by Schroeder in Vorderasiatische Schriftdenkmäler, Vol. XII (Leipzig, 1915), No. 195. Translated by J. A. Knudtzon, Die El-Amarna-Tafeln (Leipzig, 1915), Part I, pp. 969-75; Rogers, op. cit., pp. 131-35; Ebeling in Gressmann, op. cit., pp. 210-12; and others.

[94] Ereshkigal cannot leave her post in the nether world.

to her so that she might put him to death.

Fragment No. II

26. Saying: "The go[d who] did not rise [before] my [mess]enger,
27. Bring to me that I may kill him!"
28. Namtâru went to speak to the gods.
29. The gods called him to speak with him......
30. "Behold, the god who did not rise before thee,
31. Take him before thy lady."
32. Namtâru counted them, and a god was missing(?) in the rear(?).
33. "The god who did not rise before me is not here!"
34. [....] Namtâru goes [and makes] his [re]port.
35. "[.... I counted] them,
36. [And a go]d [was missing(?)] in the rear(?).
37. [The god who did not rise before me] was not there."

Here again follow a number of badly mutilated lines. Eresh-kigal sent to the gods once more, with the inexorable demand that Nergal be extradited. When the text again becomes connected, some-one is told:

43. "Take (him) to Ereshkigal!" He[95] wee[ps and goes]
44. Before Ea, his father, (saying): "[Ereshkigal] is trying to catch me.[96]
45. She does not want me to live."[97] "Be not af[raid]![98]
46. I will give thee seven and (yet) seven de[mons(?)]
47. To go with thee: [...., Mutabriqu],[99]
48. Sharabdû, [Râbiṣu, Ṭirid, Idibtu],
49. Be[nnu, Ṣidanu, Miqit, Bêlupri],
50. Ummu, (and) [Lîbu. These fourteen demons(?) shall go]
51. With thee." [When Nergal arrives at the g]ate of
52. Ereshkigal, he calls: "Gatekeep[er! Open] thy gate!

---

[95]Nergal.

[96]Reading 1-ba-ra-an-[ni].

[97]Regarding ba-la-ṭa-an-ni as an unelided I,1 permansive form, even though this explanation is not entirely free from objections.

[98]Ea is speaking.

[99]The names of the first three demons are lost.

53. Loosen the latchstring[100] that I may enter! Before thy lady
54. Ereshkigal I am sent." The gatekeeper went
55. And said to Namtâru: "A god is standing at the entrance of
    the gate.
56. Come and inspect him, that he may enter." Namtâru wen[t out];
57. And when he saw him, he said rejoicing[101] ..[....]
58. To his [la]dy: "My lady, [it is the god w]ho [disappe]ared
59. In (one of the) prev[ious] months and did not rise [before]
    me!"
60. "Bring him in! [When he] comes in I will kill [him]!"
61. Namtâru went out [and said to Nergal]: "Enter, my lord,
62. Into the house of thy sister; [joyful(?) be] thy departure."
63. Nergal [answered and said]: "May thy heart rejoice in me."
                   (Remainder destroyed)

                      Fragment No. I
                        (Reverse)

                   (Beginning broken away)
20. [....] he[102] stationed at the third gate, Mutabriqu at the
    fourth,
21. [Shar]abdû at the fifth, Râbiṣu at the sixth, Ṭirid
22. At the seventh, Idibtu at the eighth, Bennu
23. At the ninth, Ṣîdanu at the tenth, Miqit
24. At the eleventh, Bêlupri at the twelfth,
25. Ummu at the thirteenth, (and) Lîbu at the fourteenth.
26. In the court he cut down her ....
27. To Namtâru, his warrior,[103] he gave the command: "Let the
    gates
28. Be opened! Now I will run for you!"
29. Within the house he seized Ereshkigal
30. By the hair and dragged her down from the throne
31. To the ground, to cut off her head.

_____

[100]By which doors were closed. Reading up-pí (cf. Jensen,
op. cit., pp. 391 ff., and Bezold, Babylonisch-assyrisches Glossar
[Heidelberg, 1926], p. 55).

[101]Reading ḫa-a-di-ish(!).

[102]Nergal.

[103]It would seem that Namtâru went over to the side of Nergal
(cf. Jensen, op. cit., p. 393).

32. "Do not kill me, my brother! I would speak a word with thee."
33. Nergal listened to her, and his hands relaxed, while she
    wept (and) sobbed.
34. "Thou shalt be my husband, and I will be thy wife. I will
    let thee seize
35. Sovereignty over the wide underworld. I will place the
    tablet
36. Of wisdom in thy hand. Thou shalt be lord,
37. I will be lady." When Nergal heard this her speech,
38. He took her, kissed her, and wiped away her tears, (saying):
39. "Whatever thou hast desired of me from distant months,
40. Shall now be so."

A Prince's Vision of the Underworld[104]

A large tablet from Ashur, dating back to about the middle
of the seventh century B.C. and consisting of seventy-five long
lines, contains a unique story of a prince's vision of the underworld. While the reverse is in a comparatively good state of preservation, the obverse is, unfortunately, mutilated so severely that
only a few sentences can be read with some confidence.

The central figure of the story is an Assyrian prince by the
name of Kummaya, probably a pseudonym. For an unknown reason, but
apparently in consequence of some calamity, this prince desires to
see the underworld, to which end he sacrifices to Ereshkigal and
offers up prayers to her and to Nergal. His request is at last
granted, and, in a dream, Kummaya is given a view of the lower
world. The vision which he thus receives and the effect which it
has on him and on an unnamed scribe are recorded on the reverse of
the tablet, reading as follows.

1. [Kum]maya lay down to sleep and saw a night-vision. In his
   dream ʃhe descended to the underworld(?) ....ʃ. "I saw its
   terrifying splendor. [....].
2. [Na]mtar, the vizier of the underworld, the creator of decrees,
   I saw; a man stood before him; the hair of his head he[105]

---

[104]Text published in photographic reproductions, in transliteration and translation, together with a discussion, by W. von Soden
in Zeitschrift für Assyriologie, XLIII (1936), 1-31.

[105]Namtar.

held in his left, (while) in his right [he held] a sword
[....].

3. [Na]mtartu, (his) consort(?), had the head of a kurîbu,
    (her) hands (and) feet were (those) of a human being. The
    death-god had the head of a serpent-dragon, his hands were
    (those) of men, his feet were (those) of [...].

4. The evil [Shê]du (had) the head (and) the hands of men, he
    wore a tiara (and had) the feet of a ...-bird; his left foot
    was planted on a crocodile(?). Alluḫappu (had) the head of
    a lion, (his) four hands (and his) feet were (those) of men.

5. Mukîl-rêsh-limuttí[106] (had) the head of a bird, his wings
    were spread, (and) he flew to and fro; (his) hands (and)
    feet were (those) of men. Ḫumuṭṭabal, the boatman of the
    underworld, (had) the head of Zû, (his) four hands (and his)
    fe[et were (those) of men].

6. ⌈...⌉ (had) the head of an ox, (his) four hands (and his)
    feet were (those) of men. The evil Utukku had the head of
    a lion, (his) hands (and) feet were (those) of Zû. Shulak
    was a normal lion, (but) he sto[od] on his two hind legs.

7. [Mam]metu (had) the head of a goat, (her) hands (and) feet
    were (those) of men. Nedu, the gatekeeper of the underworld,
    (had) the head of a lion, (his) hands were (those) of men,
    (his) feet (those) of a bird. Mimma-limnu (had) two heads;
    one was the head of a lion, the other the head of [...].

8. ⌈...⌉ (had) three feet; the two fore(feet) were (those) of
    a bird, the hind (foot that) of an ox; he was decked with
    terrifying splendor. (Of) two gods—I do not know their
    names—the one (had) the head, hands, (and) feet of Zû, in
    his left the hand[s ....];

9. The second had a human head, he wore a tiara, in his right
    hand he carried a club, in his left ⌈....⌉. In all(?) there
    were fifteen gods; (when) I saw them, I worshiped [them].

10. (Moreover, there was) a unique man; his body was black as
    pitch, his face was like that of Zû, he was clad with a red
    garment, in his left he carried a bow, in his right he he[ld]
    a sword, (and his) left ⌈foot was planted(?) on a serpent(?)⌉.

11. When I lifted up mine eyes, warlike Nergal sat on (his) royal
    throne, he wore a royal tiara, in his two hands he held two

---

[106] "The Supporter of Evil."

terrifying ...-weapons, each (having) two heads ⌈....⌉.

12. ⌈....⌉; from his arms(?) issued lightning; the Anunnaki, the great gods, stood bowed at (his) right (and) at (his) left, ⌈....⌉.

13. The underworld was full of terror; before the prince lay deep si[le]nce(?); he[107] took me [by] the locks of my forehead and pulled me into his presence.

14. [When I] looked at him, my legs trembled, his terrifying splendor overpowered me; I kissed the feet of his [great] divinity and prostrated myself; (when) I stood up, he looked at me and shook hi[s he]ad [at me].

15. He shouted mightily at me and roared furiously at me, like a ho[wli]ng storm; (his) scepter, such as befits his divinity, (and) which is full of terror, like a viper,

16. He dragged [toward] me to kill [me].[108] (But) Ishum, his counselor, the intercessor, who spares life, who loves truth, and so (forth), said: 'Do not kill the man, thou m[ight]y king of the underworld!

17. [Spare him(?)], that the inhabitants of all the earth may forever hear of thy greatness!' The heart of the all-powerful, the almighty, who overthrows the wicked, he quieted like clear well-water.

18. (Thereupon) Nergal [made] this statement: 'Why hast thou molested(?) my beloved wife, the queen of the underworld?

19. [At] her exalted, unalterable command, Biblu, the butcher of the underworld, shall deliver thee to the gatekeeper Lugalsula, that he may lead [thee] out through the gate of Ishtar (and) Aya.

20. Forget and forsake me not! Then I will not impose the death sentence (upon thee). (But) at the command of Shamash, shall distress, acts of violence, and insurrection

21. Come upon thee together ⌈....⌉, so that, because of their terrible noise, sleep may not spread over thee.

22. This [spirit of the dead][109] whom thou hast seen in the underworld is (the spirit of) the great shepherd to whom my father, [...], the king of the gods, granted every desire

---

[107] Nergal.

[108] Because of Kummaya's arrogant desire to see the underworld.

[109] Referring perhaps to the figure mentioned in line 10.

of his heart.

23. [It is the spirit of him w]ho from sunrise to sunset carried(?) all the lands like a load and ruled over everything;

24. [The spirit of him for whom] Ashur, in view of his priesthood, [dec]reed the celebration of the holy New Year's festival in the field of the garden of plenty, the image of Lebanon ⌈....⌉ forever,

25. And whose body Yabru, Ḫumba, (and) Naprushu protected, whose seed they preserved, (and) whose army (and) camp they delivered, so that no warrior (fighting from) a chariot(?) came nigh unto him in battle.

26. [But h]e, thy begetter, the gi[gan]tic(?), the one experienced in things, the one with a broad understanding, a wide (and) intelligent heart, who can see through the laws of the earth,

27. [Who(?)] closed his ear at his speech,[110] who has desecrated holy things (and) has crushed consecrated things under foot, ye[111] will the terrifying splendor of his majesty quickly overthrow altogether(?).[112]

28. May this word be implanted in your hearts as a thorn! Ascend to the upper world, until I shall think of thee (again)!' As he (thus) spoke to me,

29. I awoke." And like a man who has shed blood, who wanders about alone among the canebrakes, whom the bailiff has seized, that his heart pounds;

30. Vel sicut aper iuvenilis maturitatem nuper assecutus qui saluit in coniugem suam (et) cuius libido denuo excitatur, emittebat "argillam" per os et anum suum.

31. He[113] uttered a loud lamentation,[114] crying, "Woe, my heart!" Like an arrow he flew into the street and scooped up into his mouth the dust on the street (and) the market-place, as he continued to call with a loud voice, "Woe! al[as]!

---

[110] Referring to the word of some deity, perhaps Ashur (cf. line 24), the head of the Assyrian pantheon.

[111] Kummaya and his royal father.

[112] If they will not mend their ways (cf. line 20).

[113] The prince.

[114] Reading si-pit-tu (see von Soden in Zeitschrift für Assyriologie, XLIV [1938], 29).

32. Why hast thou decreed this for me?" (Thus) he called out
    before the men of Assyria (and) praised, grief-stricken,
    the might of Nergal (and) Ereshkigal, who had come to the
    aid of this very prince.

33. As for the scribe who had previously accepted bribe(s), (and)
    who had entered upon the post of his father, he took ⌈the
    words⌉ of praise to heart,

34. Because of the clever understanding which Ea had granted him,
    and thus he spoke in his heart: "In order that the evil
    curses may not draw nigh unto me, (or) press upon me,

35. I will at all times do the things [that Nergal(?)][115] has
    commanded!" He went and told (it) to the palace, saying:
    "This shall be my propitiation."

---

[115] Cf. line 20. Perhaps we ought to supply the name of
Ashur (cf. lines 24 and 27).

CHAPTER III

DEATH AND THE AFTERLIFE

Scholars on both sides of the Atlantic have long recognized
that the stories translated in the previous chapters contain numerous parallels to the Old Testament. Ever since the recognition
of this undeniable fact there have been those who have sought to
prove that the Old Testament is indebted to Mesopotamian sources,
while others have denied such indebtedness. Although this point
is no longer debated with the fervor of a few decades ago, it is
by no means a dead issue.

The following chapters will be devoted to a study of the parallels between the Mesopotamian and Old Testament materials on the
two main subjects treated in the texts presented on the preceding
pages. We shall endeavor to make a careful examination of the deluge versions of the Babylonians and Assyrians, on the one hand, and
the Hebrews, on the other, and of the beliefs current among these
peoples concerning death and the life beyond the grave, as attested
by the inscriptions of Mesopotamia and the records of the Old Testament as well as by the anepigraphic or uninscribed material brought
to light from the mounds of Palestine and the Tigro-Euphrates region.
Our purpose in undertaking this investigation will be to ascertain
how the Hebrew and Mesopotamian ideas on these two subjects compare
and to determine, if possible, the genetic or historical relationship between the concepts expressed by the materials from Palestine
and the Tigro-Euphrates Valley. Since the central theme of the
Gilgamesh Epic, which fills by far the greater part of the first
half of this book, is the problem of death, as we have observed,
we shall begin with that subject.

The Origin and Nature of Death

The destructive power of death, according to Babylonian and
Assyrian speculations, extended not only over mankind and over
plant and animal life but even over the gods. While the prover-
bially immortal gods could not die a natural death, they could
perish through violence. Apsû and Mummu were killed by Ea; Tiˀâmat
lost her life in combat with Marduk; Kingu and the Lamga deities

137

were slaughtered for the purpose of creating mankind; Ereshkigal's
husband Gugalanna met with a violent death; youthful Tammuz in some
way lost his life through Ishtar's fault;[1] and Ishtar descended to
the underworld alive but was deprived of life in that dark and
gloomy hollow.

In the realm of the gods, death existed even prior to the
creation of the universe, as we can see from the episodes about
Apsû, Mummu, and Ti'âmat. From Enûma elish, Tablet VI:120, we
learn, moreover, that the death-god, called by the Sumerian name
Uggae, already existed and ruled before the creation of man. As for
death among humankind, it was not attributed to some fall into sin
on the part of man. On the contrary, according to the main Babylonian creation story, man was formed with the blood of wicked Kingu
and therefore was evil from the very beginning of his existence.[2]
Furthermore, we read in the Babylonian Theodicy: "Narru,[3] king from
of old, the creator of mankind; gigantic Zulummar,[4] who pinched off
their clay;[5] and lady Mama, the queen, who fashioned them, have
presented to mankind perverse speech, lies and untruth they presented to them forever."[6] Death was the result of man's natural
constitution; it was one of the inexorable laws of nature, a law
divinely ordained at the time of man's creation. Gilgamesh was
told by Siduri, the divine barmaid: "When the gods created mankind, they allotted death to mankind, (but) life they retained in
their keeping."[7]

Death was not conceived as the absolute end of life or as
effecting the complete annihilation of conscious vitality. Rather,
it meant the separation of body and spirit, the decay of the former
and the transfer of the latter from one mode of life or existence
to another; while the body was laid to rest in the ground, the

---

[1]The Gilgamesh Epic, Tablet VI:46-47.

[2]Enûma elish, Tablet VI.

[3]I.e., Enlil.

[4]I.e., Ea.

[5]The clay out of which mankind was made.

[6]See B. Landsberger in Zeitschrift für Assyriologie, XLIII
(1936), 70-71.

[7]Tablet X, col. iii, 3-5 (Old Babylonian version).

spirit descended to the underworld to sojourn there throughout eternity. The evidence on this point is simply overwhelming, as we shall see in connection with the Mesopotamian burial customs. Here we shall call attention to just one brief passage. An Assyrian king declares with reference to the burial of his father: "Vessels of gold (and) silver (and) all the appurtenances of the grave, his royal ornaments which he loves, I displayed before Shamash and placed (them) in the grave with the father my begetter."[8] It is to be noted that the king uses the present tense; he says sha irammu ("which he loves"), not sha irâmu ("which he loved"). The obvious and natural deduction is that the king, though dead, lives on.

However, this separation was not so complete as would be expected, for we shall observe that the rest and comfort of the spirit was largely conditioned by the care which the body received, for which reason the spirit at all times maintained a vital interest in the body and wreaked vengeance on the survivors if they failed to accord it proper burial or if the repose of the mortal remains was disturbed.

Through sin, death could be hastened and life could be shortened. "He who does not fear his god" is broken "like a reed."[9] An inscription by Tiglath Pileser I closes with the following curse pronounced upon the future ruler who should dare to destroy the records which the Assyrian monarch had made to the glory of the gods: "(The king) who will destroy my stelae and my foundation records, (or) will overturn (them), (or) cast (them) into the water, (or) burn (them) with fire, (or) cover (them) with earth, (or) will secretly deposit (them) in the house of taboo, at a place which no one is permitted to see,[10] (or) will blot out my name which is written (thereon) and will inscribe his (own) name (in place thereof), or will devise any other evil (scheme) to put an obstacle in the way of my stelae—may Anu and Adad, the great gods, my lords, look upon him in anger and curse him with an evil curse! May they overthrow his regime, up-

---

[8]Erich Ebeling, Tod und Leben nach den Vorstellungen der Babylonier (Berlin and Leipzig, 1931), p. 57.

[9]R. Campbell Thompson in Cuneiform Texts from Babylonian Tablets, etc., in the British Museum, Vol. XVII (London, 1903), Pl. 19:6.

[10]Landsberger in Zeitschrift für Assyriologie, XLI (1933), 218-20.

root the foundation of his royal throne, (and) destroy his lordly
offspring! May they break his weapons to pieces, bring defeat upon his army, (and) set him in bonds before his enemies! May Adad
blast his land with a destructive bolt (and) bring hunger, famine,
want, (and) blood(shed) upon his land! May he not let him live
one single day, (but) may he destroy (both) his name (and) his seed
in the land!"[11]

Conversely, through fear of the gods, through sacrifice, the
building of a temple, the making of an image, or other deeds of
piety, the hour of death could be postponed and life could be
lengthened. As an old saying has it, "The fear (of the gods) be-
gets favor; sacrifice increases life.....He who fears the Anunnaki lengthens [his days]."[12] Gula, the goddess of healing, is
called "the preserver of the life of him who fears her."[13]
Nabonidus prays to Sin, the moon-god: "Me, Nabonidus, king of
Babylon, preserve from sinning against thy great divinity, and
grant me, as a gift, life to distant days. And in the heart of
Belshazzar, (my) first-born son, the offspring of my loins, establish the fear of thy great divinity, that he may commit no sin,
that he be sated with abundant life."[14] Sargon of Assyria states:
"For the gift of health, (for) length of days, [and the sta]bility
of my reign, I prostrated myself in adoration."[15] Tiglath Pileser
I says of his great-grandfather, Ashurdân I, that the deeds of his
hands and the offering of his gifts "were well-pleasing to the
great gods," wherefore he "attained to gray hair and a ripe old
age."[16] Entemena, prince of Lagash, built a shrine for Enlil and

---

[11]E. A. Wallis Budge and L. W. King, Annals of the Kings of
Assyria (London, 1902), pp. 106-8.

[12]King in Cuneiform Texts ...., Vol. XIII (London, 1901),
Pl. 30:19-23; similarly R. F. Harper, Assyrian and Babylonian
Letters (Chicago and London, 1892-1914), No. 614, rev. 8-9.

[13]Ebeling, Keilschrifttexte aus Assur religiösen Inhalts
(Leipzig, 1919-23), No. 73:26.

[14]Sir H. C. Rawlinson, The Cuneiform Inscriptions of Western
Asia, Vol. I (London, 1861), Pl. 68, col. ii, 19-31.

[15]Hugo Winckler, Die Keilschrifttexte Sargons, Vol. II
(Leipzig, 1889), Pl. 36:173-74.

[16]Budge and King, op. cit., p. 94:49-54.

presented him with a statue made in the god's likeness. Confident
that Enlil, in view of these services, would be favorably disposed
toward him, he expressed the wish that his tutelary god might "forever prostrate himself before Enlil, (praying) for the life of
Entemena."[17] Sennacherib made a drum of burnished copper and dedicated it to the service of Ashur "for the lengthening of his days,
the good of his heart, (and) the stability of [his] reign."[18]
These few examples could easily be multiplied.

Although life can thus be prolonged, no one can actually escape death. Even a superman like Gilgamesh had to experience this
bitter truth. The day will come when "the unsparing death"[19] will
overtake even the most pious of men, and that perhaps with unexpected suddenness; for it happens that "he who was (still) alive
in the evening is dead by morning."[20] The only human beings who
are said to have escaped death, thus forming an exception to the
rule, were Utnapishtim, his wife, his daughter, and the boatman
of the Babylonian ark. To these immortals, Heinrich Zimmern,[21]
followed by Bruno Meissner,[22] wanted to add the Sumerian king
Enmeduranna or Enmeduranki, of Sippar,[23] of whom it is said on a
ritual tablet from Assyria that he was summoned into the presence
of certain gods. But the context seems to indicate quite plainly
that Enmeduranki was called into the assembly of the gods only
temporarily, to teach him the mysteries of the bârû-priests, and
that he then rejoined the company of his fellow-men and transmitted
these divine mysteries to them. The purpose of this legend undoubtedly is to trace the origin of the office of the bârû-priest.
In a sense it is comparable to II Cor. 12:2-4, relating that

---

[17]C. J. Gadd and L. Legrain, Ur Excavations: Texts, Vol. I:
Royal Inscriptions, Plates (1928), No. 1, cols. 1-iv.

[18]J. A. Craig, Assyrian and Babylonian Religious Texts, Vol.
I (Leipzig, 1895), Pl. 83.

[19]Leopold Messerschmidt, Keilschrifttexte aus Assur historischen
Inhalts, Vol. I (Leipzig, 1911), No. 13, col. 1, 14-15.

[20]Rawlinson, op. cit., Vol. IV (London, 1891), Pl. 60*, C, 19.

[21]Beiträge zur Kenntnis der babylonischen Religion (Leipzig,
1901), pp. 116 ff.

[22]Babylonien und Assyrien, II (Heidelberg, 1925), 149.

[23]Cf. Thorkild Jacobsen, The Sumerian King List (Chicago,
1939), pp. 74-75.

a certain man was "caught up to the third heaven," where he heard
words which no man can utter; and in another sense it may be compared to the well-known legend of Oannes, and the six other fish-
and manlike beings which, according to Berossus, rose from the
waters of the Persian Gulf and instructed the Babylonians in the
arts and sciences and all other useful knowledge.

In striking contrast to Babylonian and Assyrian speculation,
the God of the Old Testament cannot die; he is from everlasting
to everlasting (Ps. 90:2). Heaven and earth will pass away, but
he will endure and his years will have no end (Ps. 102:26-28).[24]
But "all flesh is grass, and all its beauty is like the flower of
the field; the grass withers, the flower fades" (Isa. 40:6-7).
Like grass, man flourishes for a brief moment and then is cut off
(Pss. 90:5-10; 103:15). "Man, that is born of woman, is of few
days and full of trouble. Like a flower he comes forth and is
withered; he flees like the shadow and does not endure" (Job 14:
1-2).

This sad condition of man is due to sin, which the first
human pair brought into the world by eating of the tree of the
knowledge of good and evil. Adam was warned: "On the day that
thou eatest thereof thou shalt surely die" (Gen. 2:17). And after
he had eaten of the forbidden fruit, he was told by his Creator:
"Because thou hast hearkened unto the voice of thy wife and hast
eaten of the tree ...., to dust thou shalt return" (3:17-19). As
man came from the hands of his Maker, he was holy and therefore
free from sin, otherwise God would not have pronounced him "very
good" (1:31); much less would he have emphasized the verdict by
the solemn introduction "behold!" Man, according to Gen. 2:16-17,
clearly had the power to obey God's command to abstain from eating
of the tree of the knowledge of good and evil; he was not under
any necessity to sin. He had the power to obey and the power to
disobey. Had he observed the divine ordinance, he would, to judge
from what we learn about his state of immortality, have attained
to the state of absolute holiness, so that he could not have sinned
anymore. But he chose to sin and give up his integrity. And, to-

---

[24]All Old Testament passages are cited according to the Hebrew
text. For this reason the verse numbers of the Psalms referred to
in this chapter do not always coincide with those of the English
translation, which frequently falls short by one number, since it
does not count the superscription.

gether with that, he gave up his freedom from death. The presence
of the tree of life in the Garden of Eden shows that man was intended from the beginning to "live forever."[25] But through sin he for-
feited this privilege and at the very moment of his transgression
entered upon the road of death. Man's state before the fall was not
one of absolute immortality, or of absolute freedom from death, in
which sense God and the angels are immortal, but rather one of relative or conditional immortality. This could have been turned into
absolute immortality by man's eating of the tree of life, which
had the power, naturally bestowed upon it by its Creator (2:9), to
impart imperishable physical life (3:22). But from this, he was
prevented after the fall by being banished from the garden, since
the acquisition of imperishability by sinful man would have en-
tailed his continuance in sin forever and would have precluded the
possibility of his renewal or restoration. Contrary to F. Schwal-
ly,[26] Gen. 3:19 does not attribute the cause of death to the original composition of the human body, so that man would ultimately
have died anyway, but states merely one of the consequences of
death: Since the human body was formed from the dust of the earth,
it shall, upon death, be resolved to earth again. Nowhere in the
Old Testament is death regarded as a part of man's God-given constitution, or as the natural end of life. Nor is it indicated anywhere that death already existed before sin but became a punishment
through sin. Pss. 49:8-11 and 89:49 and Eccles. 3:19 prove nothing
at all as to man's condition before the fall.

Death consists in the separation of body and soul, or body and
spirit. It is said of Rachel that when she died her soul departed
(Gen. 35:18). Elijah, praying for the life of the widow's son,
cried: "O Lord, my God, I pray thee, make the soul of this child
return into him" (I Kings 17:21). Disappointed and downhearted,
Jonah asked the Lord: "Now, therefore, O Lord, take my soul away
from me, I pray thee; for it is better for me to die than to live"
(Jonah 4:3). And the Preacher declares: "The dust returns to the
earth as it was, and the spirit returns to God who gave it" (Eccles.
12:7 [cf. Pss. 104:29; 146:4]).

---

[25] I cannot concur in the view of those who hold that the original narrative spoke of only one tree, viz., the tree of the knowledge of good and evil. But to take up that question now would lead
us beyond the scope of this work.

[26] Das Leben nach dem Tode (Giessen, 1892), p. 83.

The separation of body and spirit is frequently described as
a lying-down with the fathers. Considering the interest attach-
ing to this phrase and considering also the strongly divergent views
which have been expressed with regard to it, we shall examine it
in some detail. The words "to lie down with one's fathers," or
"to sleep with one's fathers," as the expression is usually rendered, are applied principally to the Hebrew kings, both the pious
and the wicked (cf., e.g., I Kings 2:10; II Kings 20:21; I Kings
14:20; 22:40). Over and over we read that King So-and-so "lay
down with his fathers." Originally the phrase probably meant to
rest in the burial place of the fathers. Thus it may possibly be
used in Gen. 47:29-30. This passage can be rendered: "Bury me not,
I pray thee, in Egypt; but I will lie with my fathers, and do thou
carry me out of Egypt and bury me in their burial place," or: "Bury
me not, I pray thee, in Egypt; but when I sleep with my fathers, do
thou carry me out of Egypt" etc.[27] But in all other cases the expression clearly means "to go the way of all the earth" (Josh. 23:
14; I Kings 2:2), i.e., to die.[28] This is borne out by the following considerations.

In the first place, some of the persons to whom the words under
discussion are applied were not laid to rest in the burial places
of their fathers. Moses died on the mountain of Nebo, in the land
of Moab, and the Lord buried him there, and "no man knows his sepulcher unto this day" (Deut. 34:1-6). David was buried in Zion,
the city of David (I Kings 2:10 [cf. 8:1]). Concerning Ahaz it is
stated that, although they buried him in Jerusalem, "they brought
him not into the sepulchers of the kings of Israel" (II Chron. 28:
27). And Manasseh, the son of Hezekiah, was interred not in the
burial place of his royal ancestors but "in the garden of his
house, in the garden of Uzza" (II Kings 21:18). Yet all four,
Moses (cf. Deut. 31:16), David, Ahaz, and Manasseh, "lay down with

---

[27]Thus, e.g., S. R. Driver, The Book of Genesis (New York and
London, 1904), p. 375.

[28]The same conclusion has been reached by Wilhelm Gesenius,
Hebräisches und aramäisches Handwörterbuch über das Alte Testament
(Leipzig, 1915), p. 825, and Eduard König, Hebräisches und
aramäisches Wörterbuch zum Alten Testament (Leipzig, 1931), p. 498.
Henceforth in this chapter we shall cite these two books as Gesenius,
Handwörterbuch, and König, Wörterbuch, respectively.

their fathers."[29] In the second place, in over two-thirds of the
pertinent passages we read: "And he lay down with his fathers,
and was buried" (e.g., I Kings 14:31; II Kings 8:24; II Chron. 12:
16), or: "And he lay down with his fathers, and they buried him"
(e.g., I Kings 15:8; II Kings 13:9; II Chron. 26:23). These passages show that the phrase under investigation does not refer to
the family grave, because in each instance the person in question
"lay down with his fathers" before his body was committed to the
ground. They show, moreover, that the phrase is not used in the
sense of being laid to rest, for then it would be tautological to
add that the respective dead was interred, while not a word would
be said about the fact that the person had died. In view of the
addition "and he was buried," or "and they buried him," we expect
a statement to the effect that the person in question had departed
this life. With two inconsequential exceptions out of forty passages, such a statement is never found. This seems to indicate
that the expression "to lie down with one's fathers" is the equivalent of "to die." In the third place, the Hebrew verb שָׁכַב, "to
lie down," "to sleep," is used also by itself not only in reference
to the rest in the grave (Job 21:26; Ps. 88:6; Isa. 14:18) but also
as a euphemism for "to die" (Job 14:12; Isa. 43:17). And, in the
fourth place, in I Kings 11:21: "And when Hadad heard in Egypt
that David slept (שָׁכַב) with his fathers and that Joab was dead (מֵת),"
the phrase "to sleep with one's fathers" is paralleled with מוּת,
"to die."[30]

The first of the two exceptions referred to above is found in
I Kings 22:37-40: "So the king died (וַיָּמָת) and was brought to Samaria, and they buried the king in Samaria. And one washed off the
chariot by the pool of Samaria, and the dogs licked up his blood,
and the harlots washed (in it), according to the word of the Lord
which He had spoken. Now the rest of the experiences of Ahab and
all that he did and the ivory house which he built and all the
cities that he built, are they not recorded in the Book of the

---

[29]W. Eichrodt, _Theologie des Alten Testaments_, II (Leipzig,
1935), 113-14, begs the question when he declares that in the course
of time the phrase under examination was generalized, so that it
was applicable also in cases where the dead was not buried in the
ancestral tomb.

[30]The expression "to be gathered to one's fathers" and its
variant forms will be treated separately in this chapter.

Chronicles of the Kings of Israel? So Ahab slept (וַיִּשְׁכַּב) with his
fathers, and Ahaziah, his son, reigned in his stead." In the final
verse of this passage the writer returns to the opening verse and
resumes the story temporarily interrupted by the two intervening
verses, and, while doing so, he uses a synonymous expression for
מוּת, "to die" (employed in vs. 37). The second exception we en-
counter in II Chron. 16:13-14: "And Asa lay down with his fathers,
dying in the forty-first year of his reign, and they buried him."
Here the writer first states the fact that Asa died and then, by
way of a supplementary parenthesis, as it were, he records the time
of his death. It is obvious that these passages cannot be advanced
as a counterargument.

In all these instances, with the possible exception of Gen.
47:30, the preposition עִם ("with") is. not comitative, in which
sense it is taken by Wilhelm Gesenius,[31] but comparative,[32] as it
is employed in Job 3:13-15: "For then I would have lain down and
would be quiet; then I would have fallen asleep (and) would be at
rest, with kings and counselors of the earth, who build pyramids(?)
for themselves; or with nobles who have gold, who fill their houses
with silver."

To resume our study of the Old Testament doctrines on death—
upon the departure of the spirit, the body returns to dust, but
"the spirit returns to God who gave it" (Eccles. 12:7), to be assigned its sphere, as will become evident later." We have no proof
that the spirit was thought to remain in the vicinity of the body
for some time, at least until burial.[33] On the contrary, we shall
see in connection with such phrases as "to be gathered to one's
fathers" that the spirit left this world at the moment of death,
before burial.

---

[31]Handwörterbuch, p. 595, 2.

[32]See ibid., p. 595, 1, e.

[33]Nothing can, of course, be proved by an appeal to Job 24:12:
"From out of the city the dying (מְתִים) groan, and the soul of the
wounded cries out." This applies also to Lev. 21:1.11 (cf. 19:28);
Num. 5:2; 6:6; 9:6.7.10; Job 14:22; and Isa. 66:24 (all cited by J.
Pedersen, Israel, Its Life and Culture [London and Copenhagen, 1926],
p. 180). Job 14:22, which alone merits some comment, is probably
best rendered: "But he grieves over himself, and he mourns over
himself" (so J. M. P. Smith in The Bible, an American Translation
[Chicago, 1935]). With the translation "self" for נֶפֶשׁ compare the
parallelism and Eccles. 4:5; 5:5.

Upon first sight, Eccles. 12:7, just referred to, seems to be
flatly contradicted by chapter 3:16-22: "And further saw I under
the sun: at the place of justice[34] there was wickedness, and at
the place of righteousness there was wickedness. (Then) said I
in my heart: 'God will judge both the righteous and the wicked;
for there is a time there[35] for every purpose and for every deed.'
I said (furthermore) in my heart: '(It is) on account of the sons
of men; that God may purify them, and that they may see that they
in themselves are beasts.' For that which befalls the sons of men
befalls the beast, the same thing befalls them; as the one dies,
so dies the other; they have all the same breath; man has no advantage over the beast; for all is vanity. All go to one place;
all are from the dust, and all return to the dust. Who knows the
spirit of the sons of men which goes upward and the spirit of the
beast which goes downward to the earth?[36] And so I perceived that
there is nothing better than that a man should rejoice in his works;
for that is his portion; for who shall bring him to see what shall
be after him?"

On the surface, these lines seem to deny the immortality of
the human spirit and to teach, instead, that death means the annihilation of the spiritual element in man. But a closer examination will show quite unmistakably that such is not the case. In

---

[34]König, Historisch-comparative Syntax der hebräischen Sprache
(Leipzig, 1897), § 330, kγ.

[35]With God (Gen. 49:24). So Franz Delitzsch, Commentary on
the Song of Songs and Ecclesiastes, trans. M. G. Easton (Edinburgh,
1891), p. 266.

[36]So the Massoretic text, which thus harmonizes with Eccles.
12:7. The Septuagint read הֲעֹלָה and הַיֹּרֶדֶת, instead of הָעֹלָה and
הַיֹּרֶדֶת, respectively, and so translated this verse as follows: "And
who knows whether the spirit of the sons of men goes upward and
whether the spirit of the beast goes downward to the earth?" Since
the Massoretic punctuation of 3:21 is grammatically correct and
since the passage is thus in perfect agreement with 12:7, we prefer
the Hebrew text, instead of following the Septuagint and vocalizing
the text in a way which would bring the two passages in conflict.
The Greek translators were probably influenced by the phraseology
of 2:19: "And who knows whether he will be a wise man or a fool?"
Different constructions of the expression "Who knows whether?" are
found in II Sam. 12:22, Joel 2:14, Jonah 3:9, and Esther 4:14. The
pronoun הִיא after the participial forms in Eccles. 3:21 was added to
bring out more clearly the contrast between the spirit of man and
that of the beast and so to set the two apart more definitely
(cf. Num. 18:23).

this passage the author discusses the problem of the application
of authority to purposes of injustice rather than of justice and
righteousness. This state of affairs, he says, is only temporary,
for with God in heaven there is a fixed time for everything; the
day will come when God will vindicate the righteous and punish
the wicked, thus administering to everyone what rightly belongs
to him. In the meantime, God permits this corruption in civil
and religious life to continue and develop in order to purify the
sons of men, particularly to purge them from pride, to impress them
with the fact that, in spite of their vaunted intelligence and superiority, they are in themselves, i.e., left to themselves, apart
from his help and redeeming influence, really not any better than
the beasts. For that is what they are in themselves, as appears
with special clarity from the dissolution of their bodies. On
this point there is no difference between man and beast in that both
are inevitably and helplessly cut off from life in this world and
have no further existence on earth; both have the same transitory
breath of life and therefore both must die; both were formed from
the dust of the earth and both must return to it; the earth is the
great cemetery of all that dwell below the skies. There is, indeed,
a difference between man and beast in that the spirit of the former
goes upward and returns to God, while the spirit of the latter goes
downward and perishes with the body. But, in the first place, for
this distinction, or pre-eminence, man cannot take any credit, since
it was God who breathed into the nostrils of his inanimate form the
breath of life, as is well known from Gen. 2:7, to which verse 20
alludes, and, in the second place, in spite of man's superiority
in this respect, he knows or understands neither the immortal spirit of man nor the perishable spirit of the beast. He can fathom
the one or the other as little as can the beast. Where, then, in
the final analysis, is man's boast? There is no occasion for it!
This truth God wants to teach the children of men by letting them
follow their own perverse and wicked ways for a season and then
depriving them of life and breath and making them return to the
dust of the ground, thus treating them like the beasts of the field.
These observations confirm the Preacher in his conviction that man
is not master of the future and that there is, consequently, nothing
better for a man to do than to rejoice in his works and enjoy the
fruits of his labor during his lifetime (cf. vss. 11-13), for at
the appointed time, everyone must die, and after death no one can

return to the earth and recover lost opportunities. It is apparent
from these considerations that there is no discrepancy at all between Eccles. 3:16-22 and 12:7.[37]

The times of man are in God's hand (Ps. 31:16). His days are
determined, and the number of his months is with God. God has established his bounds, which he cannot pass over (Job 14:5). But
this is not an absolute, unchangeable decree. For through godliness
life can be lengthened, while through godlessness it can be shortened. The Decalogue enjoins: "Honor thy father and thy mother,
that thy days may be long in the land which the Lord, thy God, is
giving thee" (Exod. 20:12). "The fear of the Lord adds days; but
the years of the wicked will be shortened" (Prov. 10:27). The
psalmist, pouring out his grief to God, laments: "For we are consumed by Thine anger, and by Thy wrath are we destroyed. Thou hast
set our iniquities before Thee, our hidden (sins) in the light of
Thy countenance" (90:7-8). These same thoughts find expression in
Prov. 3:1-2; 4:10; Eccles. 7:17; Ps. 55:24; Lev. 26:25; Deut. 30:
15-18; and Isa. 1:20.

To precepts, the Old Testament adds examples. Hezekiah was
told by Isaiah to set his house in order, for he would die (II Kings
20:1; Isa. 38:1). But when Hezekiah prayed and wept before the
Lord, the same Isaiah came to him with the cheering words: "Thus
says the Lord, the God of David, thy father: 'I have heard thy
prayer (and) have seen thy tears; behold, I will add unto thy days
fifteen years'" (Isa. 38:5 [II Kings 20:5-6]). Jonah preached to
the inhabitants of Nineveh: "Yet forty days, and Nineveh shall be

---

[37]I refrain from using Eccles. 3:11b ("He has set eternity in
their hearts") as an argument because the exact meaning of that
passage is uncertain; at least, it is not clear to me.

The idea that the soul is annihilated at death was foreign both
to the Hebrews and to the Mesopotamians. When Samson says, according to the original: "Let my soul die with the Philistines" (Judg.
16:30), he naturally employs the term "soul" in a figurative sense,
as it is used so often. What Samson means to say is simply: "Let
me die with the Philistines." Here "my soul" stands for the pronoun
of the first person (cf. Pss. 30:4; 62:2.6; 124:7). Or when the
prophet declares: "Our fathers sinned and are not" (Lam. 5:7), he
wishes to state merely that they are no longer in the land of the
living. The same expression occurs in Gen. 5:24: "And Enoch walked
with God, and he was not, for God took him." Enoch "was not" on
earth, but he "was" with God in heaven, "for God took him," that is,
without death, as appears from the fact that of all the other pa-
triarchs it is said: "and he died," while concerning Enoch we read
instead: "God took him" (cf. J. Orr, The Christian View of God and
the World [New York, 1893], p. 237; König, Die Genesis [Gütersloh,
1919], p. 308).

overthrown" (3:4). But when God saw that they repented of their evildoings, he spared them (3:10).

At the same time the Old Testament recognizes that righteousness does not always prolong a person's life on earth. God may cut short also the life of a pious individual, not as a punishment but to deliver him from evil. "The righteous perishes, and there is no man who lays it to heart; and godly men are taken away, without anyone considering that the righteous is taken away from the evil to come" (Isa. 57:1). Josiah was snatched out of the midst of the living in order that he would not have to witness the desolation of Jerusalem with its attendant horrors (II Kings 22:20 [cf. 23:29]). Conversely, the Old Testament recognizes that wickedness does not invariably curtail a person's life. God may grant the wicked a prolonged opportunity to mend their ways, as was the case with the people of Noah's time, who were given a respite of one hundred and twenty years (see chap. iv); or he may let them live and permit them to prosper, and that for apparently arbitrary reasons, as Job thought in the night of affliction and the anguish of his soul (chaps. 9-10; 12; 21:7-26; 24). Nevertheless, whatever God may do, his ways are just, for the differences will be taken care of in the hereafter (Psalms 49 and 73).

But in the end, at an unknown hour (Eccles. 9:12) and perhaps with unexpected swiftness (Job 1:18-19), all will have to die (Ps. 89:49) and go the way that they will never return (Job 16:22). The only exceptions were Enoch (Gen. 5:24 [cf. Heb. 11:5]) and Elijah (II Kings 2:11), who, because of their close communion with God on earth, were translated to the realms of heaven, without having to taste death.[38]

Burial Customs

Coming now to the views current among the Mesopotamians and the Hebrews on life after death, it seems best to begin with their burial customs, as revealed by the literary material and the evidence of the tombs.

The oldest important inscriptional information on the mortuary practices of the Mesopotamians is found on a cone by Urukagina, king of Lagash. Speaking of the abuses which existed before his

---

[38]The New Testament indicates that also Moses was translated (Matt. 17:1 ff.; Jude, vs. 9).

accession to the throne, Urukagina says, among other things: "When
a dead person was placed in the grave, his beer was seven jars (and)
his bread four hundred and twenty (flat loaves); two <u>ul</u>'s[39] of grain
..., one garment, one head-support(?), (and) one bed the ÙḪ.INNANA
received;[40] one <u>ul</u> of grain the <u>lú-dim</u>$_6$<u>-ma</u> received. (And) if a
man was laid to rest in 'the reeds of Enki,' his beer was seven
jars (and) his bread four hundred and twenty (flat loaves); two
<u>ul</u>'s of grain, one garment, one bed, (and) one chair the ÙḪ.INNANA
received; one <u>ul</u> of grain the <u>lú-dim</u>$_6$<u>-ma</u> received; the craftsman
took the bread of 'the lifting up of the hands.'" These conditions
Urukagina changed. Thereafter "when a dead person was placed in
the grave, his beer was (only) three jars (and) his bread (only)
eighty (flat loaves); one bed (and) one head-support(?) the
ÙḪ.INNANA received; (only) three <u>ban</u>[41] of grain the <u>lú-dim</u>$_6$<u>-ma</u> received. (And) if a man was laid to rest in 'the reeds of Enki,'
his beer [was] (only) four jars (and) his bread (only) two hundred
and forty (flat loaves); (only) one <u>ul</u> of grain the ÙḪ.INNANA received; three <u>ban</u> of grain the <u>lú-dim</u>$_6$<u>-ma</u> received." Moreover,
"the bread of 'the lifting up of the hands' of the craftsman he
abolished."[42] The jars of beer and the flat loaves of bread were
put in the grave as a food and drink offering for the dead; but
the furniture which is mentioned here and which was used somehow
in the funeral ceremony was taken by the professional buriers, or
the like.

The dead were provided with food and drink not only at the
time of entombment but also thereafter. In a number of inscriptions
we read of monthly offerings for the dead. King Ammiditana, of the
First Babylonian Dynasty, writes to one of his officials: "Thus
(says) Ammiditana: 'Milk and butter are needed for the mortuary
offerings of the month of Ab. As soon as thou seest this my tablet,
let a man of thy command take thirty cows and one (<u>pi</u>) of butter

---

[39]A measure.

[40]<u>Or</u>: took for himself.

[41]One <u>ban</u> was the sixth part of an <u>ul</u>.

[42]Cone C, cols. v, 24-vi, 21; viii, 32-ix, 10; and x, 14-16.
Text published by Ernest de Sarzec, <u>Découvertes en Chaldée</u>, II
(Paris, 1884-1912), 111. For the interpretation of these three
Sumerian passages I am greatly indebted to Professor A. Poebel,
with whom I had the privilege of reading the inscription.

and let him come to Babylon. Until the mortuary offerings are completed, let him supply the milk. Let him not delay, (but) let him
come quickly!'"[43] Similarly, Samsuditana, the last king of the
First Babylonian Dynasty, writes that "turtles are needed for the
mortuary offerings of the month of Ab," and he issues the command
that these should be procured without delay.[44] Ashurbanipal, king
of Assyria, remarks: "The regulations concerning the food (and)
drink offerings for the spirits of the kings [my] predecessors,
which had been discontinued, I re-established. To god and man,
to the dead and the living I did good."[45] The same custom was
still observed in Neo-Babylonian times. In a rather severely damaged text, found a few miles east of Harran, the father of Nabonidus
says with reference to the deeds of piety which he performed for
the benefit of certain dead: "Monthly, without ceasing, [I put
on(?)] my costly garments (and) offered fat lambs, food, red
wine..., oil, white wine, and fruits of the orchards of Elam [as
offerings] to their spirits. Rich offerings, whose odor is pleasant, I permanently established for them and set before them."[46]
According to the closing lines of the same inscription, Nabonidus
rubbed the body of his father with oil (so it would seem) and buried
him clothed in costly garments of white linen and adorned with precious stones. Moreover, he slaughtered fat lambs and presented them

---

[43]F. Thureau-Dangin, Lettres et contrats de l'Epoque de la
Première Dynastie Babylonienne (Paris, 1910), No. 7; translated
by him in Hilprecht Anniversary Volume (Leipzig, etc., 1909), p.
161, and retranslated by A. Ungnad, Babylonische Briefe aus der
Zeit der Hammurapi-Dynastie (Leipzig, 1914), No. 80.

[44]Text published by O. Schroeder in Vorderasiatische Schrift-
denkmäler, Vol. XVI (Leipzig, 1917), No. 51, and translated by P.
Kraus in Mitteilungen der vorderasiatisch-aegyptischen Gesellschaft,
XXXV, Heft 2 (1931), 13-14.

[45]C. F. Lehmann, Šamaššumukîn, König von Babylonien (Leipzig,
1892), Pl. 33:1-2. The much-discussed lines in Rawlinson, op. cit.,
Vol. V, Pl. 4:70-73, which at first view seem to affirm that Ashurbanipal brought a human offering to the spirit of his grandfather,
Sennacherib, are of little significance for our present purposes
and can therefore be omitted. On this passage see B. Landsberger
and Theo. Bauer in Zeitschrift für Assyriologie, XXXVII (1926),
215-20; Bauer, ibid., XLII (1934), 180-81; and E. G. Kraeling in
the Journal of the American Oriental Society, LIII (1933), 344-45

[46]H. Pognon, Inscriptions sémitiques de la Syrie, de la
Mésopotamie et de la région de Mossoul (Paris, 1907), Pls. XII-
XIII, col. iii; S. Langdon, Die neubabylonischen Königsinschriften
(Leipzig, 1912), pp. 292-93.

to him. Temple records of the Kassite period show that in those
days, at least, the naturalia intended for the offerings were
brought to the temples and that the official religion then took
care of the mortuary gifts.[47] A bilingual incantation text from
Assyria refers to the return of the imprisoned spirits of the
dead to partake of these offerings in the following terms: "The
imprisoned gods come forth from the grave, the evil winds[48] come
forth from the grave, for the offering of the mortuary food offering and the pouring out of water do they come forth from the
grave."[49]

At the burial of a king, at least in some cases, special sacrifices were offered to the gods of the underworld for the purpose
of inducing them to be kindly disposed toward the dead and probably
also to grant him special favors. An Assyrian king, probably one
of the Sargonids, says concerning the burial of his father: "In
royal oil I caused (him) to rest in goodly fashion. The opening
of the sarcophagus, the place of [his] rest, I sealed with strong
bronze and uttered a powerful spell over it. Vessels of gold (and)
silver (and) all the appurtenances of the grave, his royal ornaments
which he loves, I displayed before Shamash and placed (them) in the
grave with the father my begetter. [I] presented presents to the
princely Anunnaki and the (other) gods that inhabit the underworld."[50] Similarly we read in a Sargonid letter: "The day that
we heard 'The king is dead, the people of Ashur are in mourning,'
the governor of the land caused[51] his wife to go forth from the

---

[47]A. T. Clay, Documents from the Temple Archives of Nippur
(Philadelphia, 1912), Nos. 8, 86, 108, 113, and 133; Langdon in
Babyloniaca, VI (1912), 207. On the meaning of the Sumerian ex-
pression ki-anag, which Langdon (ibid., pp. 198-206) takes in the
sense of "mortuary sacrifice," see Landsberger, Der kultische
Kalender der Babylonier und Assyrer (Leipzig, 1915), pp. 5-6.

[48]The ghosts of the dead were conceived of as windlike beings,
issuing from holes in the ground (cf. the Gilgamesh Epic, Tablet
XII:82-84).

[49]I.e., to partake of these offerings. Text published by
Thompson in Cuneiform Texts ...., Vol. XVII, Pl. 37 (K. 3372 +
5241):1-10. That this passage does not treat of the imprisoned
gods mentioned in Enûma elish is evident from the fact that these
were released after the creation of man.

[50]Ebeling, Tod und Leben ...., pp. 56 ff. (cf. also W. von
Soden in Zeitschrift für Assyriologie, XLIII, 255).

[51]Here and in the following lines the original has the present
tense instead of the preterit.

palace. She burned a kid. His (chief) officer he caused to occupy
the city prefecture.[52] His officers, clad in mourning garments
(and) wearing rings of gold, stood before the city prefect. Qisaya,
the singer, together with his daughters, sang before them."[53]
Whether the bringing of sacrifices to the gods of the underworld
was the customary practice in the case of a royal dead and whether
this custom was, at least to some extent, observed also among the
common people, we are unable to determine.

To "fear" the spirit of the departed and to take care of him
and his tomb had its rewards for time and eternity. In a rather
fragmentary Sargonid letter we read: "The departed spirit that
blesses him,[54] because he fears the spirit, (says) thus: 'Let his
name (and) his seed rule the land of Assyria!'"[55] A Babylonian inscription on a mortuary cone[56] reads: "Forever, unto the growing
old of days, unto the days of eternity, unto the days which come
after, may one see this grave and not desecrate (it), (but) restore
(it) to its former condition. The man who sees this (inscription)
and does not despise (it), (but) says: 'This grave I will restore
to its former condition,' the deed of kindness which he has done
may it be repaid him. On earth may his name be honored, in the
underworld may his spirit drink pure water."[57] A clay cylinder
contains the following mortuary inscription:[58] "The grave of
Shamash-ibnî, the Dakurean, on whom Ashur-etil-ilâni, king of As-

---

[52]Evidently to prevent a revolution.

[53]Harper, op. cit., No. 473:2-11. With the above translation
cf. von Soden's notes in Zeitschrift für Assyriologie, XLIII, 255;
also Bruno Meissner in Wiener Zeitschrift für die Kunde des Morgenlandes, XII (1898), 59-60.

[54]In this case either the king or the crown prince.

[55]Harper, op. cit., No. 614, rev. 4-7.

[56]Text published by Ungnad in Vorderasiatische Schriftdenkmäler,
Heft I (Leipzig, 1907), No. 54. The above translation has profited
from various renderings in the Assyrian Dictionary files of the
Oriental Institute.

[57]Instead of muddy water, as in the story of Ishtar's descent.

[58]Text published by Clay, Miscellaneous Inscriptions in the
Yale Babylonian Collection (New Haven, etc., 1925), Pl. XXX, and
translated by him ibid., pp. 60 ff.

syria, had mercy and whom he brought fro[m Ass]yria[59] to Bît-Dakur, his (native) land, and caused him to rest in a grave in the midst of the 'house' of Dûr-Yakin(?).[59] Whoever thou art, whether a prefect, or a ruler, or a judge, or a prince, who is established in the land, commit no sin against the grave and (its) bone(s). (But) guard its place (and) spread (thy) good protection over it. For that may Marduk, the great lord, lengthen thy reign (and) place his good protection over thee. [May he ...] thy [name], thy seed, and life for thy long days [....]! If that prince, or prefect, or ruler, or judge, or viceroy, who may arise in the land, sins against this grave and the bone(s), changes its place, removes it to another place, or (if) someone incites him to evil and he hearkens (unto it), may Marduk, the great lord, destroy his name, his seed, his offspring, and his descendants in the mouth of the people! May Nabû, ..., shorten the number of his long days! May Nergal not protect his life from pestilence, calamity, and bloodshed!"

Failure to bury the dead rendered it impossible for the spirit to gain admission to and rest in the underworld. And failure to supply the departed with food caused him to suffer the pangs of hunger. If a spirit had no one to provide for his sustenance, he was compelled to roam about the world and feed on the garbage thrown out into the street[60] or to eat clay and drink turbid water in the subterranean realm of the dead.[61] To be left unburied or unprovided for was therefore a grievous misfortune or a terrible punishment. We read in the Assyrian law code: "If a woman of her own accord drops that which is in her,[62] they shall prosecute her, convict her, impale her, (and) not bury her. If she dies from dropping that which is in her, they shall impale her (and) not bury her."[63] And Esarhaddon says concerning the treatment which he accorded the warriors of enemy peoples: "The corpses of their

---

[59]So von Soden in his translation for the Assyrian Dictionary files of the Oriental Institute.

[60]Cf. the closing passage of the Gilgamesh Epic.

[61]Cf. "Ishtar's Descent to the Underworld," line 33.

[62]I.e., if she deliberately produces a miscarriage.

[63]Schroeder, Keilschrifttexte aus Assur verschiedenen Inhalts (Leipzig, 1920), Pl. 12:92-101.

warriors unburied I gave to the jackal to eat."[64] The worst curse
that could be pronounced on anyone was: "May his body fall down
and not have anyone to bury it,"[65] or: "May his body not be buried
in the ground!"[66]

By denying the dead a safe repose in the ground, by exhuming
the body, by failing to provide the deceased with the amount of
nourishment essential to the comfort and contentment of his disembodied spirit, or by cutting off the food supply, a person could
carry his vengeance even beyond the grave. Ashurbanipal says with
reference to his treatment of the Elamite kings buried at Susa:
"The graves of their former (and) later kings, who had not feared
Ashur and Ishtar, my sovereigns, (and) who had harassed the kings
my fathers, I ravaged, destroyed, (and) exposed to the sun. Their
bones I took to Assyria. Upon their spirits I imposed restlessness
(and) cut them off from food offerings (and) libations of water."[67]

On the other hand, if the dead did not receive the proper care
and attention, his spirit would torment the living. A sick person
who feels himself afflicted by the ghost of some unknown dead prays
to his ancestral spirits: "Ye spirits of my family, creators of
the grave(?)! (Spirits) of my father, my grandfather, my mother,
my grandmother, my brother, my sister, my family, my people, and
my relationship, as many (of you) as rest in the earth, I have
brought you food offering(s), I have poured out water for you, I
have taken care of you, I have praised you, I have honored you;
now stand before Sham[ash] (and) Gilgamesh, plead my cause, and
secure a (favorable) decision for me! The evil things which are in
my body, my flesh, (and) my sinews, deliver into the hand of Namtar,
the vizier of the underworld! May Ningizzida, the herald of the
wide underworld, place a strong watch over them! [May] Nedu, the
chief gatekeeper of the underworld, [turn] their faces![68] Take

---

[64]Thompson, The Prisms of Esarhaddon and Ashurbanipal (London,
1931), Pl. 9, col. v, 6.

[65]King, Babylonian Boundary-Stones and Memorial-Tablets in the
British Museum. Plates (London, 1912), Pl. 99, col. vi, 54-55.

[66]V. Scheil in Délégation en Perse: Mémoires, Vol. VI (Paris,
1905), Pl. 10, col. vi, 21.

[67]Rawlinson, op. cit., Vol. V (London, 1884), Pl. 6, col. vi,
70-76.

[68]The faces of the personified "evil things."

ye him and cause ye him[69] to go down to the land of no return!
(But) may I, your servant, be restored to life and health!"[70]
Someone else finds himself in even greater distress, for he cries
out:[71] "O Shamash, the terrifying ghost, which for many days has
been bound on my back and cannot be loosened, which pursues me all
day (and) terrifies me all night, whose persecution continues un-
abated[72] (and) which makes the hair of my head to stand on end,
which attacks(?) my forehead (and) makes my face to glow, which
dries my palate (and) drugs my flesh, which dries out my whole
body, be it a ghost of my family or of my relationship, be it
the ghost (of a man) who died a violent death, (or) be it a
wandering ghost, this one (or) that one, O Shamash, in thy presence
I entreat (thee) concerning him. Garments for his wear, sandal(s)
for [his] feet, a leather girdle for his loin(s), a waterskin for
his drink, (and) malt I have delivered to him, food for (his)
journey I have given him. Let him go to the setting of the sun;
let him be intrusted to Nedu, the chief gatekeeper of the underworld, that Nedu, the chief gatekeeper of the underworld, may keep
strong watch over him; may his key close[73] the lock!"

Turning next to the evidence of the tombs, it will not be necessary for our purpose to enter upon a discussion of the various
Mesopotamian graveyards that have been excavated. Most of the necessary material can be derived from the cemeteries unearthed at Ur
and Kish; for the graves discovered there represent almost every
important method of interment known from the Tigris-Euphrates region. We shall therefore focus our attention chiefly on these two

---

[69]The ghost.

[70]Ebeling, Keilschrifttexte aus Assur religiösen Inhalts, No.
227, rev., col. iii, 8-21. Translated by Ebeling in his Tod und
Leben ...., pp. 131-32.

[71]Text published by King, Babylonian Magic and Sorcery (London,
1896), No. 53:6-22; translated by Thureau-Dangin in Revue d' Assyriologie, XVIII (1921), 187-88, and others. Duplicate published by
Ebeling, Keilschrifttexte aus Assur religiösen Inhalts, No. 267
reverse, and transliterated and translated by him in his Tod und
Leben ...., pp. 140-41.

[72]Reading ri-du-su ittanazazzu[zu]. On the verbal form see
Poebel, Studies in Akkadian Grammar (Chicago, 1939), p. 95. A
similar reading and translation have been suggested by von Soden
in Zeitschrift für Assyriologie, XLIII, 269.

[73]Lit.: seize.

centers and treat the graves from other places merely as subsidiary
sources of information.

The most interesting of all burials are the royal sepulchers,
which so far have been found in only three localities—Ur, Kish, and
Ashur. At Ur, C. L. Woolley[74] discovered eighteen such sepulchers,
sixteen dating from early dynastic times (ca. 2800-ca. 2350 B.C.)[75]
and two from the Third Dynasty of Ur. The former differed from
the contemporary common graves not so much in the treasures which
they contained as in the peculiarities of structure and ritual.
The shaft of a royal grave was usually rectangular, extending to
a depth of thirty feet or more and measuring as much as forty
feet by twenty-eight, and was entered by a sloping or stepped passage. At the bottom of the pit, or at a somewhat higher level,
the tomb was built. This was a vaulted or domed structure of stone
or brick containing one or more rooms and occupying either the whole
area of the pit or only a part thereof. The body was inclosed in a
wooden coffin or laid on a wooden bier and was placed inside the
tomb chamber. The dead was provided with vessels containing food
and drink, with clothing, jewelry, gaming boards, and weapons—in
short, with much that he had required on earth for his use or amuse-
ment.

A royal funeral was accompanied by the death and interment of
the departed person's bodyguard, menservants, women, and, in a few
cases, even draft animals yoked to the chariot.[76] The number of

---

[74] Ur Excavations, Vol. II: The Royal Cemetery: Text (London
and Philadelphia, 1934), esp. pp. 33-134.

[75] On the dating of this period and the royal tombs see ibid.,
pp. 208-27, and Henri Frankfort, Archeology and the Sumerian Problem (Chicago, 1932), esp. pp. 5-9 and Table I. Frankfort fixed
the upper limit of the early Sumerian dynastic period at about
2900 B.C. and the lower at about 2500 B.C., the latter being the
period to which the reign of Sargon of Akkad was still assigned
at the time when Frankfort published his study. On the date of
the tombs see also Jacobsen, op. cit., p. 181.

[76] The correctness of this interpretation of the evidence has
been disputed by Sidney Smith in the Journal of the Royal Asiatic
Society, 1928, pp. 849-68, and F. Böhl in Zeitschrift für Assyriologie, XXXIX (1930), 83-98, both of whom hold (or, at least, held)
that these were not royal funerals at all but rather that they
formed part of so-called sacred marriage ceremonies. However, the
view here expressed has been ably defended by Woolley, op. cit., pp.

people who followed their king or queen to the underworld might
range from a mere half-dozen to eighty. On the manner of their
death nothing certain is known; however, there seem to be indications that they died in consequence of some deadly potion. Some
of the attendants, as a rule, had their place inside the royal sepulchral chamber, while the rest of the human victims were interred
outside, either within the same pit or in one adjoining it. The
skeletal remains of the draft animals were found lying in the same
pit in which the royal chamber was located. If the building in
the burial pit had a number of rooms, one served as the resting-
place of the principal body, while the others were occupied by the
bodies of the retinue. The attendants were not laid out as for rest
but were interred in a crouched position as for service.

The same custom prevailed at Kish, where two cemeteries, denominated A and Y, respectively, have been excavated. The lowest
level of cemetery Y has yielded a number of royal burials roughly
synchronizing with the early royal tombs of Ur. A few of these
graves contained chariots, the skeletons of draft animals, the remains of several human beings in the same pit, and, of course, a
certain amount of mortuary equipment. Unfortunately, these tombs,
like all the common graves in that stratum, collapsed under the
weight of the great mass of earth piled upon them for millennia,
so that a description of them is rather difficult. It can be said,
however, that they were less imposing as to both structure and equipment than was the corresponding type of tomb at Ur and that their
ritual was less elaborate.[77] To date, the early royal tombs of Ur
and those of Kish are the only ones to afford evidence for the
burial custom just described.

The meaning of the co-interment of the retinue at the funeral
of a royal person seems obvious. It undoubtedly was an expression
of the belief in the continuity of the earthly way of life even
after death. A man's status in the hereafter was determined by

---

37-42. A reference to this burial practice may be contained on a
Sumerian fragment dealing with the death of Gilgamesh (see S. N.
Kramer in the Bulletin of the American Schools of Oriental Research,
No. 94 [April, 1944], pp. 3-12). The same rite was practiced in
ancient China and among Indo-Europeans (cf. L. B. Paton, Spiritism
and the Cult of the Dead in Antiquity [New York, 1921], esp. pp. 47
and 131-34).

[77] L. C. Watelin and S. Langdon, Excavations at Kish, IV (Paris,
1934), 17-34.

his status on earth; his requirements were thought to correspond
to his requirements on earth. A royal dead, accordingly, needed
not only food, drink, raiment, and the like but also the services
of his or her retinue, teams, and chariots, wherefore it was necessary that these should follow him or her in death. The men and
women who thus accompanied their master or mistress may have done
so voluntarily, in order to continue their services and so to assure
for themselves a more desirable existence than was the lot of those
commoners who passed through the gates of death in the ordinary manner. Neither at Ur nor at Kish were the bodies of the attendants
supplied with burial equipment, evidently because of a belief that
their master or mistress would provide for them in death as he or
she had done in life.[78]

The two royal tombs of the Third Dynasty of Ur, to which reference has been made above, belonged to Shulgi (or Dungi) and Bûr-
Sin. They were great subterranean mausoleums constructed on the
site of the big cemetery at Ur; over them were built funerary
chapels following the pattern of the private houses of the living.
Both mausoleums had been quite thoroughly plundered by the time
they were excavated. In three of the chambers were found scattered
bones representing two, three, and five bodies, respectively.
Whether this points to the custom just described is not easy to
decide, especially since the tombs had been rifled.[79]

The royal burials discovered at Ashur, the ancient capital
of Assyria, were located underneath the old palace floor.[80] They
were vaults built of brick or partly of brick and partly of stone.
Among them are the vaults of Ashurnaṣirpal II (883-859 B.C.)
and Shamshi-Adad V (823-811 B.C.). The bodies were buried in stone
sarcophagi consisting of dolerite, basalt, or limestone. The dolerite sarcophagus of Ashurnaṣirpal measured about twelve and a half
feet in length, six feet in width, and six feet in height, and was
covered with a slab of the same stone about half a foot thick. The

---

[78]Ibid., p. 19; Woolley, op. cit., p. 42.

[79]Woolley, op. cit., pp. 17 and 40-41.

[80]Some of the early rulers of Babylonia were interred "in the
palace" (King, Chronicles concerning Early Babylonian Kings, II
[London, 1907], 52-56).

sarcophagus of Shamshi-Adad, made of basalt, was considerably
smaller, measuring only about eight feet in length, three and a
half feet in width, and the same in height. All the burials had
been thoroughly plundered and severely damaged so that little can
be said about them apart from the location, construction, and appearance of the tombs and the sarcophagi.[81]

The oldest private burials at Ur were discovered in two super-
imposed strata dating from the al-ʿUbaid period,[82] so far the
earliest period in Babylonia of which we definitely have archeological remains. In the graves of both series, the skeletons lay
stretched out on their backs, with the hands crossed over the pelvis.
This attitude does not appear to have been encountered anywhere else.
Each body was provided with a certain amount of mortuary equipment,
such as vessels containing food and drink for the dead. In the
upper and somewhat later layer this equipment consisted of at least
a cup, one or more open plates, and one or more chalices. From two
burials were recovered maceheads of limestone and steatite; from one,
a hammer ax of stone and from another a copper spearhead of the
harpoon type. The graves in the lower level were a little more
elaborate. But here no weapons or any chalices were present. Instead, there were encountered a number of nude female figurines of
terra cotta, undoubtedly representing some fertility goddess. The
cups and plates, occurring in both layers, bear unmistakable witness
to the existence of a belief, already in this early period, in the
continuity of life after death.[83]

The next group of private graves at Ur have been dated by
Woolley[84] to the Jemdet Naṣr period, representing the third era
in the development of Babylonian culture as known today and antedating the early royal tombs. In these graves were found abundant
vessels of stone and cups of lead, most of which originally doubt-

---

[81] W. Andrae, Das wiedererstandene Assur (Leipzig, 1938), pp.
136-40 (cf. also p. 16).

[82] The date for this period, as well as for the Jemdet Naṣr
period, to be mentioned shortly, cannot as yet be established.

[83] Woolley in the Antiquaries Journal, X (1930), esp. 337-38.

[84] In the Antiquaries Journal, X, 327-28, and XIV (1934),
363-64.

less contained food and drink deposited by the survivors for the
benefit of the dead. The body occupied a lateral position and the
hands, frequently holding a cup or some other vessel, were brought
close to the face, while the back was often curved with the head
bent forward over the breast; the legs were contracted so violently
that the knees were on a level with the chin and the heels almost
touched the pelvis. In other words, the dead were buried in the
so-called embryonic position. This was invariably the position in
which the dead were entombed in cemetery Y at Kish around the time
of the Dynasty of Akkad.[85] To inter the body in this attitude was
"probably a preparation for rebirth."[86] It would appear as if here
we had an indication either of the rather widespread belief among
primitive peoples that the dead man returns to the earth as a new-
born child or of the belief that death is birth into a life in the
great beyond.

By far the greatest number of private graves at Ur come from
what Woolley has called the "royal cemetery" and are considerably
later than those just discussed; they date from about 2600 B.C. to
around 2000 B.C. Since during all the centuries covered by these
graves the fashion of the common burials at Ur underwent but minor
changes, we shall treat them as a whole; only one small group shows
peculiarities meriting special attention.

On the private graves from the royal cemetery we fortunately
have some rather detailed information. A typical burial of this
kind was a rectangular shaft measuring on the average about five
feet by two. The bottom of the pit and the walls up to a height
of about two feet were often lined with a coarse reed matting. The
dead was laid on the floor of the grave wrapped in a matting roll
or placed in a coffin made of matting, reeds, wickerwork, wood, or
clay. The body reclined on its side, either the right or the left,
with the back straight or slightly curved, the knees flexed in vary-
ing degrees, and the hands in front of the chest. This seems to
show quite clearly that the position of the body was intended to
imitate the position of a person asleep, reminding us of the following statement in one of the Sargonid letters: "The people who are

---

[85]Watelin and Langdon, op. cit., IV, 49-50.

[86]G. van der Leeuw, Religion in Essence and Manifestation
(New York, 1938), p. 212.

dead are at rest,"[87] and of the Gilgamesh Epic, Tablet XII:29:
"She who rests, she who rests, the mother of Ninazu, she who rests."
There was no religious principle determining the orientation of
the body; it could face any point of the compass. As regards the
evidence of the tombs, there is no indication that the Babylonians
and Assyrians had any conception of a particular direction in
which the soul of the deceased would go on the way to the abode
of the dead. As in the case of the royal burials, the dead was
furnished with food and drink and various personal effects, such
as he apparently would need in the life to come, the wealth and
nature of the objects placed in the tomb being determined doubtless by the wealth and position of its occupant.[88]

    A few of the bodies, seemingly belonging to the First Dynasty
of Ur, were partially cremated after having been placed in the
grave, the burning being almost invariably confined to the skull
and its immediate area. The occupants of these graves, which for
the most part were poorly equipped and were restricted to one part
of the cemetery, perhaps were members of a different race from the
bulk of the inhabitants, or they may have been adherents of a different religion; perhaps they were prisoners of war. At any rate,
these burials were exceptional at Ur.[89] However, at Surghul[90] and
El-Hibba cremation was the rule, at least according to Robert
Koldewey, one of the excavators of these two sites.[91] With reference to pre-Sargonic times, this is said likewise to have been the

---

[87]Harper, op. cit., No. 716:18.

[88]Woolley, op. cit., esp. pp. 135-80.

[89]Ibid., pp. 142-43.

[90]Dr. I. J. Gelb identifies this with Shurgula (written
sur-gu-la), occurring on an Old Akkadian tablet. Dr. Gelb has
promised to publish a note on this point sometime in the future.

[91]See Koldewey's article in Zeitschrift für Assyriologie, II
(1887), 403 ff. (cf. also H. V. Hilprecht, Explorations in Bible
Lands [Philadelphia, 1903], pp. 282-88). Koldewey probably went
too far when he asserted that both places must be regarded as
"fire necropoles" and that the houses were the dwellings of the
dead (cf. Pinhas Delougaz, The Temple Oval at Khafājah [Chicago,
1940], p. 143).

case in Nippur.[92] In Ashur cremation was practiced but rarely.[93]
At Surghul, El-Hibba, and Nippur food, drink, and various objects
were deposited both with the body to be cremated and with the remains subsequently committed to the ground.[94] Cremation was thus
not motivated by the belief that death ends all; the vessels accompanying the ashes rather point in the opposite direction.

In addition to the tombs excavated in the royal cemetery at
Ur, Woolley found a number of brick-built vaults underneath the
floors of houses, some dating from the days of the Third Dynasty
of Ur and others from the Kassite period.[95] At Ashur the early
private graves, dating from about the period of the Third Dynasty
of Ur, were either simple pits cut into the ground or brick-built
family vaults below the house floors; but in either case the dead
was provided with the accouterments of life. If buried in a vault,
he was laid to rest either in a clay coffin or without any special
protective casing.[96] At Khafajeh the majority of burials, going
back to pre-Sargonic times, were simple graves dug under the floors
of the houses. Some of the graves were covered by vaults of sun-
dried bricks. The houses continued to be used for ordinary domestic
purposes.[97] The dead thus remained close to the survivors, who
provided for them, while their graves were protected from desecra-
tion.

The private burials in the earliest tomb stratification of
cemetery Y at Kish lay in the rooms of the houses in which the departed used to live.[98] For the sake of economy, the tomb was ordi-
narily built in a corner, since this method necessitated the construction of only two sides, the walls of the room providing the
other two. The floor was paved and the whole structure covered by
a vault. The dead, wrapped in matting, was interred in a lateral
position, in the attitude of a person asleep, without any rule of
orientation, and was equipped with a variety of things ostensibly

---

[92]Hilprecht, op. cit., esp. pp. 454-58.

[93]Andrae, op. cit., p. 169.

[94]Hilprecht, op. cit., esp. pp. 448-49, 454-58, and 466-67.

[95]Woolley in the Antiquaries Journal, XIV, 357.

[96]Andrae, op. cit., pp. 14 and 126-27.

[97]Delougaz, op. cit., pp. 137-38.

[98]This stratum, perhaps antedating somewhat the royal cemetery
at Ur, was the same in which the royal sepulchers were found.

for his use in the hereafter, especially receptacles containing
food and drink. Of particular interest is the fact that the hands,
placed close to the mouth, held a cup as if the dead were about to
drink from it.[99] This feature was observed also in a number of
burials of cemetery A at Kish,[100] in tombs at Fâra,[101] and in some
graves at al-'Ubaid (or Tell el-'Obeid).[102]

The Neo-Babylonian burials in cemetery Y were of two types:
The dead was placed either in a clay coffin or simply in the ground.
In the former case the body lay normally on its back, either on the
floor of the coffin or on the earth with a coffin inverted over it;
but, since the coffin was never long enough for the body, the knees
were drawn straight upward. However, in the case of the second type,
the corpse was laid out at full length.[103]

The burials of the Parthian period, unearthed at Kish, Nippur,
Babylon, Ashur, and elsewhere, and characterized chiefly by slipper-
shaped clay coffins, are too late to be of much value for our purposes. But it is interesting to note that even in this late period
the dead were still interred with various objects used in daily life.

The epigraphic and anepigraphic evidence presented on the preceding pages shows that life was believed to continue after death
and that the relation between a man and his relatives and acquaint-
ance was not severed altogether at the grave. It shows, moreover,
that the living and the dead were interdependent. The welfare of
the dead depended principally on the attention which they received
from the living, while that of the living was determined to a great
extent by the care which they bestowed upon the departed, the respect which they showed them, and the help and consideration which
they received from them.[104]

Turning now to the Hebrews, we find that among them, as among

---

[99]Watelin and Langdon, op. cit., IV, 17 ff.

[100]E. Mackay in Field Museum of Natural History: Anthropology,
Memoirs, I, No. 1 (1925), 13.

[101]Ernst Heinrich, Fara, Ergebnisse der Ausgrabungen der
Deutschen Orient-Gesellschaft in Fara und Abu Hatab 1902/03, ed.
Andrae (Berlin, 1931), p. 17.

[102]H. R. Hall and C. L. Woolley, Ur Excavations, Vol. I:
Al-'Ubaid (Oxford, 1927), 173.

[103]Watelin and Langdon, op. cit., IV, 52-54.

[104]Cf. Langdon in Babyloniaca, VI, 213-14.

their Mesopotamian neighbors, the prevailing method of disposing of the dead was the interment of the body. This treatment was accorded even to criminals who had been hanged (Deut. 21:22-23), to suicides (II Sam. 17:23), and to national enemies who had been captured and put to death (Josh. 8:29; 10:26-27). Although there is no Old Testament proof that burial was considered essential to the comfort of the departed[105] or to the safety of the survivors,[106] as was the case in Babylonia, Assyria, and other countries, it was nevertheless regarded as a deed of kindness to bury the dead (II Sam. 2:5), while it was a disgrace to be left unburied (I Kings 14:11-13; 16:4; 21:24; Jer. 16:4; 25:33; Ps. 79:3; Eccles. 6:3) or to be exhumed (Isa. 14:19; Jer. 8:1-2). Men of means might have family tombs, as we read of Abraham (Gen. 23:3-20; 49:29-32), of Kish, the father of Saul (II Sam. 21:14), and of the family of the disobedient prophet who was slain by a lion (I Kings 13:22); poor people, on the other hand, might be buried in a public cemetery, called "the graves of the children of the people" (II Kings 23:6). The dead were buried outside the city (Gen. 23:20; 35:8.19) or inside the city. Interment beyond the confines of the city was probably the lot of the common people, while burial within the city walls would appear to have been reserved for outstanding personages. Thus David and most of the kings of Judah, as well as the high priest Jehoiada (II Chron. 24:16), were buried in Jerusalem. Samuel, Joab, and King Manasseh were interred in their houses (I Sam. 25:1; I Kings 2:34; II Chron. 33:20). The house naturally included the

---

[105]In answer to the assertion by R. H. Charles, _A Critical History of the Doctrine of a Future Life_ (London, 1913), pp. 34-35, that unless a person received an honorable burial he was "thrust into the lowest and most outlying parts" of the underworld, it is sufficient to point out that in Ezek. 32:23, on which Charles bases his argument, the phrase "in the farthest (i.e., the lowest) parts of the pit" (בוֹר ־ בְּיַרְכְּתֵי) refers quite clearly to the grave (קֶבֶר), mentioned immediately before this phrase and again a few words thereafter (this time, however, the author using the term קְבֻרָה). This is recognized also by Gesenius, _Handwörterbuch_, under יְרֵכָה . However, in Isa. 14:15 the same phrase is applied to the nether world. This could easily be done, since the term bôr ("pit"), as we shall see, is employed not only in reference to the grave but also the underground realm of the spirits.

[106]The dead referred to in Ezek. 39:14 are given burial for sanitary reasons, not because of any fear that their spirits might still be moving about on the face of the earth and might molest the inhabitants of the land unless the bodies be interred.

court belonging to it and evidently also other enclosures. Since
the graves were ceremonially unclean and since contact with them
rendered a person likewise unclean (Num. 19:16), we may assume that
all three of these men were laid to rest in enclosures belonging
to their houses, and in such a way that defilement could easily be
avoided. In fact, II Kings 21:18, being more specific than II
Chron. 33:20, states expressly that Manasseh was "buried in the
garden of his house, in the garden of Uzza." Similarly, it is
said of Amon, his son and successor: "And they buried him in his
sepulcher in the garden of Uzza" (II Kings 21:26). In I Sam. 25:1,
I Kings 2:34, and II Chron. 33:20, the word בַּיִת ("house") may denote
simply a piece of property with a house on it, in which sense the
corresponding Babylonian and Assyrian term bîtu occurs quite frequently (cf. also Gen. 15:2 and 39:4 and Esther 8:1, where "house"
means as much as "possessions," Besitz or Besitztum).[107]

The body was carried to the grave on a bed or couch, which in
some instances, at least, seems to have been buried with the corpse
(II Sam. 3:31; II Chron. 16:14). Coffins were used either not at
all or but rarely among the ancient Hebrews, to judge from archeological finds in Palestine and from the Old Testament silence on
the matter;[108] the coffin in which the embalmed remains of Joseph
were committed to the ground (Gen. 50:26) is the only one mentioned
in the records of the Old Testament and bears witness to Egyptian
rather than Israelite usage.

At the interment of a royal personage fragrant materials were
burned. Concerning Asa, king of Judah, it is said: "They laid

----

[107]We have an interesting parallel to this in the word rancho
as it is used in American Spanish. This term designates, first, a
rude hut for herdsmen or farm laborers and, second, a large grazing
farm or ranch. Hence the statement "Fué sepultado en su rancho"
could, in itself, mean either "He was buried in his house on the
ranch" or "He was buried on his ranch."
The eight burials found by E. Sellin and C. Watzinger underneath the floors of houses and courtyards in Jericho and discussed
in their volume Jericho (Leipzig, 1913), pp. 70-71 and 190, were
Canaanite and therefore do not concern us here. Watzinger himself
states that the objects recovered from the tombs are of the same
type as those unearthed in the area surrounding the "palace." But
the "palace" belonged to City III and therefore was Canaanite. Also
City IV, resting on City III and having been destroyed by the in-
vading Hebrews, was Canaanite (cf. C. C. McCown, The Ladder of Progress in Palestine [New York and London, 1943], pp. 68 ff.).

[108]II Kings 13:21 presupposes a burial without a coffin.

him in a bed which had been filled with divers kinds of spices,
mixed with expert skill in mixing spices, and they burned for him
a very great burning" (II Chron. 16:14). And Zedekiah is assured:
"Thou shalt die in peace; and according to the burnings of thy
fathers, the former kings, who were before thee, shall they burn
for thee" (Jer. 34:5). There is no evidence at all that these
"burnings" were sacrifices for the dead, as some have asserted;
the custom of burning aromatic spices at a royal funeral was undoubtedly nothing more than an expression of the general honor
and esteem in which the deceased was held (cf. II Chron. 21:19),[109]
the fires thus corresponding to our flowers.

The Old Testament is silent on the question of whether or not
the dead were buried with some of their personal effects and were
provided with food and drink, as in Egypt and Mesopotamia.[110]
Josephus,[111] indeed, reports that an immense amount of silver,
furniture of gold, and other precious goods were buried with David,
and the excavations have shown that the custom of burying the dead
with numerous objects used in daily life was observed also both in
Canaanite and in Israelite Palestine.[112] But, in the first place,
of all the graves unearthed in Palestine, there are few of which
it can be said with confidence that they represent ancient Hebrew
(and not Canaanite) burials. And, in the second place, while in
Mesopotamia definite remnants of food have been found in the vessels
accompanying the body,[113] there is no proof, according to G. E.
Wright,[114] that a single clear remnant of food or drink has been
discovered in any of the dishes, jugs, and jars placed in the tombs
which have so far been excavated in ancient Israelite Palestine,

---

[109] Thus also König, Geschichte der alttestamentlichen Religion
(Gütersloh, 1915), p. 88.

[110] On Deut. 26:14 see below.

[111] Antiquities of the Jews, vii. 15. 3; xvi. 7. 1.

[112] See P. S. P. Handcock, The Archaeology of the Holy Land
(London: "first published in 1916"), pp. 302-26; R. A. S. Macalister,
A Century of Excavation in Palestine (New York and Chicago, 1925),
pp. 256-65; P. Thomsen in Reallexikon der Vorgeschichte, IV (Berlin,
1926), 473-85; H. Vincent, Canaan d'après l'exploration récente
(Paris, 1907), esp. pp. 284-96.

[113] See Woolley, op. cit., esp. pp. 151, 203, and 409-10.

[114] In the Biblical Archaeologist, VIII (1945), 17.

although there does not appear to be any reason why remnants of
such things could not have been preserved in at least some of the
graves, considering what has been found preserved in ruined Palestinian houses.[115] The objects discovered in supposedly Hebrew tombs
may have been placed there not in the belief that the departed would
use them in the hereafter but partly for sentimental and partly for
symbolical reasons (to indicate that life would continue beyond the
grave). Referring to the purpose of the pottery vessels put in the
tombs, Wright says: "We know that a feast was provided for the
family and friends assembled for the funeral (cf. Jer. 16:7; Hos.
9:4). Perhaps the vessels in the graves were those used by the
mourners. But why should they be placed in the tombs? To me the
more probable answer is that this custom is an old survival from
prehistoric times. Food may once have been placed in the tombs,
but from the fourth millennium[116] on in Palestine the vessels are
only a symbolic and/or traditional survival of the primitive custom."[117] In the case of the Mesopotamian burials there can be
little doubt as to the purpose of the vessels placed in the tombs,
since we have inscriptional evidence to show that the living provided the dead with nourishment, both at the time of interment and
thereafter, and since remains of food have been found in Mesopotamian tombs; but in the case of presumably Hebrew graves we cannot
at all be sure.

Another method of disposing of the dead was cremation. This
method, however, was employed only in exceptional cases. Thus the
bodies of Saul and his three sons were burned, evidently to prevent

---

[115]According to Handcock, op. cit., pp. 311-18, and Macalister,
op. cit., p. 260, remains of food were found in tombs at ancient
Gezer, but those were pagan burials.

It is, of course, quite possible that throughout the Old Testament dispensation there were those in Israel who supplied the dead
with food and drink, but whether that was orthodox Hebrew practice
is a different question. At Beth-zur were discovered three (presumably Hebrew) burials of the Persian or the Hellenistic period
which showed not even a trace of mortuary equipment (see O. R.
Sellers, The Citadel of Beth-Zur [Philadelphia, 1933], pp. 21-22,
and his remarks in the Biblical Archaeologist, VIII, 16).

[116]It may not be amiss to call attention to the fact that the
dates for Near Eastern history are still subject to change.

[117]In the Biblical Archaeologist, VIII, 17.

their being further disgraced at the hands of the Philistines; but
the cremation was only partial, for we read of the subsequent burial of their bones (I Sam, 31:6-13; II Sam. 21:12-14). Perhaps
for sanitary reasons cremation was employed during an epidemic
(Amos 6:10). Achan and his family were stoned and then burned with
all their belongings (Josh. 7:24-25), as a punishment for their
aggravated transgression (cf. Lev. 20:14; 21:9) and for the purpose
of completely removing the evil from the midst of Israel (cf. Josh.
7:12-13).

The Realm of the Dead

The dwelling-place of the departed was localized by the Babylonians and Assyrians within the earth. It was the place into
which Gilgamesh's pukku and mikkû fell and to which Enkidu subsequently descended to bring up these objects for his master, but he
was unable to ascend until Nergal had made a hole in the ground to
let him come up. Ishtar likewise descended to this gloomy realm
but was not able to return to the upper world until Ea had liberated
her from the clutches of Ereshkigal.

The Mesopotamians conceived of the underworld as beginning at
a short distance below the surface of the earth. This is obvious
from the fact that Gilgamesh tried to recover his pukku and his
mikkû from the nether world first with his hand and then with his
foot, but he could not reach them. Moreover, when Nebuchadrezzar
wished to describe the great depth to which he had carried the sub-
structure of the royal palace, of Marduk's stage-tower, or of a
quay wall, he declared that he had established their foundations
"on the breast of the underworld" (ina irat kigalli). The grave,
accordingly, either lay within the confines of the underworld or it
formed a passage leading into it.[118] However, the underworld proper,
that is, the dwelling-place of the chthonic deities and the discarnate spirits, was situated in the lowest part of the earth. A
text from Ashur[119] divides the earth into three layers; the first
was occupied by man, the second constituted the domain of Ea, and
the third was the underworld.

---

[118]Cf. Thompson in Cuneiform Texts ...., Vol. XVII, Pl. 37
(K. 3372+5241): 1-10.

[119]Published by Ebeling in Keilschrifttexte aus Assur
religiösen Inhalts, No. 307:34-37.

The names by which the abode of the dead was known among the inhabitants of the Tigris-Euphrates region are numerous. The opening lines of the Sumerian version of Ishtar's descent to the nether world call it kigal, "the great place below," which in itself can refer also to the pedestal of a statue. This term forms one of the elements composing the name Ereshkigal, "the lady of the great place below," that is, the queen of the underworld. In Semitic Babylonian it is found, e.g., in the phrase irat kigalli, "the bosom or breast of the underworld," an expression denoting, as we have seen, the area upon which were laid the foundations of large buildings and massive walls (as of a quay). Since the gathering place of the dead was situated within the earth, the Sumerians referred to it also as kur and the Semites in Babylonia as irṣitu, both words signifying "earth." Kur is the regular designation for the lower world in the Sumerian recension of Ishtar's descent, while irṣitu occurs, e.g., on the twelfth tablet of the Gilgamesh Epic and in the name Bêlit-irṣitim, which in the Semitic version of Ishtar's descent is the Babylonian designation for the queen of the nether world. Other names which the Babylonians assigned to the realm of the dead are irṣit lâ târi (in Sumerian: kurnugia or kurnugi), "the land of no return"; arallû or aralû (Sumerian: arali), whose etymology is still obscure; mûshab irkalla or shubat irkalla, both expressions signifying "the dwelling of Irkalla," or simply irkalla or irkallum; kûtû, derived from the name of the Babylonian city Kûtû (the biblical Cuthah), the sacred city of Nergal, who, as a chthonic deity, was the king of the underworld; and urugal (Sumerian), meaning literally, "the great city."[120]

The entrance to the land of the dead, according to an incantation text quoted above (p. 157), was located in the distant west, at the place where the Babylonians saw the sun descend. Through this entrance, as is indicated by the text just referred to, an incantation priest could banish a molesting spirit to the nether world. This was probably also the passage through which certain deities, such as Tammuz and Ishtar, descended to the underworld. But other entrances could be made anywhere; every grave constituted such an entrance.

---

[120]For a fuller and well-documented discussion of the Babylonian names of the nether world see Knut Tallqvist in Studia Orientalia, Vol. V, No. 4 (1934).

After entering the great below, the dead had to cross the
river Ḫubur,[121] where he was greeted by Ḫumuṭṭabal ("Take away
quickly!"), the boatman of the nether world. This four-handed
being, with a face like that of Zû, the divine storm-bird,[122]
ferried the dead to the other side of the river. From there
the departed proceeded to the city of the nether world. To this
city, at least at one time during its history, was undoubtedly
applied the term urugal, "the great city," which in the inscriptions,
obviously by an extension of its meaning, is employed with reference to the entire "land of no return." It was a great metropolis
surrounded by seven walls, each wall pierced by a gate,[123] and each
gate guarded by a demon.[124] Within the walls were the lapis lazuli
palace of the queen of the lower world[125] and the palace of justice,
called Egalgina, where the Anunnaki dwelt.[126]

This vast city of the dead and the adjoining territory were
ruled by a goddess known variously as Ereshkigal, Allatu, Irkalla,
and Bêlit-irṣiti(m). She appears as the wife of Ninazu ("The Lord
of Healing"), of Gugalanna, and of Nergal, the god of plague and
pestilence, of war and death.[127] Befitting her station, Ereshkigal
was surrounded by numerous attendants, who were ever at her beck
and call. There was the grim plague-god Namtar, her vizier, who
put her orders into execution. There was Bêlit-ṣêri, her scribe,
who read to her,[128] presumably such things as the names of the new

---

[121]Ebeling, Tod und Leben ...., p. 128:5-8; Craig, op. cit.,
I, 17:3 and 44:17 (cf. Landsberger in Zeitschrift für Assyriologie,
XLIII, 46:17).

[122]See "A Prince's Vision of the Underworld," rev. 5.

[123]So in the story of Ishtar's descent and in a bilingual incantation published by Thompson in Cuneiform Texts ...., Vol. XVI
(London, 1903), Pl. 13:46-47.

[124]Mentioned by their names in Ebeling, Keilschrifttexte aus
Assur religiösen Inhalts, No. 142, col. iv, 12-15.

[125]Sumerian recension of Ishtar's descent, line 72.

[126]Babylonian version of Ishtar's descent, rev. 31-33.

[127]Tallqvist, Akkadische Götterepitheta (Helsinki, 1938), p.
307 (under Ereshkigal), equates Gugalanna with Nergal, but without
giving any reason for the identification. His reference on p. 259
(under "Allatum") is, of course, insufficient.

[128]Gilgamesh Epic, Tablet VII, col. iv, 51-52.

arrivals, which had been announced by the gatekeeper and had in all
likelihood been recorded by her (for she is also called "the bookkeeper of heaven and earth" and "the bookkeeper of the great
gods").[129] Moreover, there were the seven great gatekeepers guard-
ing her palace, and the Anunnaki, the seven dreaded judges of the
underworld. And, finally, there was the host of demons who, like
Namtar, spread disease and suffering among mankind and so brought
ever new subjects to her gloomy domain. In the purported vision
of the underworld published in the preceding chapter, Ereshkigal's
attendants are portrayed as composite beings, reminding us of
Egyptian demonology.

The Hebrew beliefs on the realm of the dead were in some respects quite similar, in others they were diametrically opposed to
those of the Mesopotamians.

The common Hebrew designation for the place of the dead is
Shě'ôl. The etymology of this word is still obscure, despite the
numerous efforts that have been made to determine its root and to
discover its basic meaning. Friedrich Delitzsch[130] identified it
with a supposed Babylonian term shu'âlu. But this view has long
since been abandoned, following Peter Jensen's[131] demonstration that
Delitzsch's idea was based on a misunderstanding of the Babylonian
lines in question and that no such word for the Babylonian underworld can be derived from them.

Shě'ôl is generally translated with "the realm of the dead."
It denotes the subterranean spirit world, the grave, the state or
condition of death, and the brink of death, or the like.

In the first-mentioned sense Shě'ôl is met with in Num. 16:

---

[129]See von Soden in Zeitschrift für Assyriologie, XLI, 233-36.
Bêlit-şêri evidently also reduced Ereshkigal's decrees to writing.

[130]Wo lag das Paradies? (Leipzig, 1881), p. 121; Prolegomena
eines neuen hebräisch-aramäischen Wörterbuchs zum Alten Testament
(Leipzig, 1886), p. 145, n. 2.

[131]Die Kosmologie der Babylonier (Strassburg, 1890), pp. 222-
24. On the unsuccessful attempts made by Morris Jastrow, Jr., to
defend Delitzsch's position see his article in the American Journal
of Semitic Languages and Literatures, XIV (1897/98), 165-70, and his
book The Religion of Babylonia and Assyria (Boston, 1898), pp. 558-
60. The signs URU.KI, which caused Jastrow such difficulties, can
together stand also for âlu ("city"). See, e.g., Rawlinson, op. cit.,
Vol. V, Pl. 25:32, and G. Dossin in Textes cunéiformes, Vol. XVII
(Paris, 1933), No. 1:4.11.

30-33, dealing with the fate of Korah, Dathan, and Abiram. As
Enoch and Elijah went up alive into heaven, to dwell with the celestial spirits, so Korah and his company went down alive into the
underworld, to be with the spirits residing in that dark and gloomy
place. In the same meaning Shĕ'ôl is employed very plainly also
in Deut. 32:22: "A fire is kindled in mine anger and shall burn
to the very depths of Shĕ'ôl, so that it shall consume the earth
and its produce and set the foundations of the mountains on fire."
Ps. 139:8: "If I ascend up into heaven, Thou art there; if I make
my bed in Shĕ'ôl, Thou art there (also)"; and Amos 9:2: ."Though
they dig into Shĕ'ôl, thence shall my hand take them; and though
they mount up to heaven, thence will I bring them down," refer to
the subterranean spirit world, as shown by the contrast between
heaven and Shĕ'ôl, the two extremes. The same place is meant in
Isa. 14:13-15: "Thou saidst in thy heart: 'The heavens will I
ascend, above the stars of God will I set up my throne; I will sit
on the mount of assembly, in the farthest parts of the north. I
will rise above the heights of the clouds, I will make myself equal
to the most High.' But thou shalt be brought down to Shĕ'ôl, to
the farthest (i.e., the lowest) parts of the pit"; in 7:11; 57:9
(where the statement "and didst debase thyself unto Shĕ'ôl" is
used hyperbolically); in Job 11:8; 26:6; Ps. 49:16; and Prov. 15:
11.24.

But in other passages Shĕ'ôl applies to the grave. This is
true of Isa. 14:11, where the prophet, in his exultation over the
fall of Babylon, declares: "Brought down to Shĕ'ôl is thy pomp,
(and) the noise of thy harps; underneath thee maggots are spread,
and worms are thy covering" (cf. Job 21:26); and Ezek. 32:26-27:
"There (is) Meshech-Tubal, with all his multitude round about his
graves, all of them uncircumcised, slain by the sword, for they
caused terror in the land of the living. They lie not with the
mighty, who have fallen of the uncircumcised, who went down to
Shĕ'ôl with their weapons of war, whose swords are laid under their
heads; their sins are (come) upon their bones, for they were the
terror of the mighty in the land of the living." The mention of
pomp, worms, and maggots, in the first instance, is a very clear
indication that the reference is to the grave,[132] while the state-

---

[132]Although the fallen king of Babylon was not to be accorded
the customary royal honors and was not to be buried in his own tomb

ment "whose swords are laid under their heads," in the second passage, removes all doubt that the "weapons of war" are conceived of
not as descending to the realm of the spirits, deep in the bosom
of the earth, but as being put in the grave, and that this is the
place to which the mighty are pictured as going. Almost every
statement in these two passages favors this interpretation. Such
is also the signification in which Shě'ôl is employed in Job 24:
19-20: "Drought and heat snatch away snow-waters; (so does) Shě'ôl
(those who) have sinned.[133] The womb forgets him, the worm feasts
on him," and in Ps. 141:7: "As when one plows and cleaves the
earth, (so) our bones are scattered at the mouth of Shě'ôl." The
obvious meaning of the second passage is: "As one plows up the
land and, in doing so, cleaves the earth and scatters the clods,
so our graves have been 'plowed up' and our bones have been cast
out and scattered at the mouth or margin of the grave, there to
lie in disgrace." There is no ground for believing that the char-
acteristics of the grave and those of the underworld have been con-
fused in these passages.[134] In the sense of the future resting-
place of the body, Shě'ôl occurs also on an Aramaic papyrus from a
Jewish community in Egypt. The document, probably part of a story,
treats of a certain Bar Punesh, who apparently had rendered some
distinguished service for which he is rewarded by the king. In
one line the king addresses Bar Punesh with these words: "Thy
bones shall not go down to Shě'ôl (שׁאול), and thy spirit[135] [shall

in the royal cemetery to be united with his own, he was nevertheless to be buried. Together with the slain on the field of battle
he was to be thrown into a hole and covered with a heap of stones
(cf. Josh. 7:26; 8:29; II Sam. 18:17). For the prophet says: "All
the kings of the nations, all of them, lie in honor, everyone in his
house. But thou art cast down away from thy grave, like an abomi-
nable branch, clothed with slain men thrust through by the sword,
those who go down to the stones of the pit, like a trampled corpse.
Thou wilt not be united with them in burial" (Isa. 14:18-20).

[133]Cf. Ps. 55:24: "Bloody and deceitful men will not live out
half their days."

[134]The fact that the common Old Testament designation for the
grave is קֶבֶר is no proof at all that Shě'ôl cannot have the same
meaning. קֶבֶר is the general word for "grave" while Shě'ôl is used
primarily in poetry, occurring only eight times in prose, out of a
total of sixty-five passages.

[135]Lit.: thy shadow.

not ....]."[136] That Shĕ'ôl in this case signifies "the grave" is
clear not only from the express mention of the bones, i.e., the body
(pars pro toto), but also from the contrast between "bones" and
"spirit." Cowley, in the work just cited, is therefore correct in
rendering Shĕ'ôl simply with "the grave."

In the Aramaic text just quoted, the words "Thy bones shall
not go down to Shĕ'ôl (i.e., the grave)" mean in reality "Thou
shalt not go down into death but shalt live forever."[137] This
figure of speech is found also in the Old Testament. In Prov. 23:
13-14 we read: "Withhold not chastisement from a child; for if thou
beatest him with the rod, he will not die. Beat him with the rod,
and thou shalt save his soul from Shĕ'ôl." Beating a child with
the rod will not cause him to die but will correct the child and so
will accomplish the opposite, namely, it will deliver him (lit.:
his soul) from Shĕ'ôl. The contrast shows quite plainly that the
reference is to death, as is recognized by the Septuagint, which
here translates Shĕ'ôl with θάνατος ("death"). Administering cor-
poral punishment to a disobedient son while there is hope (19:18)
will save him from an early death (29:1).[138] This interpretation
of Shĕ'ôl is also favored, if not required, by the parallelism in
Ps. 89:49: "Who is the man (that) will live and not suffer death,[139]
(but) deliver himself from the power of Shĕ'ôl?" Furthermore, when
David instructs Solomon that he should not let Joab's gray hairs[140]
go down to Shĕ'ôl (i.e., the grave) in peace and that he should
bring the gray hairs of Shimei down to Shĕ'ôl with blood (I Kings
2:5-9), he undoubtedly means nothing more than that Solomon should
not let these men go down into death in the normal way, that he
should not let them die a natural death. Or when Jacob tells his

---

[136]A. Cowley, Aramaic Papyri of the Fifth Century B.C. (Oxford,
1923), No. 71:15.

[137]Cf. I Kings 1:31; Neh. 2:3; Dan. 2:4; 3:9.

[138]C. H. Toy, A Critical and Exegetical Commentary on the Book
of Proverbs (New York, 1908), p. 314, goes too far when he declares
that in the Book of Proverbs Shĕ'ôl stands throughout for physical
death. In 15:11.24 more than this is implied.

[139]Lit.: see death (cf. Ps. 90:15: to see evil, i.e., to
suffer evil).

[140]In this and the following instances, the words "the gray
hairs of someone" signify simply, by metonymy, "a person as an
aged man."

sons: "My son shall not go down with you; for his brother is dead, and he alone is left. If harm were to befall him on the way that ye go, ye would bring my gray hairs down to Shĕ'ôl in sorrow" (Gen. 42:38), he probably wants to say merely that he would die of grief. To this same category belong a number of passages in which Shĕ'ôl is used as a figure of speech to denote extreme misfortune, seemingly inescapable death, the brink of death, or the like (Pss. 30:4; 86:13; 88:4; Jonah 2:3 [=2:2 in the English translation]).

These are the meanings in which the term Shĕ'ôl is employed in the Old Testament. In some cases it is quite clear which of the values listed above is to be assigned to the word under discussion, while in others it is impossible to come to a definite decision. There is nothing peculiar about the fact that Shĕ'ôl has all these values. As an analogy we may mention the word "death," which in the Bible denotes not only physical death (to which man and beast alike are subject) and pestilence (i.e., one of the causes of physical death), but also spiritual death (cf. Rom. 8:6; Eph. 2:1) and the condition of the damned souls or spirits; in fact, it denotes even the subterranean realm of the dead, as we shall see presently. Here again it is not always easy to determine the intended meaning.[141]

Synonyms for Shĕ'ôl, particularly in the sense of "the grave," are 'abaddôn, "destruction," "place of destruction" (Job 26:6; 28:22; Ps. 88:12; Prov. 15:11);[142] shaḥath, "pit" (Job 33:18-30; Pss. 30:10; 55:24; Isa. 38:17; 51:14; Ezek. 28:8; etc.); and bôr, "pit" (Pss. 28:1; 30:4; 88:5; Isa. 14:15.19; 38:18; Lam. 3:55; Prov. 28:17). In some passages, such as Job 38:17, also the word mâweth ("death"), designating the underground spirit world, occurs as a synonym for Shĕ'ôl; but such cases are not so numerous as has been asserted.

---

[141]Contrary to the opinion of some, there is no proof that Shĕ'ôl served at any time in Israel as the designation of the goddess of the underworld (see König, Geschichte der alttestamentlichen Religion, p. 53). The arguments produced by W. C. Wood in the Journal of Biblical Literature, XXXV (1916), 268, to show that Shĕ'ôl appears as "the god of the underworld" also in Hebrew history rest for the most part on his precarious interpretation of the names Shā'ûl, Gib'ath-Shā'ûl, Methûshā'ēl, and Mishā'ēl, and on the poetic personification of Shĕ'ôl in certain Bible passages, and as such are far too weak to sustain his claim. On the meanings of the names in question see König, Wörterbuch.

[142]Once also 'abaddô (Prov. 27:20).

This term may stand for an original môshab māweth, "the dwelling
of Death," i.e., the dwelling of the death-god, as is suggested
by the Babylonian phrases mûshab irkalla and shubat irkalla, "the
dwelling of Irkalla," and by the appearance of the death-god's
name as Môt on the tablets from Ras Shamra and as Mûtu in Babylonian.[143] If such is the origin of this Hebrew designation for
the realm of the dead, there can scarcely be any room for doubt
that the expression was taken over from the Canaanites. It should
be noted, however, that in the Old Testament this designation contains no allusion to the death-god.

The Old Testament localizes the realm of the dead, or, rather,
the realm of certain disembodied human spirits, within the innermost parts of the earth, below the sea. This is evident from such
passages as Deut. 32:22; Ps. 139:8; Isa. 14:13-15; Amos 9:2, which
have been quoted above, and Job 26:5: "The shades are made to quake
beneath the waters and their inhabitants."

The assertion is frequently made that Shĕ'ôl, i.e., the subterranean spirit world, was entered through gates in the west.
While it is true that the Old Testament refers in a general way
to "the gates of Shĕ'ôl" (Isa. 38:10) and "the bars of Shĕ'ôl" (Job.
17:16), there is no proof that these gates were thought to be in
the west.[144] Furthermore, there are reasons for believing that
neither Isa. 38:10 nor Job 17:16 treats of the underworld at all,
but that both passages deal with the grave.

To begin with Job 17:16 and to quote this passage in its context, Job says: "My days are past, my plans are broken, the desires of my heart. They[145] want to turn night into day, (and) in
the face of darkness (they declare) light (to be) near! If I wait
for Shĕ'ôl as my house, (if) I have (virtually) spread out my couch

---

[143]See von Soden in Zeitschrift für Assyriologie, XLIII, 16:43,
and Harper, op. cit., No. 977, rev. 4. Whether the death-god appears also in the Hebrew personal name אֲחִימוֹת (I Chron. 6:10 [= 6:
25 in the English version]), is by no means certain. This name
could be rendered "My brother is the death-god" or "A brother of
death." On the latter interpretation the thought may possibly be
analogous to that expressed in Isa. 28:15. König, Wörterbuch, p.
12, does not hazard a translation.

[144]König, Geschichte der alttestamentlichen Religion, pp. 501-2.

[145]The friends of Job.

in the darkness, (if) I have (already) called to corruption:[146]
'Thou art my father,' (and) to the worm: '(Thou art) my mother
and my sister,' where then is my hope? And who will see my hope?
It[147] will go down to the bars of Shĕ'ôl, when (our) rest together
is in the dust" (17:11-16). That up to verse 16, exclusive, Job
speaks of the grave is too obvious to demand proof. Nor do we have
to spend much time trying to demonstrate that this holds good also
of verse 16b: "when (our) rest together is in the dust." It is
therefore reasonable to inquire whether also verse 16a: "It will
go down to the bars of Shĕ'ôl," does not perhaps refer to the
resting-place of man's mortal remains. This question can, I believe, be answered in the affirmative, partly in view of the context
and the fact that Shĕ'ôl occurs also as a synonym for the grave,
and partly in view of similar imagery found elsewhere in the Old
Testament. The expression "the bars of Shĕ'ôl" is comparable to
the "bar(s) and doors" of the sea (Job 38:10) and "the bars" of
the earth (Jonah 2:7). In both passages "the bars" refer to the
walls of the basin of the sea,[148] not to the underworld. We may
therefore conclude that "the bars of Shĕ'ôl" designate the confining
barriers of the sepulchral chamber,[149] particularly if "the chambers of death," mentioned in Prov. 7:27 and paralleled with Shĕ'ôl,
denote the burial chambers.

Somewhat similar reasons confirm the view that also Isa. 38:10
is concerned solely with the habitation of the body. In this passage Hezekiah is quoted as stating: "I said: 'In the middle of my
days must I enter the gates of Shĕ'ôl, deprived of the rest of my
years.'" In Pss. 9:14 and 107:18 and Job 38:17, we meet also the
expression "the gates of death." In the first two instances this
phrase is employed as a figure of speech for mortal peril or for

---

[146]The original has שַׁחַת, which usually signifies "the pit."
Even if in this verse we take the word in the latter sense, it still
points to the grave and not the underworld, as is shown by the
second half of the verse. On שַׁחַת see König, Wörterbuch.

[147]On the troublesome verbal form in this line see Gesenius'
Hebrew Grammar, edited and enlarged by E. Kautzsch and translated
by Cowley (Oxford, 1910), § 47, k.

[148]C. F. Keil, Die zwölf kleinen Propheten (Leipzig, 1888),
p. 292.

[149]The fact that Job 17:16 has בַּד while the other two passages
use בְּרִיחַ is of no consequence.

seemingly inescapable death, while in the last-named case it denotes the underworld, i.e., the gates stand for the whole realm
(pars pro toto). Parallels to this usage are found, e.g., in
Deut. 12:12 and 15:7, Jer. 14:2, and Pss. 87:2 and 122:2, where
the gates stand for the city. It must therefore be admitted as
a distinct possibility that "the gates of Shĕ'ôl" in Isa. 38:10
may simply be a designation for Shĕ'ôl itself. Moreover, since
there is no conclusive evidence that the souls of pious persons,
among whom Hezekiah must be numbered, were believed to descend to
Shĕ'ôl in the sense of the subterranean spirit world, while there
are passages which state clearly that the souls of the righteous
ascended to heaven, as we shall see, it is reasonable to assume
that Hezekiah uses Shĕ'ôl in the sense of "the grave" and that he
wants to say merely that he was afraid he would die.

There is no reason why "the gates of Shĕ'ôl" must be taken
any more literally than such figurative expressions as "the hand
of Shĕ'ôl," i.e., the power of Shĕ'ôl (Pss. 49:16; 89:49; Hos.
13:14), "the mouth of Shĕ'ôl" (Ps. 141:7; Isa. 5:14), the "mouth"
of the earth (Gen. 4:11), "the belly of Shĕ'ôl" (Jonah 2:3), "the
door of my lips (Ps. 141:3), "the gate of heaven" (Gen. 28:17),
"the gates of Hades" (Matt. 16:18), "the keys of death and of Hades"
(Rev. 1:18), or "the keys of the kingdom of heaven" (Matt. 16:19).
The mere fact that other nations of the ancient world, such as the
Babylonians and the Assyrians, pictured the realm of the dead as
having gates in the literal sense of the term proves as little for
Israel as a certain belief or practice in the Roman Catholic church
would prove for Protestantism.

It has, furthermore, been asserted that the Old Testament describes the underground realm of the spirits as a land of dust and
darkness, as it was pictured in Mesopotamia. The principal passages
on which this idea is based are Job 10:21-22, in which Job speaks
of going to "the land of darkness and blackness"; Job 38:17: "Have
the gates of death been revealed to thee? Or hast thou seen the
gates of darkness?" and Dan. 12:2, stating that in the last days
many will awake from the 'admath ʿāfār, some to everlasting life
and others to everlasting shame and disgrace.

This view is partly correct. In Job 38:17, which without
doubt treats of the nether world, as we can see from the context,[150]

---

[150]Cf. König, Das Buch Hiob (Gütersloh, 1929), p. 403.

the subterranean abode of the spirits of the departed is conceived
as a place of darkness,[151] but the other two passages do not admit
of this interpretation. In the first place, it must be remembered
that in neither one of them do we find the term Shĕ'ôl nor any of
its synonyms noted above. Furthermore, the context shows that Job
speaks of the grave. He says: "Wherefore hast Thou brought me
forth from the womb? Would that I had expired and no eye had seen
me! I should (then) have been as though I had not been; from the
womb to the grave I should have been carried. Are not my (remaining)
days few? Then cease (and) turn from me, that I may be cheerful
(yet) a little while, before I go—and do not return—to the land of
darkness and blackness; a land of darkness, as darkness (itself),
of darkness and without order, and when it shines, it is like darkness" (10:18-22). In verse 19: "from the womb to the grave I
should have been carried," Job makes express mention of the grave.
That this term is here not synonymous with the underworld is obvious from his remark that he would have been "carried" to the
grave; no one is "carried" to the realm of the spirits within the
depths of the earth.[152] Since there is no indication that Job has
changed the subject, the natural conclusion is that also in the
next verses he speaks of the grave rather than of the abode of the
spirits. In a similar way William Cullen Bryant, in his Thanatopsis,
speaks of "breathless darkness, and the narrow house" and pictures
that "great tomb" and "mighty sepulcher" into which the lifeless
forms of men are laid as a "mysterious realm" coextensive with the
face of the earth. And in German we speak of Grabesdunkel ("sepulchral darkness") and Grabesnacht ("sepulchral night"). It cannot
be argued that the picture in Job 10:21-22 does not fit the grave.

And as regards Dan. 12:2, why must 'admath 'âfâr be translated
"the land of dust"? The first meaning of 'adâmâ is simply "the surface of the earth," "the ground" (Gen. 4:11; Amos 3:5), while 'âfâr
denotes not only "the dust" but occurs quite frequently also in the
sense of "the earth" (Job 28:2; 41:25 [= 41:33]; Ps. 103:14; Isa.
2:10; etc.). What, then, is there against rendering 'admath 'âfâr

---

[151]No matter whether we read צַלְמָוֶת ("the shadow of death") or
צַלְמָה ("blackness," "darkness"), the picture is the same.

[152]There is, of course, not the slightest reason for assuming
that Job had in mind a "carrying" by spiritual beings, such as is
mentioned in Luke 16:22.

by "the surface of the earth"? Gesenius[153] translates this phrase
with "the earth consisting of dust" (die aus Staub bestehende Erde).
Both he[154] and König[155] see in this passage a reference to the
grave.[156] Because of the very nature of its location, the Hebrews
might of course have thought of the underworld as a place or land
of dust, but we have no Old Testament warrant that they actually
did so.

    While the Babylonian nether world had its own pantheon, the
Old Testament Shĕʾôl was under the control of the same God who
governed heaven and earth and all that is therein. For we read:
"Whither shall I go from Thy spirit? Or whither shall I flee from
Thy presence? If I ascend up into heaven, Thou art there; if I
make my bed in Shĕʾôl, Thou art there (also)" (Ps. 139:7-8); "Shĕʾôl
(lies) bare before Him, and ʾAbaddôn has no covering" (Job 26:6);
"Shĕʾôl and ʾAbaddôn (lie open) before the Lord, how much more the
hearts of the sons of men" (Prov. 15:11); "Though they dig into
Shĕʾôl, thence shall my hand take them; and though they mount up
to heaven, thence will I bring them down" (Amos 9:2); and: "A fire
is kindled in mine anger and shall burn to the very depths of Shĕʾôl,
so that it shall consume the earth and its produce and set the
foundations of the mountains on fire" (Deut. 32:22). God's power
extends from the heights of heaven to the depths of Shĕʾôl. He is
the only ruler of Shĕʾôl recognized in the Old Testament. The contention that in the early period of Hebrew history Shĕʾôl was
thought to be beyond the limits of God's control or jurisdiction
lacks biblical confirmation.[157]

---

[153]Handwörterbuch, p. 11 (under אֲדָמָה).

[154]Ibid., p. 608 (under עָפָר).

[155]Wörterbuch, p. 341 (under עָפָר).

[156]After these lines had been written, I noticed that K. Budde,
Das Buch Hiob (Göttingen, 1896), p. 104, had already rendered
ʾadmath ʿāfār, in Dan. 12:2, by Erdboden ("the surface of the earth").

[157]Just as indefensible and altogether unnatural is Charles's
affirmation (op. cit., p. 138) that even according to as late a
passage as Dan. 12:2-3 God cannot influence the inhabitants of
Shĕʾôl for good or evil as long as they are there but that "they
must first through resurrection return to earth and come within the
bounds of the divine rule" before he can punish or reward them.
The mere fact that God can raise the dead from Shĕʾôl is undeniable
evidence that his power extends thither and that Shĕʾôl is within
"the bounds of the divine rule"; and if his power is strong enough

We have seen that the term She'ôl is employed both of the
grave and of the underground spirit world. The former place is
"the house of assembly" (Job 30:23 [cf. Eccles. 3:20]), "the
house of eternity" (Eccles. 12:5 [cf. Isa. 14:18-19]), in which
all living, good and bad alike, must appear eventually.[158] But
what of the latter place? Is it reserved for the souls of all or
only for those of a certain type or group?

That the souls of men do not all go to the same place is, in
general, attested in Psalm 73. Here the author is troubled by the
prosperity of the sinners and the sad lot of the righteous. Although the wicked mock and defy God in heaven, things turn out
well with them. "They are not in trouble like (other) men, nor
are they plagued like (other) people" (vs. 5). But the psalmist,
though he has kept his heart pure and has washed his hands in innocence, is plagued all the time and chastened every morning (vss.
13-14). He tried to solve the problem presented by the apparent
inversion of right and wrong, but it defied all solution until he
went into God's sanctuary and there (as he listened and observed)
learned the ultimate fate of the ungodly. The psalmist says:
"Surely Thou dost set them in slippery places; Thou dost lay them
in ruins. How they become a desolation as in a moment! They are
utterly consumed with terrors. As (one despises) a dream upon
awakening, (so,) O Lord, when Thou dost bestir Thyself, wilt Thou
despise their image" (vss. 18-20). The wicked will be cast off
and so will be banished from God's gracious presence. But the
righteous will forever be with God and enjoy unbroken communion
with him; even in the hour of death, God's right hand will hold

---

to raise the souls from She'ôl, why can he not influence them otherwise while they are still there?

[158]The same or similar designations for the grave appear in
the literatures of other nations. Sennacherib referred to his sepulcher as his "abode of eternity" (Messerschmidt, op. cit., Nos.
46 and 47); the architect of the Egyptian king Sesostris I called
the royal tomb which he was commissioned to build "an eternal seat"
(J. H. Breasted, The Dawn of Conscience [New York and London, 1934],
pp. 224-25); in other Egyptian passages, as well as on Palmyrenian
Aramaic, Syriac, and Punic inscriptions, the tomb is alluded to
under the phrase the "house of eternity" (see John A. Wilson in the
Journal of Near Eastern Studies, III [1944], 208; M. Lidzbarski,
Handbuch der nordsemitischen Epigraphik, I [Weimar, 1898], 235-36);
and on Latin inscriptions it is termed domus aeterna.

them and take them to heaven. For the psalmist continues: "Yet
I am always with Thee; Thou holdest my right hand. Thou dost
guide me with Thy counsel, and afterward Thou wilt receive me to
glory.[159] Whom have I in heaven (but Thee)? And having Thee, I
desire nothing on earth. When my flesh and my heart fail, God
(will still be) the refuge of my heart and my portion forever"
(vss. 23-26).[160]

And as regards Shĕ'ôl, in particular, we have evidence that
it, in the signification of the subterranean realm of the spirits,
applies to the habitation of the souls of the wicked only. This
can be gathered from Psalm 49, which, like Psalm 73, deals with
the problem of divine retribution. In verses 8-11 the speaker declares physical death to be the inevitable lot of all men, saying:
"A brother can by no means redeem a man, he cannot give to God a
ransom for him—for the redemption of their soul(s) is too costly,
and he must desist from it forever—, so that he should live forever, (and) not see the pit. For he sees (that) even wise men die,
(that) they perish together with the fool and the brutish person,
and leave their substance to others." The term "man" (ש׳א) designates a person of means, as evident from the context,[161] while the
"brother" denotes his wealthy peer. Not even a rich man, who, if
anyone, should have the means to do so, can save his rich fellow-
man from eventual death, in spite of the fact that the latter would
naturally also spend his substance.[162] No amount of wealth, however
great it may be or however wisely it may be applied, can achieve
that end. For the "brother" must see that even the wise among the
rich, i.e., even those who make the wisest use of their wealth,
must perish.[163] Then in verses 15-16 the psalmist continues:

[159]Or: "Thou wilt receive me with honor." The ultimate sense
is the same.

[160]Cf. Charles, op. cit., pp. 76-77; König, Die Psalmen
(Gütersloh, 1927), pp. 602-12.

[161]Note the chiasm in vs. 3.

[162]For a fine discussion of vs. 8 see König, Die Psalmen,
pp. 593-94.

[163]This interpretation is demanded by the general context
(cf. ibid., pp. 594-95). Charles (op. cit., p. 76, n. 2) overstates
the case when he declares that in the Psalms the terms "wise man"
and "fool" are always used in a religious or ethical sense. In the
Psalter the words for "wise" (חָכָם), "to be wise" (חָכַם), "wisdom"

"Like sheep they[164] turn[165] to Shĕ'ôl; death shall shepherd them;
the upright shall rule over them in the morning; and their forms
shall be consumed by Shĕ'ôl, so that they have no habitation. But
God will redeem my soul from the power of Shĕ'ôl, for He will receive me." As sheep turn to the shepherd, upon the latter's call,
to be led out to the pasture grounds (cf. Ps. 23; John 10:4), so
the wicked turn to Shĕ'ôl, only to be shepherded by death until
the dawn of the resurrection morning (Ps. 17:15; Dan. 12:2), when
the righteous will rule over them (cf. I Cor. 6:2-3) and their
forms will be consumed by Shĕ'ôl, the place of torment.[166] The
righteous, on the other hand, will be saved from the power of
Shĕ'ôl and will live with God. In view of what the psalmist says
in verses 8-11 about the inevitability of death, the term Shĕ'ôl
refers, of course, not to the grave but to the underground abode
of the spirits; from this, God will redeem the righteous. The
Hebrew verb for "to redeem" is pādâ. This word occurs also in
verses 8-10, quoted above. There it is used in the sense of pre-
serving someone from something, of freeing someone from the necessity of having to go through a certain experience (cf. Job 33:28).
There is no reason why a different meaning should be attributed to
it in verse 16. Rather, the contrast drawn between the lot of the
godly and that of the ungodly and the fact that Shĕ'ôl is here portrayed as penal in character, argue for the retention of the meaning which pādâ has in verse 8. The psalmist wants to say that God
will save the righteous from what we would call going to hell. God
will, instead, take the righteous to himself. Since we seem to
have here an allusion to Gen. 5:24, the Hebrew term lāqaḥ ("to take
or receive") has been interpreted in the sense of a bodily translation to heaven, as lāqaḥ is employed in Gen. 5:24 and II Kings
2:9-10. But that interpretation is precluded by verses 8-11, according to which all men must submit to physical death. Moreover, if

---

(חָכְמָה), "fool" (כְּסִיל), and "folly" (כֶּסֶל, כִּסְלָה), all of which together
occur around twenty times in that book, have only in the bare majority of cases a religious or ethical signification.

[164]The wicked.

[165]With this meaning of the verb שׁע cf. Job 10:20: "Turn
(from me)." On the form שֻׁעו see König, Wörterbuch, p. 497.

[166]Cf. Franz Delitzsch, Biblical Commentary on the Psalms,
II (New York, n.d.), trans. D. Eaton, 136; König, Die Psalmen,
pp. 598-99 and 601.

the psalmist meant to say that he personally, because of highly exceptional piety, was not going to "see the pit," or sink down into
the grave, how much good would that do others? If he expected to
be carried to heaven, that would solve his own problem, but how many
other God-fearing people would it help solve their problem? And yet
as is indicated in the opening lines, his solution concerns not only
them but all the inhabitants of the earth.[167] The meaning of verse
16 is, rather, that upon death God will take the souls of the righteous to the realms of heaven.[168] The psalmist thus represents Shĕ'ô
in the sense of the subterranean spirit world, as the future abode
of the wicked only and represents heaven as that of the righteous.[16]
As a place of punishment Shĕ'ôl appears already in the story about
Korah, Dathan, and Abiram (Num. 16:1-35), whose fate is wished upon
the wicked oppressors in Ps. 55:16.

Contrariwise, there is no passage which proves that Shĕ'ôl was
ever employed as a designation for the gathering-place of the departed spirits of the godly. But it will be asked: "Did not Jacob,
according to Gen. 37:35, expect to go down to Shĕ'ôl to be joined
there with his son Joseph?" Considering that Shĕ'ôl, as we have seen
can denote also the state or condition of death and that in Gen. 42:
38 Jacob probably uses Shĕ'ôl in precisely this sense, it is likely
that Jacob meant to say nothing more than that he would die of a
broken heart because of the loss of his son—that this loss would
cause him to enter the afterworld, where his son already found himself and where he apparently expected to find him. In using the

---

[167]To assume with R. Kittel, Die Psalmen (Leipzig, 1929), p.
182, that according to this psalm only the godless will have to die
while the righteous will be spared and will instead be translated,
is tantamount to denying that the psalmist, who must have seen daily
that not even righteousness is a guaranty against physical death,
possessed even an average measure of intelligence.

[168]In this connection it is not without interest to note that
in Gen. 5:24 the Septuagint renders lāqaḥ with μετατίθημι and that
this Greek term is employed in the Wisd. of Sol. 4:10 of the translation of the soul.
Neither Psalm 49, as König affirms in his commentary on the
Psalms (p. 601), nor any other passage in the Old Testament teaches
an intermediate state or sojourn (status medius or intermedius) for
the righteous after death.

[169]Cf. Charles, op. cit., pp. 74-76; C. A. Briggs, A Critical
and Exegetical Commentary on the Book of Psalms, I (New York, 1906),
411; and E. Sellin in Neue kirchliche Zeitschrift, XXX (1919),
283-84.

expression "to go down to Shĕ'ôl," Jacob is probably just as indefinite on the particular sphere in which he hoped to move and
have his being as we are when we speak of "going down into death,"
or when we refer to the "great beyond," or the "afterworld."

The same indefinite idea which, so it seems to me, is conveyed
by Jacob's statement characterizes the well-known formulas: "to
be gathered to one's people," "to be gathered to one's fathers,"
"to go to one's fathers," and "to go to the generation of one's
fathers," which some will probably invoke to show that, while the
later writings of the Old Testament occasionally refer to a celes-   c
tial dwelling-place for the godly, the earlier books consign the
souls of all men alike to the underworld.

These expressions call for a somewhat detailed examination.
The first expression is applied to Abraham (Gen. 25:8), Ishmael
(25:17), Isaac (35:29), Jacob (49:29.33), Aaron (Num. 20:24),
and Moses (27:13; 31:2; Deut. 32:50); the second to Josiah (II
Kings 22:20; II Chron. 34:28) and the God-fearing generation under
the leadership of Joshua (Judg. 2:10); the third to Abraham (Gen.
15:15); and the fourth to the soul of the earthly-minded rich person (Ps. 49:20). In two passages, Num. 20:26 and 27:13b, referring
to Aaron, we find also the shortened form "to be gathered," either
to one's people (cf. 27:13a) or to one's fathers. If we may include
Ishmael among the godly (cf. Gen. 21:9-21), the first three of the
phrases just mentioned occur only of pious individuals. But considering that the fourth expression, whose wording is almost identical with that of the first three, is applied to the wicked, we
cannot attach any special significance to this fact.

That these figures of speech do not refer to the interment in
the grave of the fathers, or the ancestral tomb, as has been maintained, is clear from the fact that Abraham, Aaron, and Moses were
not united with their fathers in the grave.[170] Nor do they have
reference to burial in general, for in the stories of the "gather-

---

[170]John Skinner, A Critical and Exegetical Commentary on
Genesis (New York, 1910), p. 352, goes beyond the evidence by asserting that "the popular conception of Sheôl as a vast aggregate
of graves in the under world enabled the language to be applied to
men who (like Abraham) were buried far from their ancestors."
There is no Old Testament proof that the grave was thought to be
located within the nether world. Equally indemonstrable is the
view put forth by Charles (op. cit., p. 33) that in the course of
time "all the graves of the tribe or nation were regarded as united
in one" and that to this aggregate the designation Shĕ'ôl was given.

ing" of Abraham and Isaac it is expressly added that they were buried (Gen. 25:8-9; 35:29); moreover, Jacob was "gathered to his
people" (Gen. 49:33) several months before his body was committed
to the ground (50:1-13). Unlike the phrase "to lie down with one's
fathers," which we considered above, they do not even mean simply
"to die," for in some instances they are preceded by the express
statement: "And he gave up the ghost and died" (Gen. 25:8.17;
35:29)—a statement which describes both the process and the conclusion of the process. To be gathered to one's people or fathers
is a sequel of death, as appears with special clarity from Deut.
32:50: "And die on the mountain whither thou goest up and be gathered unto thy people." It denotes something that follows upon
death but precedes burial.[171] There can be no doubt that the figur
of speech under discussion have reference to the immortal element
in man. A clear indication of that we seem to have in Ps. 49:19-20
"Though in his lifetime (a man) blesses his soul, and (men) praise
thee that thou doest well unto thyself, it shall go to the generation of his fathers; they will not see light forever." The subject of the verbal form tābô ("it shall go") is nafshô ("his soul")
While the word nefesh ("soul"), in composition with the pronominal
suffixes, can stand also for "self,"[172] there does not appear to be
any valid reason why in this case it should not be taken in the
more literal sense. But, regardless of how the term nefesh must
be interpreted in this particular instance, the expressions under
consideration cannot mean anything else than that the soul or spirit
of a certain person leaves this world at death and enters the after
world, in which his fathers or certain of his kindred already find
themselves.[173] But there is no justification for concluding on the
basis of these formulas that those who have gone before are thought
of as assembled in Shĕ'ôl in the sense of the subterranean spirit
world and that the dead will join them in that dark and gloomy

---

[171]Num. 20:26c is to be rendered: "And Aaron shall be gathered
(to his people) by dying there."

[172]In such cases "my soul" = "I"; "thy soul" = "thou"; etc.
(cf. Pss. 25:13; 30:4; 62:2.6; 124:7; Isa. 51:23; etc.).

[173]Much the same view has been expressed by König, Die Genesis
p. 555; Theologie des Alten Testaments (Stuttgart, 1922), pp. 227-
28, and by the Spanish exegete Lino Murillo, El Génesis (Rome,
1914), pp. 633-34.

abode; this is true particularly since the word Shĕ'ôl is never
found in connection with any of these phrases. The expressions themselves designate a person's condition in the other world neither
as happy nor as miserable, thus leaving the reader to infer or sur-
mise the individual's ultimate fate from the context or from whatever information on his life is available. They are as little
informative on the ultramundane whereabouts of the soul as are the
words of David, uttered at the loss of his child: "I shall go to
him, but he will not return to me" (II Sam. 12:23), or the formula
"to go the way of all the earth" (Josh. 23:14; I Kings 2:2).

It will probably be argued further that our view on Shĕ'ôl is
incompatible with the story of the conjuring-up of Samuel, where it
is expressly said that Samuel came up. But in reply to this argument, attention may be called, first of all, to the much-debated
question whether the apparition described in I Sam. 28:3-20 was
the real Samuel or whether it was an evil spirit who had assumed
the outward appearance of Samuel and had arrayed himself in the
kind of garments worn by the prophet in his lifetime, the case thus
being comparable, in a sense, to the assumption of human form and,
of course, human dress by angels (cf. Gen. 18:1-8; Judg. 13:2 ff.).
I believe that the whole affair was a demonic delusion, reminding
one of II Thess. 2:9-12. This opinion is not proved wrong by the
fact that the biblical writer speaks throughout of the appearance
of Samuel himself (cf. vss. 12.14—16.20), and not of some de-
ceiving ghost or the like, for the writer may simply be referring
to the spirit by the name which the woman gave it, without indicating his personal position, thus presenting the matter from the
viewpoint of the witch and the king,[174] or without deeming it necessary (in view of his remark in verse 6) to go beyond her terminology.[175] But irrespective of the identity or reality of the
apparition, does not the narrative show beyond doubt that the witch
and the king believed Samuel to be in the subterranean spirit world,

---

[174]Cf. Matt. 2:16: "Then Herod, when he saw that he had been
duped by the Magi (i.e., from his viewpoint), was very angry."

[175]No argument for the reality of the prophet's appearance can,
of course, be derived from the fulfilment of the prediction. There
are other agents, besides prophets, that can fortell events. Nor
can one adduce I Sam. 15:35: "And Samuel came no more to see Saul
until the day of his death." From this passage it follows as little
that Samuel came to see Saul after his death (i.e., the prophet's
death) as it follows from II Sam. 6:23 that Michal had a child after
her death.

even though he was a prophet of God? Granting that this is correct,
are we to judge Old Testament theology by the views of a benighted
and outlawed witch and a distracted, Godforsaken, and desperate king
who was, at the same time, perhaps not much less benighted than the
witch herself? Even assuming, for the sake of argument, that Samuel actually appeared, the narrative still does not prove that his
spirit resided in Shě'ôl. It may show merely that he came by way
of some passage through which spirits were believed to come.[176]
When the apparition asks: "Why hast thou disturbed me by bringing
me up?" (vs. 15), it may simply be using the technical expression
(probably borrowed from paganism by the practitioners of the black
art) for bringing the spirits of the departed back into the sphere
of mortals for the purpose of obtaining information from them, the
spirit employing this terminology in the same manner in which people
today speak of the "rising" and the "setting" of the sun, although
they may be thoroughly convinced that the sun stands still and that
it is the earth that moves. Furthermore, the words of Samuel,
"Tomorrow shalt thou and thy sons be with me" (vs. 19), need not
mean more than that by the end of the next day Saul and his sons
would be in the realm of death, i.e., that they, like Samuel, would
be dead. As far as our present purposes are concerned, this story
is devoid of all argumentative value.

Another point which appears to militate against the view on
Shě'ôl presented on these pages is offered by Eccles. 12:7, which
states that the departed spirits of all men return to God. But
even this consideration is far from conclusive. The passage does
not state that the souls of men will be absorbed by the spirit of
God, nor that all of them will remain with God, while Ps. 73:26
says explicitly that even after death God will be the "portion" of
the righteous "forever." How the passage in question is to be understood is evident in part from Psalms 49 and 73 but particularly
from its context, from 11:9: "Rejoice, young man, in thy youth,
and let thy heart cheer thee in the days of thy prime, and walk in
the ways of thy heart and in the sight of thine eyes, but know that
for all these (things) God will bring thee into judgment,"[177] and

---

[176]Cf. A. Lods, La Croyance à la vie future et le culte des
morts dans l'antiquité israélite (Paris, 1906), I, 253-54 (cf. also
the Gilgamesh Epic, Tablet XII:79-84).

[177]Also in his pleasures, man is to comport himself in such a
manner that he can face his God with a clear conscience.

12:14: "For God will bring every work into judgment, with regard
to every secret thing, whether it be good or evil." In the light
of the retributive work of God mentioned in the two verses just
quoted, and in the light of Psalms 49 and 73, the natural interpretation is that, after their departure from this life, all men
must present themselves before God in judgment, to be assigned
their respective places, the pious to remain with God and the wicked
to be banished to Shě'ôl. Thus, already according to the Old Testament, there was "a great gulf fixed" (Luke 16:26) between the souls
of the blessed and those of the damned.[178]

The Condition of the Dead

As the departed, according to Mesopotamian beliefs, arrived
at the first gate of the city of the dead, he was met by Nedu,[179]
the chief gatekeeper. Nedu announced the name of the new victim
to Ereshkigal and, upon word from her, admitted him into her presence and into that of the Anunnaki. As we can conclude from various
references in Babylonian literature,[180] judgment was now pronounced
on him, the only judgment of which there is a clear indication in
Babylonian eschatology.[181]

Tablet XII:87-153 of the Gilgamesh Epic gives us some idea of
the rules by which the judges in the underworld were guided and of
the treatment which the dead were accorded. If a man had died on
the field of battle, his father and his mother would support his
head and so provide, to some degree, for his comfort. If a man had
two sons, he was assigned quarters in a brick structure, where he

---

[178]The translations of Enoch (Gen. 5:24) and Elijah (II Kings
2:11) are exceptional cases and therefore cannot serve as evidence
pro or con, any more than the translation of the Babylonian Noah
and certain members of his household. The assumptions of Enoch and
Elijah show merely that exceptionally pious individuals can at the
end of this mundane life be transferred body and soul to the realms
of heaven; but they contain no indication as to what will happen to
the common sort of men after death.

[179]In the Sumerian account of Ishtar's descent to the underworld he is called Neti.

[180]Cf. the Sumerian version of Ishtar's descent and Meissner,
op. cit., II, 146-47.

[181]Contrary to Friedrich Delitzsch, Das Land ohne Heimkehr
(Stuttgart, 1911), p. 22, some time elapsed between death and judgment, as evidenced by the fact that the spirit could not even enter
the underworld until the body had been interred.

could eat bread. If he had three sons, he was permitted to drink
water out of the waterskins of the deep. If he had four sons, he
was granted privileges that made his heart rejoice. If he had
five sons, he received an honorable position in the palace of the
nether world; like that of a good scribe, his arm was bared and
ready for action, and straightway he entered the palace to take
up his duties. On the other hand, if he had none of these or similar points to his credit, or had even committed some crime, his
lot was dismal. The man with only one son lay prostrate at the
foot of the wall and wept bitterly. The curse which in the epi-
logue of the Code of Hammurabi is pronounced on any ruler who in
days to come would ignore or pervert the laws of Hammurabi contains
the following sentence: "Below, in the underworld, may he (i.e.,
Shamash) deprive his spirit of water!"[182]

Life after death was, accordingly, more or less a continuation
of life on earth. Moreover, a person's status and condition in the
hereafter were determined by his position and his deeds and achieve-
ments on earth. This is in full harmony with the evidence of the
tombs excavated at Ur and Kish, particularly the royal tombs. In
my estimation, this evidence points quite definitely to a belief
that the dead would have much the same needs as they had on earth
and would enjoy similar honors and prerogatives. It was undoubtedly
for these reasons that the kings took with them their courts, their
teams and chariots, and the furniture of their palaces.

In some respects, this conception of the conditions in the
lower world is in distinct contrast with what we read on Tablet
VII of the Gilgamesh Epic. According to this tablet, which perhaps contains material of later origin, the Mesopotamians pictured
the realm of the dead as the house from which no one ever went
forth, where people were clad like birds with garments of wings,
where over door and bolt dust had spread; the house of darkness
whose occupants were bereft of light, where dust was their food
and clay their sustenance, unless they received nourishment from
the living.[183] Here dwelt the mighty rulers of the past, the very

---

[182] Harper, The Code of Hammurabi (Chicago and London, 1904),
Pl. LXXIX:37-40.

[183] Cf. "Ishtar's Descent to the Underworld," lines 31 ff.;
and some of the passages quoted under the heading "Burial Customs."

representatives of Anu and Enlil, deprived of their crowns and, instead of being served, having to serve and wait on tables. Here also dwelt high priest and acolyte, incantation priest, ecstatic, and the attendants of the lavers of the great gods. Yea, here dwelt even Etana, the famous king of Kish who had ascended to the skies on the wings of an eagle, and Sumuqan, the god of cattle and vegetation. This kind of continuity of existence may well be called a curse rather than a blessing; total annihilation would have been an incomparably better lot. [184]

While there were moments of violent emotional outbursts, the nether world was, under ordinary circumstances, a place of silence, [185] where the dead "rested," [186] for which reason Enkidu was warned not to make a sound in the underworld. But the shades were active enough to eat and drink and to perform various duties. In fact, since they partook of the nature of the gods, as we shall presently see, they could even be invoked and worshiped and, in turn, could benefit or injure the living. [187]

On the condition of the dead, as on the realm of the dead, the beliefs of the Hebrews again differed widely from those of the Mesopotamians.

The Old Testament pictures the dead as resting or sleeping. Job says: "Why did I not die at birth, coming forth from the womb and expiring? Why did knees receive me? Or why breasts, that I should suck? For then I would have lain down and would be quiet; then I would have fallen asleep (and) would be at rest..... There the wicked cease (their) raging; and there the weary are at rest. (There) the captives are at ease together; they hear not the voice of the taskmaster" (3:11-13, 17-18). Answering his friends, Job declares: "Man lies down and does not rise (again); until the

---

[184]The Ur-Nammu composition, published by Langdon, Sumerian Liturgical Texts (Philadelphia, 1917), No. 6, has been left out of consideration, pending a new translation of this difficult poem. A very brief summary of the more intelligible lines has been given by Kramer in the Bulletin of the American Schools of Oriental Research, No. 94, p. 6, n. 11.

[185]See "Ishtar's Descent to the Underworld," line 11 (Assyrian recension).

[186]See above, pp. 162-63.

[187]See the material adduced under the heading "Burial Customs."

heavens are no more, they will not awake, nor be aroused from their
sleep" (14:12). And, speaking of his hope, he says: "It will go
down to the bars of Shĕ'ôl, when (our) rest together is in the dust"
(17:16). The psalmist prays: "Look (upon me and) answer me, O Lord,
my God; lighten mine eyes, lest I sleep the (sleep of) death" (13:
4). In another passage the psalmist exults: "Despoiled are the
stout of heart, they have slumbered away into their sleep; and none
of the men of war have found their hands. At Thy rebuke, O God of
Jacob, both chariot and horse have sunk into a deep sleep" (76:6-7).
In the same vein Jeremiah prophesies concerning the fate of the
Babylonians: "They shall sleep a perpetual sleep and never awake,
says the Lord" (51:39). In Dan. 12:2 we read that those who "sleep
in the ground of the earth shall awake." In verse 13 of the same
chapter Daniel is told: "But thou, go thy way till the end (comes);
for thou shalt rest and stand in thy lot at the end of the days."
The Proverbs warn: "The man who wanders from the way of wisdom will
rest in the assembly of the dead" (21:16). And in Isa. 57:1-2 the
prophet laments: "The righteous perishes, and there is no man who
lays it to heart; and godly men are taken away, without anyone considering that the righteous is taken away from the evil to come.
He enters into peace, they rest on their couches, whoever walks
straight before him." By being swept away, the righteous finds
rest in the grave, while the wicked is spared for the penal evil
to come and is gripped by the unrest of the times. In all these
cases the reference is without doubt to the rest or sleep of the
body; in fact, in some instances this idea is brought out unmistakably.

The dead dwell in silence (Pss. 94:17; 115:17), in the place
of destruction (Job 26:6; 28:22) and the land of forgetfulness
(Ps. 88:13; Eccles. 9:5; Job 14:21), and therefore do not praise
the Lord or give him thanks. We read: "In death there is no remembrance of Thee; in Shĕ'ôl, who praises Thee?" (Ps. 6:6); "What
profit is there in my blood, when I go down to the pit? Will the
dust praise Thee? Will it declare Thy faithfulness?" (30:10);
"Wilt Thou do wonders for the dead? Or will the deceased rise
to praise Thee?[188] Selah. Will Thy lovingkindness be recounted

---

[188]The dead will not return to this world and praise God in
the land of the living (cf. Job 7:19-10; Isa. 38:11).

in the grave, Thy faithfulness in the place of destruction
(ʾabaddôn)?" (88:11-12); "The dead do not praise the Lord, nor any
who go down into silence" (115:17); "Shĕʾôl does not thank Thee,
death does not praise Thee; those who go down to the pit cannot
hope for Thy faithfulness" (Isa. 38:18). Ps. 6:6 may refer either
to the world of the condemned spirits, whither the psalmist may
have feared he would be banished because of his sins (cf. vss. 2
and 5: "Return, O Lord"), or to the grave, in which case the
thought would be analogous to that expressed in John 9:4. All
these passages, with perhaps the exception of Ps. 6:6, can be interpreted without difficulty as referring to the condition of the
body in the grave. In fact, this interpretation is clearly required
in the case of Ps. 30:10. Man was made of the dust of the ground
(Gen. 2:7; Ps. 103:14), and at death he returns to dust, or becomes
dust, and therefore is correctly designated as "dust" (Gen. 3:19;
Ps. 104:29; Eccles. 3:20; Job 34:15). His voice is stilled into
silence, and his moldering dust no longer remembers, nor does God
remember it in His deeds and help it with His protecting hand (Ps.
88:6), for the dust is not the object of His loving care. Accordingly, Eccles. 9:10 exhorts: "Whatsoever thy hand finds to do, do
(it) with thy might; for there is no work or device or knowledge or
wisdom in Shĕʾôl (i.e., the grave), whither thou art going."

Eight times in the Old Testament (Isa. 14:9; 26:14.19; Ps.
88:11; Prov. 2:18; 9:18; 21:16; Job 26:5) the dead are also designated as rĕfāʾîm, which today is generally regarded as the plural
of rāfè, meaning "weak." If the etymology is correct, it is natural to assume, in the light of the above observations, that this
term is applied to the departed because they have been deprived of
their physical strength by the hand of death (cf. Isa. 14:10: "All
of them will speak up and say unto thee: 'Thou also hast become
weak [or sick unto death, חָלִיתָ] even as we'"; Job 14:10: "When a
man dies he is powerless").[189]

In contrast, the spirit of Samuel conjured up from the dead
is called ʾelohîm, which is the ordinary Hebrew term for "God" or
"gods." To Saul's question as to what she had seen, the witch of
Endor answered: "I have seen ʾelohîm coming up out of the earth"
(I Sam. 28:13). Since the participle ʿolîm ("coming up") is in the
plural, one might be inclined to see in this an indication that the

---

[189]Cf. van der Leeuw, op. cit., pp. 128-29.

woman saw more than one spirit. But since Saul immediately refers
to the apparition in the singular and since only one ghostly figure
is described in the following verses, the agreement between noun
and verb must be regarded as grammatical rather than logical.[190]
The word 'elohîm is employed elsewhere also with reference to men
in authority, as God's representatives on earth. (Ps. 82:6; Exod.
4:16; 7:1).

In a bilingual incantation text from Assyria, the ghosts of
the dead are called "gods" (ilâni), as we have seen (p. 153). To
judge from this passage and a number of personal names from Mesopotamia,[191] it does not appear to have been uncommon to refer to
the discarnate spirits as "gods." For the explanation of this
practice we do not have to go far afield. According to various
creation stories from the land of the two rivers, man was created
partly with divine blood and so received the immortal spirit of the
gods and was able to partake of divine understanding, as Berossus
informs us. At death, this element in man left the body and entered upon a divine mode of existence, with powers to benefit or
injure the living; therefore it was accorded divine honors, although not in the same measure in which these were accorded the
gods. Similarly we read in Gen. 2:7: "And the Lord God formed
man from the dust of the ground, and breathed into his nostrils
the breath of life, and man was a living soul." In at least some
circles among the ancient Hebrews this verse was without doubt interpreted to signify that the spirit in man was of a divine nature.
It was therefore but a simple step if certain individuals in Israel
designated the departed human spirits as gods.[192]

But in what sense did the witch of Endor take the term 'elohîm?
Did she mean a god, a spiritual being, or someone who exercised
authority while still on earth? The second meaning can, I think,
be dismissed without any further consideration, since from the
viewpoint of the necromancers and doubtless also that of Saul it

---

[190]H. P. Smith, A Critical and Exegetical Commentary on the
Books of Samuel (New York, 1904), p. 241; Gesenius' Hebrew Grammar,
§ 132, h.

[191]See J. J. Stamm, Die akkadische Namengebung (Leipzig, 1939),
pp. 283-84.

[192]Cf. the Roman di manes, "the good gods," i.e., the deified
souls of the departed.

was self-evident that she had seen a ghost. The first meaning is
likewise highly improbable; for if the witch considered this apparition to be a god, the probability is that the ghosts of the departed in general were regarded as such by the necromancers. In
that case, however, it would again have been self-evident that the
woman had seen a god. Saul would therefore not have been particularly interested in this point. But what was of vital importance
to him was to know whether the apparition answered the description
of Samuel, the judge and the prophet of God, as it was evidently
for the purpose of communicating with the spirit of Samuel, and of
no one else (cf. I Sam. 28:8.11), that he had come to Endor. When
therefore Saul heard the witch call the ghost an 'elohîm and describe him as an old man and as being covered with a mantle, obviously such as Samuel was accustomed to wear, Saul concluded that
he was at last once more in the presence of this man of God, this
former representative of God on earth, who could give him absolutely
reliable information, as he had demonstrated in his lifetime; and
so he prostrated himself before the alleged Samuel, partly as an
expression of awe and reverence and partly for the purpose of gaining his good graces. In my opinion, there can be little doubt that
the word 'elohîm must here be understood in the last-named signification. However, should it be intended to mean "god," we must
not forget that there is no way of determining how generally among
the Hebrews (apart from the necromancers and their dupes) this
appellation was applied to the departed spirits. Nor can we tell
for certain whether orthodox Hebrew theology sanctioned or condoned
the application of this title to the spirits of the dead; for we
must remember that it was a witch who used the term in this sense
and that her theological views, like her practices, were unquestionably at a decided variance with those of the religious leaders in
Israel.

  R. H. Charles maintains that the relations and customs of this
earthly life were perpetuated in Shě'ôl.[193] Samuel, he says, was
"distinguished by his mantle" (I Sam. 28:14), "kings by their crowns
and thrones" (Isa. 14:9), and "the uncircumcised by his foreskin"
(Ezek. 32:18-32). "Indeed," he continues, "the departed were regarded as reproducing exactly the same features as marked them at
the moment of death," so that, e.g., those who were slain with the

---

[193]Op. cit., pp. 40-41.

sword will forever bear the tokens of a violent death in Shĕ'ôl
(Ezek. 32:25).

But in the first place, while Saul and the witch at Endor apparently thought that the customs of the mundane life were perpetuated in the hereafter, it may well be asked whether that was
orthodox Hebrew theology.

In the second place, Isa. 14:9: "Shĕ'ôl beneath is stirred
on account of thee to greet thy coming; it has stirred up for thee
the departed, all the rams[194] of the earth; it has raised up from
their thrones all the kings of the nations," is taken from a satire,
in which the prophet depicts the dead kings and princes as being
in commotion over the arrival of the fallen king of Babylon, the
supposedly or seemingly invincible ruler of the world. And since
this passage forms part of a satire, there is no occasion for taking
it literally. Incidentally, the text mentions only the thrones of
the kings, not their crowns; but the latter are doubtless understood, in view of the reference to the thrones. According to the
Gilgamesh Epic, Tablet VII, column iv, line 41, the kings in the
underworld did not wear their crowns, neither did they sit on
thrones.

In the third place, the idea that the uncircumcised was recognized in Shĕ'ôl by his foreskin, is based on an unnecessarily literal interpretation of the term "uncircumcised," occurring repeatedly in Ezek. 32:18-32. To be circumcised, in the biblical sense
of the term, implied far more than the act of removing the foreskin;
it meant, above all, to embrace the faith of Israel (Gen. 17:1-11).
Conversely, to be uncircumcised meant to be not a member of God's
convenant but to be a heathen (Gen. 34:14; Judg. 14:3; 15:18; I Sam.
17:26.36; etc.) and therefore to be outside the pale of God's grace
and its blessings (Exod. 4:24 ff.). Consequently, to die uncircumcised meant to die a godless person and to share the fate of the
godless. Moreover, Ezek. 32:18-32 treats almost exclusively of the
grave and not of the spirit world, as is evidenced by such state-
ments as these: "His graves are round about him, all of them slain,
fallen by the sword" (vs. 22); "with all her multitude round about
her grave, all of them slain, fallen by the sword" (vs. 24); "with
all his multitude round about his graves, all of them uncircumcised,

---

[194]The princes, the leading goats of the herds of peoples (cf.
Jer. 50:8; Zech. 10:3).

slain by the sword" (vs. 26); "they have laid their swords under
their heads" (vs. 27); and as further evidenced by the phrases "to
be laid with the uncircumcised" (vs. 19) and "to be laid with them
that are slain by the sword" (vs. 28). The only lines that deal
with the realm of the spirits are verse 21a: "Out of the midst of
Shĕ'ôl the strong among the mighty shall speak of him with his
helpers," and verse 31a: "These shall Pharaoh see and be comforted
over all his multitude." But neither one of these verses contains
any allusion to the foreskin. To these two passages a person may
be inclined to add verses 18 and 24, because of the phrase "the
nether parts of the earth." But in the light of verse 19, particularly the expression "to be laid with the uncircumcised," there
can be little doubt that the grave is meant in verse 18. In verse
24 the context again supports the latter interpretation. The situation in Ezek. 32:18-32 is simply this: Since the enemies spoken
of in this passage are God's enemies, they will go down to Shĕ'ôl
body and soul, that is, their bodies will go down to Shĕ'ôl in the
sense of the grave, and their souls or spirits will descend to
Shĕ'ôl in the sense of the realm of the condemned spirits, and so
these enemies will receive the full reward of the godless.

     And, finally, there is no Old Testament authority for the
opinion that the departed bear the same features in the hereafter
which marked them at the moment of death. That idea is due largely
to the failure to differentiate between the resting place of the
body and the habitation of the spirit.

     On the shape or form of the spirits in the great beyond, the
Old Testament is silent. G. van der Leeuw[195] sees indications in
the Book of Isaiah that the dead were conceived of as birds, similarly as they are portrayed in the Gilgamesh Epic, Tablet VII,
column iv, and in "Ishtar's Descent to the Underworld," line 10.
He derives this idea from 8:19: "And when they say unto you: 'Consult the 'obôth and the yiddĕ'ônîm, that peep and mutter,' (thus
shall ye say unto them): 'Should not a people consult its God?
(Should one consult) the dead on behalf of the living?'"[196] To
this passage, on van der Leeuw's principle, we could add 29:4:

[195]Op. cit., pp. 292-93.

[196]Cf. König, Das Buch Jesaja (Gütersloh, 1926), pp. 127-28,
and A. Dillmann, Der Prophet Jesaja, rev. and ed. by Kittel
(Leipzig, 1898), pp. 85-86.

"Then low from the earth shalt thou speak, and muffled shall thy
speech sound from the dust; and thy voice shall be like unto (that
of) an 'ôb from the earth, and thy speech shall peep out of the
dust."[197]

In trying to determine the validity of van der Leeuw's argument, our first concern must naturally be to ascertain the meanings
of the words 'ôb and yiddĕ'ônî, the latter being invariably coupled
with the former. Van der Leeuw, like others,[198] understands these
designations to refer to the spirits of the dead brought up from
the underworld by the necromancer. But we actually have no proof
that the terms in question were ever so employed in the Old Testament. According to Lev. 20:27a, the 'ôb and the yiddĕ'ônî were
in[199] the person practicing the occult arts. The passage reads:
"And a man or a woman, if there is in them an 'ôb or a yiddĕ'ônî,
shall surely be put to death." Moreover, this verse seems to carry
the implication that the 'ôb or yiddĕ'ônî was in these individuals
not just momentarily but that he resided there, like the spirit of
divination which Paul cast out of a certain woman in Philippi (Acts
16:16 ff.). From these observations it follows that the 'ôb and
the yiddĕ'ônî were not talismans, as held by some,[200] but that they
were spirits of some kind. Concerning the witch of Endor, it is
said that she was "the mistress (or possessor) of an 'ôb," i.e.,
she had or controlled an 'ôb (I Sam. 28:7). Since such a spirit
was at her command, Saul approached her with the request: "Divine
for me, I pray, with the help of the 'ôb, and bring up for me whom
I shall name unto thee," or "bringing up for me whom I shall name
unto thee" (vs. 8). The definite article in the expression "with
the help of the 'ôb" refers, of course, to the particular 'ôb who

_____

[197] With Ps. 90:10 (: "we fly away") cf. 91:5; Job 5:7; 20:8;
Isa. 11:14; 60:8; etc.

[198] E.g., Driver, A Critical and Exegetical Commentary on
Deuteronomy (Edinburgh, 1902), pp. 225-26, and König, Geschichte
der alttestamentlichen Religion, pp. 89-90.

[199] This is the most natural interpretation of the preposition
ב. The ב denoting proximity ("at" or "by"), which has also been
suggested in this connection, occurs but rarely and appears to be
used in a somewhat different way (see I Sam. 29:1; Ezek. 10:15.20,
with which is to be compared 1:3).

[200] So H. P. Smith, op. cit., pp. 239-40, and similarly A.
Jirku, Die Dämonen und ihre Abwehr im Alten Testament (Leipzig,
1912), pp. 5-11.

dwelt in her, or whom she controlled. In the light of these three
passages it is clear that the 'ôb and the spirit of Samuel were two
separate entities, and that the witch allegedly raised the ghost of
the prophet (vss. 11 ff.) with the aid of her 'ôb, that is, the
demon at her command. Since the term yiddĕ'ônî is always used by
the side of the 'ôb, it follows that the two are synonymous words;
but it is impossible to determine just how they differ from one
another.

Interesting parallels to the problem before us are found in
the stories of the raising of Enkidu and Ishtar. In each case Ea
(or Enki), the god who does the raising and who therefore corresponds, in a sense, to the human necromancer, sends at least one
being to the underworld to effect the release of the dead for whose
return he has been entreated. According to the Babylonian versions,
Nergal is sent out in the first story and Aṣushunamir in the second;
according to the Sumerian recensions, Enki sends out Utu (i.e.,
Shamash) in the first instance and kurgarra and galatur in the second. In neither case is the agent one of the dead. Nergal and Utu
are gods, while Aṣushunamir is a mere mortal, as are probably also
kurgarra and galatur; the last three were created for the purposes
at hand.

As already indicated, a woman who had a spirit of divination
was called "the mistress of an 'ôb." Designations such as "the
mistress of a yiddĕ'ônî," "the lord of an 'ôb," and "the lord of
a yiddĕ'ônî" probably also existed, although they are not found in
the Old Testament.[201] Since the spirits of divination were in the
wizards, the latter, by metonymy, were themselves called 'obôth
and yiddĕ'ônîm (cf. I Sam. 28:3.9; II Kings 23:24).[202] In Isa.

---

[201]The expression ba'al 'ôb occurs only in post-biblical Hebrew.

[202]Thus also in Deut. 18:11b: "one who consults a medium or a
wizard." With the force of the participle sho'ēl may be compared
vs. 10: "There shall not be found among you one who makes his son
or his daughter pass through (ma'abîr) the fire"; Gen. 4:14 (מֹצְאִי)
and 9:6. The objection raised by H. P. Smith, op. cit., p. 239,
that the feminine plural form of the 'ôb "makes it doubtful whether
it can be referred to necromancers," carries no weight (cf. Gesenius'
Hebrew Grammar, § 122, r; Dillmann, Grammatik der äthiopischen
Sprache, rev. and enlarged by C. Bezold [Leipzig, 1899], § 133, a).
Equally untenable is his argument derived from the statement wĕ-'āśâ
'ôb wĕ-yiddĕ'ônîm, in II Kings 21:6 (= II Chron. 33:6). These words
can quite easily be translated: "And he appointed mediums (or necromancers) and wizards." For 'āśâ (עָשָׂה) in the sense "to appoint"
see I Kings 12:31; 13:33; II Kings 17:32.

8:19 the two terms under discussion are probably to be taken in
the sense of "mediums" and "wizards," respectively. König's argument that these words must here be understood as applying to the
spirits of the dead, because of the parallelism with the last part
of the verse, lacks cogency.[203] The prophet may quite well have
meant mediums (or necromancers) and wizards, for with their aid a
person could actually consult the dead, according to the devotees
of this practice. In Isa. 29:4 the word 'ôb is perhaps best rendered with "demon." The voice of the wizard, if he was a ventrilo-
quist, probably sounded as if it rose from the ground and was therefore alleged to be that of a demon. This passage need not
necessarily refer to necromancy but may allude to some other
inquiry.[204] The 'ôb appears in connection with necromancy in only
three passages—in Deut. 18:11; I Sam. 28:7 ff.; and Isa. 8:19; in
all the other cases he is mentioned in connection with witchcraft
or wizardry in general.[205]

Another important word in the study of Isa. 8:19 and 29:4 is
the verb ṣāfaf, or ṣifṣēf (if a quadriliteral). In Isa. 10:14 and
38:14, the only other instances of its occurrence in the Old Testament, this verb is employed with reference to the chirping or
peeping of birds. In a Jewish-Aramaic passage it is applied to
the squeaking of mice,[206] while in Ezek. 17:5 a kind of willow tree
is called ṣafṣāfâ, which undoubtedly received its name from the
sound made by the wind as it rustles or whispers through the leaves.
Finally, in Isa. 8:19 the verb under discussion is paralleled with
"to mutter or murmer." Even if it could be shown that the 'obôth
and the yiddĕ'ônîm referred to the spirits of the dead, the last-
mentioned two points and the further consideration that nowhere
else in the Old Testament are the dead depicted as birds, although

---

[203] Das Buch Jesaja, p. 127.

[204] Cf. van der Leeuw, op. cit., p. 382.

[205] In Deut. 18:11: "Or a charmer, or one who consults an 'ôb
or a yiddĕ'ônî, or one who inquires of the dead," the last statement probably refers to those who consult the dead directly, without the aid of a diviner, as by incubation, i.e., by spending the
night in a grave in the hope of receiving a revelation from the
dead (cf. Isa. 65:4 and Lods, op. cit., I, 251).

[206] Jacob Levy, Wörterbuch über die Talmudim und Midraschim
(Berlin and Vienna, 1924), IV, 212.

that concept was widespread in the ancient world, would make it
manifestly too hazardous to restrict the usage of the verb in question to the vocal sounds of birds and to derive from the above-
quoted passages in the Book of Isaiah the idea of a bird soul.[207]
In these verses ṣāfaf probably means simply "to whisper," as interpreted by Gesenius[208] and König,[209] or "to murmur," "to mutter."[210]
The spectacle which the ungodly present, according to Isa.
66:24, is ghastly: "Their worm will not die, nor will their fire
be quenched; and they will be an abhorrence to all flesh." The
prophet, foretelling the final victory of God over his enemies,
here speaks, without qualification, of a worm that will not die
and a fire that will not be quenched and therefore will continue
beyond the end of time (cf. Judith 16:17; Mark 9:43-44). The lot
of the ungodly will consist not merely in the deprivation of all

---

[207]The doctrine of winged angels (Isa. 6:1-6) does not prove
anything for the appearance of the human soul after death, contrary
to van der Leeuw, op. cit., p. 293, since the angels form a different order of spirits. Not even in the New Testament do we find an
indication that the saints in bliss are or will be angels. Matt.
22:30 states merely that in the resurrection the dead will be like
unto the angels in heaven in that they will not marry or be given
in marriage.

[208]Handwörterbuch, p. 693.

[209]Wörterbuch, p. 394.

[210]Granting, for the sake of argument, that in Isa. 8:19 and
29:4 the terms ʾoḇôṯ and yiddĕʿônîm refer to the ghosts of the departed, it cannot even be proved that the prophet himself ascribed
or conceded to the dead the ability to utter sounds audible to man.
The first passage contains a quotation from the speech of the idol-
aters followed by a twofold answer (in the form of rhetorical questions), which the prophet gives the believers. In the first part of
his reply the prophet castigates the devotees of necromancy by
pointing out that such occult practice is a disregard of God's sovereignty, the implication being that this is unnatural and impious
and therefore condemnable; in the second part he heaps ridicule
upon them by emphasizing the folly of consulting the dead on behalf of the living and thus making the dead the instructors of the
living. "To the law and to the testimony!" he continues in the
next verse. Instead of confirming the claims of the adherents of
necromancy (assuming for the moment that the ʾoḇôṯ and the
yiddĕʿônîm designate the dead), his answer implies a denial. As
for the second passage (not cited by van der Leeuw but added by us),
it does not necessarily mean any more than that the prophet uses
the phraseology of the witches or wizards in the same way in which
we might say: "He sounds like a voice from the grave," i.e., as a
voice from the grave is supposed to sound.

happiness but will entail actual pain and suffering.

Consonant with this passage, we read in Dan. 12:2-3 that on
resurrection day the godly will rise to "everlasting life" and the
ungodly to "utter contempt, to everlasting abhorrence. And those
who are wise will shine like the brightness of the firmament, and
those who have led many to righteousness like the stars forever and
ever." Here the term "wise" is used, of course, in a religious and
ethical sense, denoting the pious; these will rise in radiant
beauty.[211]

According to these passages, death has nothing but horror,
torment, shame, and disgrace in store for the wicked; their continued existence beyond the grave will thus be death in its ugliest
form. For the righteous, on the contrary, death is the gateway to
everlasting life and highest honor. Their lot, as we read elsewhere, will be a life of unalloyed happiness in the presence of
God. The psalmist says: "Thou wilt show me the path of life; fulness of joy is in Thy presence, pleasures are in Thy right hand for
evermore" (16:11). Again: "I shall behold Thy face in righteousness; I shall, upon awakening, be sated with (beholding) Thy form"
(17:15). The righteous will be taken to glory (73:24).

There is nothing in the Old Testament to show that the living
can in any way improve the lot or condition of the dead. While
among the Babylonians and Assyrians it was the duty of the surviving
relatives to supply the departed with food and drink to quench their
thirst and still their hunger, we have no Old Testament evidence
that this practice was in vogue also among the Hebrews. Its existence in Israel has indeed been asserted by some, but most of the
passages adduced in support of this view hardly merit attention.
The only one deserving to be considered is Deut. 26:14. In connection with the triennial charity tithe (cf. 14:28-29), the person
ultimately responsible for the delivery of the consecrated things
had to declare before God: "I have not eaten of it in my mourning;
neither have I taken away from it as one unclean; nor have I given

---

[211]Whether the sacred writer is in any way indebted to Babylonian, Egyptian, or other pagan sources for his imagery that certain dead will be clad in firmamental or siderial splendor (Sellin
in Neue kirchliche Zeitschrift, XXX [1919], 261-63), we have no
means of determining. Moreover, it seems quite unnecessary to look
for foreign influence of any kind. With the imagery here employed
may be compared Exod. 24:10; Num. 24:17; and Matt. 13:43; also I
Cor. 15:40-42 and Rev. 2:28.

any of it on account of a dead person; (but) I have hearkened unto
the voice of the Lord, my God, (and) have done according to all
that Thou hast commanded me."

The part of this declaration which engages our attention is
the statement: "nor have I given any of it on account of a dead
person (lĕmēth)." The interpretation of this line pivots on the
preposition lĕ. Does it mean "to" or "for," i.e., "on account of"
(cf. Gen. 4:23; Lev. 21:1; Deut. 14:1), as we have rendered it?
Taking it in the first meaning, the allusion would be to the widely
prevalent practice among peoples of antiquity, including perhaps the
later Jews (cf. Tob. 4:17; Sir. 30:18 [Greek text]), of placing
food in the grave with the dead.[212] This superstition, though not
otherwise authenticated in the Old Testament, may have prevailed
also among certain groups in Israel, and we may have in this passage a condemnation of it.[213] On the other hand, if lĕ is to be
taken in the second meaning noted above, "the allusion will be to
the custom of the friends of a deceased person testifying their
sympathy with the mourners assembled in the house by sending to
them gifts of bread or other food, for their refreshment" (II Sam.
3:35; Jer. 16:7; Ezek. 24:17).[214] Since food consumed at a funeral
meal was ceremonially unclean (Num. 19:14; Hos. 9:4), it was ille-
gitimate to devote any part of the tithe to such use, inasmuch as
that would have rendered the remainder of the tithe equally unclean.
In the absence of literary or archeological proof that the ancient
Hebrews provided a dead person with food, and in view of the custom
prevailing among them of sending food to the mourners for their refreshment, the second interpretation of the line under examination

---

[212]If this custom existed also among the Jews of the inter-
testamental period, it may owe its observance by them to Greek
influence.

[213]Ps. 106:28: "They joined themselves to the Baal of Peor,
and ate sacrifices (offered to) the dead," may refer to the par-
taking of the offerings made to Baal and related deities, whose
real existence the psalmist probably denies, thus regarding them
as dead or lifeless images (cf. Num. 25:1-3; Pss. 115:4-7; 135:
15-17; Wisd. of Sol. 13:10-19; Briggs, op. cit., II, 351), or it
may refer to the eating of offerings which in connection with that
worship were actually made to the dead. In either case, however,
we are dealing with a pagan rite which the psalmist condemns.

[214]Driver, A Critical and Exegetical Commentary on Deuteronomy,
p. 291.

is by far to be preferred. The Old Testament contains no evidence
that the dead were at all in need of nourishment.

Whether they are in heaven or in Shĕʾôl, the dead are not
"cognizant of aught that passeth here" (Robert Southey). The sons
of a dead man "come to honor, and he knows it not; or they sink into insignificance, and he does not perceive them. But he grieves
over himself, and he mourns over himself" (Job 14:21-22). Whatever
pain and grief the dead man will have to suffer, he will suffer on
his own account; the woe of his surviving kinsmen will not affect
him. In a petition for help, the prophet addresses God in the words:
"For Thou art our Father; for Abraham does not know us, and Israel
does not recognize us" (Isa. 63:16). King Josiah is told by God,
through the mouth of the prophetess Huldah: "Behold, I will gather
thee unto thy fathers, and thou shalt be gathered to thy grave in
peace; and thine eyes shall not see all the evil[215] which I am
about to bring upon this place" (II Kings 22:20). The dead are,
accordingly, completely removed from earthly affairs and are no
longer active in the history of men. In the words of Eccles. 9:6,
"they no longer have a share forever in anything that is done under
the sun." They do not return, as in Babylonia and Assyria, to molest the living, nor are they in any way responsive to the petitions
of the living.[216] These are some of the reasons why the Old Testament does not recognize or legitimize ancestor worship.[217]

What has been said about the removal of the dead from things
terrestrial is not at all contradicted by Jer. 31:14: "Hark! in
Ramah is heard lamentation, bitter weeping! It is Rachel weeping
for her children, refusing to be comforted for her children, because
they are no more." For here we are plainly dealing with a mere
rhetorical mode of expression, comparable to such poetic figures
of speech as we find in Ps. 98:8: "Let the rivers clap (their)
hands; let the mountains be joyful together," and Isa. 55:12: "The
mountains and the hills shall break forth before you into singing,

---

[215]"Shall not see all the evil" = shall not see any of the evil
(cf. Ps. 103:2: "Forget not all His benefits" = forget not any of
His benefits).

[216]Job 4:12-16 contains no indication that a human spirit is
meant.

[217]See König, Geschichte der alttestamentlichen Religion, pp.
84-96; Theologie des Alten Testaments, pp. 32-34; Eichrodt, op. cit.,
II, 115-18.

and all the trees of the field shall clap (their) hands." We can
see this quite clearly from the fact that the picture before us is
that of a mother who is still among the living and who is steeped
in sorrow because her children have departed this life and are no
longer with her. Rachel appears not as one who has already joined
the company of the dead but as one who is still in the land of the
living.[218]

The Resurrection of the Dead

According to Babylonian and Assyrian thought, there were various kinds of returns from the subterranean "house" of eternal gloom
and darkness. There was, e.g., a real resurrection of the gods.
Tammuz annually died at the height of summer and rose again with
the arrival of spring. Ishtar descended to the nether world and
there was deprived of life; but she was revived and set free from
the realm of death.[219] Moreover, in the case of human beings, the
spirit of the dead could be temporarily recalled to the upper world
for the purpose of gaining information from him, as is illustrated
by the case of Enkidu and as is indicated by the title mushêlû
eṭimmu,[220] "he who causes the spirits of the dead to rise," "the
necromancer"; or a famished spirit, who had none to care for him,
could ascend to the land of the living and feed on the garbage
thrown into the street; or, again, like the Roman manes, the spirits
could come up and smell the burning incense and partake of the offerings made to the deceased.

---

[218]Nor would the idea that the dead are ignorant of events on
earth necessarily be contradicted by the epithet yiddě'ônîm, "those
who know much" (rather than merely "the knowing ones"), or "those
who impart knowledge," if it could be demonstrated that this title,
at least in some passages, was employed with reference to the spirits
of the dead. For we could assume that the word yiddě'ônî originated
in paganism, that from here it was taken over by the practitioners
of the black art among the Hebrews, and that it was employed by the
religious leaders in Israel in the same way in which we use the word
"soothsayer," i.e., true-sayer or truth-sayer (cf. the German
Wahrsager), although we may scoff at the soothsayer's claim that
he can foretell events.

[219]See "Ishtar's Descent to the Underworld." On the question
of Marduk's death and resurrection see Jensen in Orientalistische
Literaturzeitung, XXVII (1924), cols. 573-77, and Zimmern in Der
alte Orient, Vol. XXV, Heft 3. (1926).

[220]Rawlinson, op. cit., Vol. II, Pl. 51, No. 2, rev. 51.

Theoretically it was possible also for the dead among mankind
to rise from the grave; for Ishtar threatens that she will "cause
the dead to rise that they may eat as the living, that the living
may be more numerous than the dead." But there is no evidence that
an actual resurrection of a human being from the dead was believed
to have taken place at any time; nor is there any indication of a
belief in some future resurrection of the flesh. According to
Diogenes Laërtius, a Greek writer of about the third century A.D.,
such a doctrine was apparently ascribed to the Babylonian Magi by
the Greek historian and rhetorician Theopompus (fourth century B.C.);
for Diogenes writes: "The last named author [Theopompus] says that
according to the Magi men will live in a future life and be immortal,
and that the world will endure through their invocations."[221] But
the available cuneiform documents offer no reason for believing
that the Mesopotamians looked for the resurrection of the body.
On the contrary, Gilgamesh's question: "(And) I, shall I not like
unto him lie down and not rise forever?"[222] implies a negation of
this idea.

There are passages in Babylonian literature, particularly in
hymns and prayers, which at first sight seem to demonstrate beyond
doubt that the Babylonians believed in the resurrection of the dead.
A very clear proof for such a belief seems to be found at first
glance in the well-known epithet muballiṭ mîti, "the one who makes the
dead to live," or "the one who restores the dead to life," a title
bestowed upon such gods as Marduk, Nabû, Ninurta, and Shamash, and
upon Gula, the goddess of healing.[223] But we must guard against a
too literal interpretation of this phrase. All that these two words
imply is that through the interposition of a given deity those already on the brink of death, or those virtually dead, are given a
new lease on life. This we can see quite plainly from Enûma elish,
Tablet VI:153-54. There Marduk is called the one "who restored all
the ruined gods, as though they were his own creation; the lord who
by his holy incantation restored the dead gods to life" (uballiṭu
ilâni mîtûti). The reference is, of course, not to gods who had

_____

[221]Vitae philosophorum 1. 9 (trans. R. D. Hicks, "Loeb Classical Library").

[222]Tablet X, col. iii, 31, and col. v, 22 (Assyrian version).

[223]Tallqvist, op. cit., pp. 67-68.

actually died but to gods who had been delivered from destruction.[224]
The same applies to Enûma elish, Tablet VII:26, according to which Marduk
is "the lord of the holy incantation, who restores the dead to life"
(muballiṭ mîti). These "dead," as is evidenced by the following
lines, were "the vanquished gods" who had gone over to the side of
Ti'âmat but whose lives were spared and who were then set free. The
meaning of the phrase under consideration stands out even more clearly in the following two selections from the Sargonid letters:
"After the city Birat was devastated and its gods were carried off,
I was a dead man (mîtu anâku). But when I saw the golden seal of
the king, my lord, I was restored to life (abtaluṭ). But now, when
I sent my messenger (to inquire) concerning the welfare of the king,
my lord, I did not see the seal of the king, my lord,[225] and so
was not restored to life (ul abluṭ); I am a dead man (mîtu anâku).
Let the king, my lord, not forsake me!"[226] "With the many deeds
of kindness, which from the beginning the king, my lord, has shown
(me) and manifested (toward me), who was but a dead dog, the son
of a nobody, the king, my lord, has restored me to life (ubal-
liṭanni)."[227] The same general idea of extricating someone from
extreme misfortune or sore distress and restoring him to the enjoyment of life is, of course, intended when it is said of Ninurta:
"The body of him who has been brought down to the underworld (ana
arallê) thou dost restore (tutarra)."[228] Similarly, Cyrus, employing the Babylonian phrase under discussion with reference to a nation, called himself "the lord who by his power has restored the
dead to life" (sha .... uballiṭu mîtûtân),[229] meaning the Babylonians, whom he freed from the rule of Nabonidus. In like manner,
the Hittite king Shuppiluliumash says in a treaty: "The dead
(mîta) land Mitanni I cause to live (uballazu) (and) restore it to

---

[224]See Enûma elish, Tablet VI:45 ff.

[225]That is, I did not receive a sealed document from the king,
my lord.

[226]Harper, Assyrian and Babylonian Letters, No. 259, rev. 1-10.

[227]Ibid., No. 521:4-7.

[228]King, Babylonian Magic and Sorcery, No. 2:22.

[229]Rawlinson, op. cit., Vol. V, Pl. 35:19.

its former estate."[230]   It is manifest from these observations that
no argument for a Babylonian belief in the physical resurrection
of the dead can be derived from the phrase in question. As far as
available cuneiform evidence is concerned, the coinage of this
phrase, suggested probably by the so-called death and resurrection
of nature, is as close as the Babylonians and Assyrians ever got
to the idea of a resurrection of the human body.

It is quite different in the Old Testament; there we have definite proof for a belief in the revivification and renovation of
the dead. There are passages which treat of individual resurrections and others which deal with mass resurrections. As regards the
first group, we are not so much concerned with the resurrection stories recorded in I Kings 17:17-24 and II Kings 4:33-36 and 13:21,
according to which certain dead people were restored to life through
the instrumentality of the prophets Elijah and Elisha; for although
the mere existence of these stories, recorded as history, testifies
to a faith among the Hebrews in the immortality of the human spirit
and, at least, the possibility, under certain conditions, of a
renovation of the body after death, not only are they strictly exceptional cases but in each instance the dead was brought to life
before burial. We are concerned, rather, with those passages in
which an individual expresses his belief that at some time after
death and decay his body will be raised to communion with God.

Such a passage is Ps. 17:15: "As for me, I shall behold Thy
face in righteousness; I shall, upon awakening, be sated with (beholding) Thy form." In this verse the psalmist (not the community)[231] expresses his conviction that he will awake from the sleep
of death (Pss. 13:4; 76:6; Jer. 51:39.57) and rise from the grave
(cf. Dan. 12:2); that he will then be permitted, as one who is
righteous in God's sight, to stand in the presence of God and to
behold his very face and form, the beholding of God's form being
a privilege which, in a measure, was granted only to Moses (Num.
12:8; cf. also Deut. 4:12.15). In this vision the psalmist will
find true gratification and satisfaction, which will compensate

[230]H. H. Figulla, E. Forrer, and E. F. Weidner, Keilschrifttexte aus Boghazköi, Vol. I (Leipzig, 1923), No. 1, rev. 22.

[231]See H. Gunkel, Die Psalmen (Göttingen, 1926), p. 56, and
R. H. Pfeiffer, Introduction to the Old Testament (New York and
London, 1941), p. 634.

him for the ills suffered on earth below.[232] As death is elsewhere
called a "sleep," so the resurrection is here portrayed as an
awakening from sleep (cf. Job 14:12; Dan. 12:2). Accordingly, the
psalmist expects the same body to rise which had previously fallen
"asleep." It will be a resurrection, or rising again, in the true
sense of the term.

Without question the best-beloved passage belonging to this
category, one which has been sung into the hearts of millions, is
Job 19:25-27: "But I know: My Redeemer lives, and as the last
will He arise[233] on the dust. And behind my skin,[234] (now) thus
struck to pieces,[235] and that from out of my flesh, I shall behold
God, whom I shall behold for my good, and mine own eyes shall see
Him and that not as another. My reins fail with longing in my
bosom."[236]

These lines require somewhat detailed consideration. The
Hebrew term which we have rendered with "Redeemer" is gô'ēl, the
active participle qal of the verb gā'al, "to redeem," "to buy back."
In the Old Testament this word finds a variety of applications.
If a person had made a special vow involving the offering of his
services to the Lord, he could redeem himself from the obligations

---

[232]On this interpretation see Franz Delitzsch, A Commentary
on the Book of Psalms, Vol. I (New York, n.d.), trans. D. Eaton
and J. E. Duguid, pp. 304-6, and Kittel, Die Psalmen, pp. 57-59.

[233]I.e., appear (cf. Exod. 1:8; Deut. 34:10; Judg. 5:7).

[234]This, in the final analysis, is tantamount to saying: "And
surrounded with my skin," as will appear later.

[235]More literally: "(which) they have thus struck to pieces."
The third person plural of the active voice here corresponds idio-
matically to our passive, as in Job 4:19, 6:2, 7:3, and 18:18. On
this point and on the absence of the relative particle 'asher see
Gesenius' Hebrew Grammar, §§ 144, g, and 155, f-m. The feminine
demonstrative pronoun zôth is in the accusative and really means
"into this" (cf. ibid., § 117, 11); strictly speaking, it never signifies "thus," not even in Job 33:12, where it denotes "in this,"
or "on this point." The rendering "thus" is somewhat free. In
German I would translate vs. 26 as follows: "Und hinter meiner Haut,
(die) man zu dem da zerschlagen (oder zerfetzt) hat, und zwar von
meinem Fleische aus, werde ich Gott schauen."

[236]Translated in essentially the same way by Budde, Das Buch
Hiob, pp. 102-7, and N. Peters, Das Buch Job (Münster, 1928), p.
194, but on a different interpretation.

of the promise by paying the price at which such services were val-
ued by the priest in charge; or if he had devoted an animal, a
house, or a field to the Lord, he could under certain conditions
buy them back from the sanctuary (Leviticus, chap. 27). If an im-
poverished person had to sell something from his possessions, it
could be redeemed either by the former owner or by a kinsman; or
if someone had to sell himself into bondage because of poverty, he
could be redeemed by one of his relatives, unless he was able in
some way to redeem himself (Lev. 25:25-55). Again, the law of the
levirate marriage enjoined that if a man died without issue, his
brother or nearest kinsman should marry his widow and that the
firstborn of this union should be regarded and registered as the
son and rightful heir of his mother's first husband, to perpetuate
his family and to keep its property in its possession (Deut. 25:
5-10; Ruth, chaps. 3-4). Finally, if a person had killed someone,
it devolved upon the nearest kinsman to pursue the slayer and, if
he overtook him before the latter had reached one of the cities of
refuge, to put him to death and so to avenge the blood of him who
had been killed and to restore his honor as well as that of the
family (Num. 35:9-28; Deut. 19:1-13; Joshua, chap. 20). In all
these instances the man who performed the act of redemption or
vengeance was called the gô'ēl.

But the real gô'ēl in the Old Testament is God himself. In
over forty cases out of about one hundred, the verb gā'al, "to
redeem," is applied to God (or the Messiah). He is the defender
of the lowly or downtrodden, who pleads their cause (Prov. 23:10-11;
Ps. 119:154; Jer. 50:34; Lam. 3:58). He it is who delivers his
people from their enemies, from sin, death, and corruption (Exod.
15:13; Pss. 69:19; 72:14; 74:2; 77:16; 103:4; etc.; Isa. 35:9; 43:14;
44:22; 47:4; 48:20; 49:7.26; 59:20; 63:16; etc.; Jer. 31:10; Hos.
13:14; Mich. 4:10). Wherever the verb gā'al appears in the psalter
or the prophets, God (or the Messiah proceeding from God) is the
cause of the redemption.

This is the case also in Job 19:25. Here the gô'ēl is God
himself, as is evident from the context. It is the same concerning whom Job had said in 16:19: "Behold! even now there is a
Witness for me in heaven, and He who testifies for me is on high."
The gô'ēl is Job's witness to his innocence, against the accusations
leveled at him.

In Job 19:25 some commentators have understood gô'ēl in the

sense of a kinsman avenger of blood.[237] But since in Job's case
no slaying at the hands of man is involved, this thought is out of
the question.[238] Nevertheless, attempts have been made to defend
the idea of blood revenge by an appeal to Job 16:18, where Job
says: "O earth, cover not my blood, and let there be no (resting-)
place for my cry!" But here Job merely compares his expected
death with the shedding of blood; he compares the ebbing of his
vitality with the flowing-out of blood.[239] And with this picture
or figure of speech in mind, he calls upon the earth not to swallow or cover his blood but to let it lie bare on the ground and so
to allow its voice a free and unobstructed passage to his Witness
in heaven (vs. 19). Job's cry is here identical with the voice of
the blood, for the reference to the latter presupposes that Job
will be dead by the time that this cry ascends to heaven. The cry
proceeds from the blood as from a poured-out soul, which was lodged
in the blood (Lev. 17:11), the latter being even called the soul
itself (Deut. 12:23). Abel's blood cried to God for vengeance or
punishment (Gen. 4:10). But Job is not concerned about vengeance;
he is concerned, rather, about vindication. He wants to be freed
from the reproach which men have heaped upon him in consequence of
the unparalleled misfortune which has befallen him at the hands of
God and which will lead him to the grave (7:6-8; 13:15; 17:1.11-16;
30:32). He wants God himself to bear witness that he has thus been
afflicted not because of some special sin, or sins, committed by
him, but for some other reason. In 9:33-35; 13:3.13-28; 23:1-10;
and 31:35-37 Job longs for justification in the present life, but
in all these passages, with the exception of chapter 13, he clearly
indicates that it is futile to entertain such hope; while in 19:25
ff. he obviously looks for it in the life to come, as is attested
not only in the text itself but also in the preceding verses, where
Job, convinced of the imminence of death, expresses the fervent
but unattainable wish that he could leave to posterity an indestruct-
ible and indelible testimony of his innocence, so that the charges
which will continue to be brought against him after his departure

---

[237]Thus Friedrich Delitzsch, Das Buch Hiob (Leipzig, 1902),
p. 58.

[238]The slaying of Job's servants (1:15-17) does, of course,
not enter into consideration here.

[239]König, Das Buch Hiob, pp. 169 and 193-94.

would not pass unchallenged.[240]   The thought that Job speaks of
blood revenge not only finds no confirmation in 16:18 but, since
Job regards God as the cause of his disaster and his imminent death,
even though he was hardly aware of the fact that Satan had brought
this calamity upon him by God's express permission (1:6-2:7), this
view would lead us inevitably to the absurd conclusion that God
was here portrayed as Job's murderer, i.e., as the one who pur-
posely took the life of a human being without having the right or
the authority to do so, and that Job expected God to avenge his
death on God!

        The plain import of our passage is rather this: Job's three
friends have attributed his extraordinary suffering to extraordinary
sins on his part. Against this groundless and uncharitable charge
Job unwaveringly maintains his innocence and solemnly affirms that,
although all other hope is vain, God himself, his Redeemer, will
vindicate him and free his name from reproach. Death and corruption are not the end, but beyond the gates of death and decay
stands the ever living Redeemer, who as the last (cf. Isa. 44:6;
48:12) holds out over everything (cf. Ps. 102:26-28).[241] The day
will come when He will appear upon the dust, i.e., on earth,[242]
to speak the final decisive word, to vindicate Job against his ac-
cusers by declaring publicly that this was not an exceptionally
great sinner who had received the just reward of his heinous deeds.[243]

---

[240]Cf. S. R. Driver and G. B. Gray, A Critical and Exegetical
Commentary on the Book of Job, I (New York, 1921), 170.

[241]That 'aḥarôn ("the last") is here to be taken in the absolute sense is evident from the fact that in Job 19:23-27 the scene
is laid in the life to come.
     In this connection may be mentioned a probably purely acciden-
tal parallel to the first part of Job 19:25 found in a myth from
Ras Shamra which deals, among other things, with the death and
resurrection of Aliyn Baal, the Canaanite god of life and fertility.
The words in question read: "And I know that Aliyn Baal is alive,"
i.e., that Baal has risen from the dead. For the text see Ch.
Virolleaud in Syria, XII (1931), 212:8 and Pl. XL, or J. A. Mont-
gomery and Z. S. Harris, The Ras Shamra Mythological Texts (Philadelphia, 1935), p. 53:8. Translation by C. H. Gordon, The Loves
and Wars of Baal and Anat (Princeton, etc., 1943), p. 10. On this
parallel see also E. G. Kraeling, The Book of the Ways of God (New
York, 1939), p. 89.

[242]Budde, Das Buch Hiob, p. 104.

[243]Franz Delitzsch, Biblical Commentary on the Book of Job,
trans. F. Bolton, I (Edinburgh, 1881), 353-54.

This He will do, as we learn from the following verses, by resur-
recting Job's body and by elevating him to blessed communion with
God;[244] a sinner would never be raised to such honors (cf. Job
13:16).

In our interpretation of verse 26 it seems best to begin with
the expression ʿênai ("mine eyes") in verse 27. In view of the
fact that this phrase precedes the verb, thus occupying an emphatic
position, and in view of the express mention of skin and flesh in
verse 26 (which can, of course, be understood only of physical skin
and flesh), it would be most unnatural to take ʿênai in the sense
of the eyes of the spirit (as in Job 34:21; Pss. 11:4; 33:18; Prov.
15:3). The phrase ʿênai is therefore to be understood of Job's
physical eyes (cf. Job 42:5). And, since it occupies an emphatic
position, it is to be translated "mine own eyes."

But if Job expected to behold God in the hereafter with the
eyes of his body, it follows that the min of mibbĕśārî in verse 26
is not privative but local, so that mibbĕśārî cannot possibly mean
"without my flesh" but must mean "from out of my flesh." With
this usage of min may be compared Ps. 33:13-14: "The Lord looks
down from out of (min) the heavens. He sees all the sons of men.
He looks forth from (min) the place of His dwelling upon all the
inhabitants of the earth" (cf. also Cant. 2:9 and 5:4, where in
English, however, we use "through" instead of "from"). These considerations indicate, moreover, that 'aḥar in verse 26a serves as
a preposition and not as an adverb or a conjunction; the parallelism between min and 'aḥar requires that. The picture in verse 26a
is that of someone striking or beating a person with a stick or a
rod until the skin bursts. This imagery is quite appropriate in
the case of leprosy, with wh'ch Job is generally believed to have
been afflicted; for this malady is called also "the stroke of
leprosy" (Lev. 13:2.9.20.25), or simply "the stroke" (Lev. 13:3/22).
The imagery accords well with Job's statement in 19:21: "The hand
of God has struck me" (cf. II Kings 15:5), and with his petition
in 9:34: "Let Him take away His rod from me" (cf. also 21:9). In
the resurrection Job will be surrounded with this same skin and

---

[244]A somewhat parallel thought finds expression in Rom. 4:25:
Jesus was "raised for our justification," i.e., for the declaration
of our justification. Moreover, an appeal to justification in the
hereafter is contained also in an Egyptian composition of about
2000 B.C., which has been called "The Dialogue of a Misanthrope with
His Own Soul" (Breasted, op. cit., pp. 168-78).

will behold God from out of his own flesh. It will be the same
Job whom his friends condemned and of whom this might have been
thought impossible, but it will be a Job restored to health and
honor. This view is supported by the emphatic expression of the
pronoun "I," the phrase "mine own eyes," and the addition "and
that not as another" (vs. 27).

Against the view here presented it has been objected, however,
that the idea of the resurrection of the flesh would stand in contradiction to Job's own utterance in 14:7-14: "There is hope for
a tree; if it is cut down, it will sprout again, and its shoots
will not cease. Even if its root becomes old in the earth, and
its trunk dies off in the ground, at the scent of water it will
bud, and bring forth shoots like a young plant. But when a man
dies, he is powerless; yea, when a man expires, where is he? The
waters depart from the sea, and a stream parches and dries up; so
man lies down and does not rise (again); until the heavens are no
more, they will not awake, nor be aroused from their sleep. O that
Thou wouldest hide me in Shě'ôl, that Thou wouldest conceal me till
Thy wrath be past, that Thou wouldest set me a time and then remember me! If a man dies, will he live (again)? All the days of my
warfare would I wait, until my change should come."[245]

But a careful examination of this passage will show unmistakably that it does not in any way militate against our interpretation
of Job 19:25-27. If a tree is cut down, the stump left in the
ground sends up new shoots, or if the roots of the tree become old
and its trunk consequently dies, it may be revived by means of
water, and so in either case the tree rises from the dead, as it
were, and reappears above the earth. But with man it is not so.
He is like the water that evaporates from the sea and then, in the
form of clouds, travels to distant places; or like the water of a
stream that dries up and never returns again to its channel. Man
lies down and is not aroused from his sleep until the heavens exist
no more. This does not imply that the heavens will always exist
and that the dead, therefore, will never rise, for, according to
Ps. 102:26-28 and Isa. 34:4 and 51:6, the time will come when even

---

[245]Until the time would come that he would be relieved of his
post in Shě'ôl. The imagery is, of course, taken from military
life.

heaven and earth will pass away.[246] Then will the dead awake and
come forth (cf. Dan. 12:1-4;13), but not in order to return to
this earthly life. For once a man has been summoned from the land
of the living, the present world will never see him again. But
how Job wishes that it were otherwise! O that God would temporarily hide him in Shĕ'ôl until his wrath be past! There he would
wait patiently until God would turn from his fierce anger and would
remember him in mercy, i.e., would release him from the grave and
permit him to return to this earthly life. But Job knows that to
cherish such hope is vain. For there is no path that leads from
Shĕ'ôl back to earth, so that a man might enter again upon his
former way of life. As far as the dead are concerned, the mundane
life is a thing of the past forever. This same thought Job had
already expressed with even greater clarity in 7:9-10: "A cloud
dissolves and it is gone; so is he who goes down to Shĕ'ôl; he will
not come up (again). He will not return again to his house; and
his place knows him no more."[247]

The God who, for reasons unknown to Job, had so sorely afflicted this paragon of piety (1:8; 2:3) that even his friends,
who had come to sympathize with him and to comfort him (2:11), interpreted his suffering as a divine retribution for some extraordinary sin, or sins, this same God is Job's Redeemer, who will
vindicate him against the charges of his friends by raising him

---

[246] This is not opposed to Eccles. 1:4 and Ps. 148:6, for the
expressions "forever" and "forever and ever" are used also in a
relative or limited sense, denoting merely a long or very long
period of time. To maintain with Dillmann, Hiob (Leipzig, 1891),
p. 124, that the conception of the eternal duration of the heavens
and the celestial bodies as set forth in Pss. 72:5-17 and 89:30-38
is of a popular nature while the idea of the ultimate destruction
of the heavens (and their host) according to Isa. 51:6 and 65:17
and Ps. 102:27 is of prophetic origin, and that the latter group
of passages therefore do not enter into consideration at this point,
is not only insisting on a meaning for the expressions dôr dôrîm
("throughout all generations"), lĕ'ôlām ("forever"), and lā'ad
("forever") which they do not necessarily have in these passages
but also making an arbitrary distinction, in these instances, between popular and prophetic beliefs.

The cuneiform literature of the Babylonians and Assyrians does
not contain any references to the final destruction of heaven and
earth. However, Seneca (ca. 4 B.C.-A.D. 65) reports that, according to the Babylonian priest Berossus, the earth would be destroyed
through a conflagration followed by a deluge (Quaestiones naturales
iii. 29).

[247] In this sense are to be explained also Pss. 78:39 (cf.
103:15-16) and 88:11.

to blissful communion with God. It is for the dawn of this glorious day and the realization of this blessed vision that Job's reins
within him pine away with longing.   There is here no reason for
assuming that Job gave utterance to a merely momentary emotional
feeling and not to a firm and abiding conviction, on the ground
that his despondency would otherwise be difficult to understand.
For in the long black night of affliction it sometimes happens even
to staunch believers that they lose sight of the glory which shall
be revealed in them (Rom. 8:18) and that the burden becomes so
heavy and oppressive to them that they sink into the depths of sad-
ness. Job at times faltered and gave way to a degree of gloom
which was quite unworthy of him, but in all that he was only human.
Moreover, a careful reading of this book of the Old Testament will
show that after the sublime expression of faith recorded in 19:25
ff. Job behaves differently; he is more composed and his words are
no longer filled with that despair which characterized so many of
his former speeches.[248] Though his outward condition remains un-
changed and though his mind is as perplexed as before by the problem of his extraordinary suffering, his inward agitation subsides,
and his heart, far from cursing God to his face (2:5), is drawn
closer to God and attains to peace through the conviction that some
day, in the life to come, the clouds which now obstruct his vision
of God will break and he will behold his divine Redeemer for his
good, and all will be well again. The lesson of immortality and
blessed resurrection has thus accomplished its purpose.[249]

    We shall next consider some passages which speak of a mass
resurrection. We shall begin with Isa. 26:19. In this passage
the seer speaks of the time when God's dead, i.e., those who died
in the Lord, will rise from the grave and join the living faithful

---

[248] Franz Delitzsch, Biblical Commentary on the Book of Job,
I, 372, and Dillmann, Hiob, p. 177.

[249] W. H. Green, The Argument of the Book of Job Unfolded (New
York, 1881), pp. 211-13. The Christian church has since early times
applied the term gô'ēl, or Redeemer, in Job 19:25, to the Messiah,
Jesus of Nazareth, the second person of the Godhead, who will raise
the dead on Judgment Day (I Thess. 4:13-17; I Cor. 15:20-22; John
5:26-29; Matt. 25:31-46) and through whose redemptive work man has
access to God (Rom. 5:1-2; Eph. 2:18; Heb. 7:25; I Pet. 3:18).
Since this point belongs in the field of messianic prophecies, and
since a discussion of it would probably carry us rather far afield,
those particularly interested in it are directed to the commentaries
on Job and to the works on messianic prophecies.

(cf. I Thess. 4:15-17). Identifying himself with God's cause and God's people, the prophet regards the dead as his "dead bodies" and declares: "Thy dead will live (again), my dead bodies will rise—awake and rejoice, ye that dwell in the dust!—for Thy dew is a dew of light, and so the earth will bring forth (the) deceased." At first sight, these lines seem to stand in contradiction to verse 14: "(The) dead will not live (again), (and the) deceased will not rise; for this purpose hast Thou visited and destroyed them, and hast wiped out all remembrance of them." It is to be noted, however, that this passage is concerned with the question of the return to their previous state and condition of the former oppressors of the Jews (vs. 13). These tyrants will never return to the earth to usurp authority over God's people (cf. Isa. 43:17; Jer. 51:39); their despotic rule was the very reason why God destroyed them. God's dead will rise indeed; but it will be through the power of God. They will be revived by his life-giving dew.[250] As the dew of the night falls upon the vegetation of the earth and revives it, so the dew of God will fall upon the graves of his dead and restore them to life.[251]

The unbelieving dead are left out of consideration in verse 19 because the prophet, at this point, is not concerned with their resurrection. However, that they also will rise, at least a certain group or type of them, appears to be implied in verse 21: "For behold! the Lord is about to go forth from His place, to visit the iniquity of the inhabitants of the earth upon them; and the earth will uncover her blood, and will no more cover her slain." We have here a picture of the final judgment, dealing with the living and the dead. On this occasion the earth will reveal the violently shed innocent blood, which she was forced to drink. This blood, now laid bare, will cry out to God for vengeance (cf. Gen. 4:10). Yea, the earth will bring forth the innocently slain persons themselves, who will bear witness against the murderers. Since the expressions "her blood" and "her slain" are general, the murderers are not to be limited to those who will still be alive

---

[250]"Light" and "life" are sometimes used as interchangeable terms (cf. Ps. 56:14; Job 3:20; 33:30).

[251]See Franz Delitzsch, Biblical Commentary on the Prophecies of Isaiah (Edinburgh, 1890), I, 444-48, and König, Das Buch Jesaja, pp. 238-41.

but must include those who have already been cast down to Shĕ'ôl.
Furthermore, since the resurrected victims will testify against
their murderers, most of whom will by that time no longer be numbered among the living, it is not at all beyond the range of rea-
sonableness to assume that Isa. 26:21 carries the implication that
also the dead criminals will be brought forth, body and soul, for
the purpose of standing trial, or hearing judgment pronounced upon
them.

This view is favored by Dan. 12:1-3: "And at that time shall
Michael stand up, the great prince who stands by the children of
thy people, and there shall be a time of trouble such as has not
been since there was a nation until that time; but at that time
thy people shall be delivered, everyone who is found written in
the book. And many, namely, those who sleep in the ground of the
earth, shall awake, some to everlasting life and others to utter
contempt,[252] to everlasting abhorrence. And they that are wise
shall shine like the brightness of the firmament, and they that
have led many to righteousness like the stars forever and ever."

In the lines just quoted, Daniel receives the revelation that
his people are moving toward a day of unparalleled distress but
that the archangel Michael will then arise and deliver his people,
i.e., the true Israel, all those whose names are recorded in the
book of life (whether living or dead). Since many members of the
true Israel will by that time have lost their lives (cf. Dan. 11:33
ff.), the question naturally arises: "How will this deliverance
affect those who will have to die before the advent of that great
day, particularly those who will have to lay down their lives because of their fidelity to God?" In order that the prophecy might
fulfil its purpose of encouraging the believers to persevere in
their loyalty to God in the dark days ahead and to suffer martyrdom
rather than to deny their faith, the angel answers this question
by stating that they will likewise share in this great salvation,
for they will be delivered from the sleep of death and will enter
upon everlasting life and the enjoyment of great rewards, while
the godless, such as the oppressors and persecutors of God's people
alluded to in verse 1, will be consigned to everlasting abhorrence.
Dan. 12:1-3 thus teaches a resurrection of both the godly and the
ungodly and clearly involves a judgment based on moral principles.

---

[252] See Gesenius' Hebrew Grammar, ᵴ 124, e.

Today it is customary to take the min of miyyĕshēnê (vs. 2)
in the partitive sense and to interpret our passage as teaching
merely a partial resurrection, i.e., a resurrection of pre-eminently
pious persons, on the one hand, and of extraordinarily wicked individuals, on the other. While it seems natural, from a philologi-
cal viewpoint, to take min in this sense, it is also possible to
conceive of it as the explanatory min,[253] found before a compre-
hensive or exhaustive apposition, which in our case means the
statement "those who sleep in the ground of the earth." Parallels
to this usage of min are found in Gen. 7:22: "Everything died in
whose nostrils was the breath of the spirit of life, namely everything (mikkol) that was on the dry land"; 9:10: "And with every
living creature that is with you—the birds, the domestic animals,
and all the wild animals of the earth (that are) with you, namely
all (mikkol) those that go forth from the ark of all the wild animals of the earth"; Lev. 11:32: "And whatsoever any of them falls
upon when dead shall be unclean, namely every (mikkol) article of
wood, (every) garment, skin, or sack, any article at all of which
use is made"; I Chron. 5:18: "The Reubenites, the Gadites, and half
of the tribe of Manasseh, namely (min) the valiant men, men able
to carry shield and sword," etc.; Jer. 40:7: "Now when all the
commanders of the forces that were in the field, they and their men,
heard that the king of Babylon had appointed Gedaliah, the son of
Ahikam, governor of the land and that he had committed to him (the)
men, women, and children, of the poor of the land, namely those who
(mê'asher) had not been carried away captive to Babylon"; and probably also Gen. 6:2: "And they took unto themselves wives—whomso-
ever (mikkol 'asher) they chose."

From a grammatical viewpoint, the preposition min in Dan. 12:2
can be regarded either as partitive or as explicative. I personally prefer the latter interpretation—and I state this very frank-
ly—only because of John 5:28-29, which clearly goes back to our
passage. On this interpretation, the contrast is not between "many"
and "all" but between "many" and "few" (cf. Matt. 20:28; Rom. 5:12-
19). It will not be a small number but a vast multitude that will

---

[253]On this min see N. Zerweck, Die hebräische Präposition min
(Leipzig, 1894), pp. 41-42 (cf. also Gesenius' Hebrew Grammar, ɛ
119, w, n. 2; and Gesenius, Handwörterbuch, s.v.). On the explanatory min in Arabic see W. Wright, A Grammar of the Arabic Language,
Vol. II (Cambridge, 1898), ɛ 48, g.

rise from the grave; in fact, there will be a _general_ or _universal_ resurrection, something which Isa. 26:19-21 neither denies nor definitely affirms.

Concluding Remarks

Our observations on the preceding pages allow of a number of interesting conclusions. To begin with, it is apparent that Mesopotamian eschatology exhibits but comparatively minor inconsistencies, if we consider the long period of time represented by our sources and if we, furthermore, consider that different races contributed toward its development.[254] It ought to be equally apparent that, while there is progress in the unfolding of the Hebrew eschatological beliefs, there is no conflict between the earlier and the later writings of the Old Testament, correctly interpreted, in the matter of death and the afterlife.[255] This is one of the reasons why no attempt has been made in this chapter to arrange the Old Testament material according to the different periods of Hebrew history.

Another obvious conclusion is the fact that the differences between the Hebrew and the Mesopotamian eschatological beliefs far outweigh the similarities. Let us briefly review the main points.

1. In Mesopotamia man was thought to have been created mortal, so that death was the natural result of his constitution; in Israel he was believed to have been created for never ending life, wherefore death was something unnatural.

2. In Mesopotamia the underworld had its own pantheon; in the Old Testament the realm of the dead is controlled by the same God who rules over heaven and earth.

3. In Mesopotamian literature all men without distinction, good and bad alike, are after death consigned to the same dark and gloomy subterranean hollow. In the Old Testament there is not one line which _proves_ that at least in the early days of Hebrew history the souls or spirits of all men were believed to go to the nether world; but there are passages which clearly and unmistakably hold

---

[254] Thus also Langdon in _Babyloniaca_, VI, 193, and Jastrow, _Hebrew and Babylonian Traditions_ (New York, 1914), p. 252.

[255] Almost the same conclusion has been reached by Sellin in _Neue kirchliche Zeitschrift_, XXX, 234.

out to the righteous the hope of a future life of bliss and happiness in heaven.

4. In Mesopotamia the dead and the living were interdependent. There it was held that the spirit of the deceased had to be fed by the living and that he was acquainted with their affairs and could return to the earth and harm or benefit them. According to the Old Testament, the dead has no knowledge of what occurs on earth; nor is there any proof that the disembodied spirit can at all affect the living, either for better or for worse, or that the living can in any way change the lot of the departed soul.

5. Even the latest Babylonian and Assyrian records reveal nothing of a resurrection of the flesh, a doctrine so clearly set forth in Daniel and Isaiah. A deity descending to the underworld may be released from the realm of darkness, but the dead among men are condemned to an eternal sojourn in the great below, cut off from all hope of entering the body again and of rising from the grave.

These differences set the eschatalogy of the Mesopotamians and that of the Hebrews as far apart as the east is from the west. It is therefore quite obvious that the eschatology of the Old Testament did not develop from that of the Babylonians and Assyrians. What similarities do exist can be attributed either to common observations (such as the inevitability of death and the impossibility of breaking the shackles of the grave and of returning to the mundane life) or to a common heritage (such as the belief in the continued existence of the spirit after death, or the idea of a judgment of some kind).

CHAPTER IV

THE STORY OF THE FLOOD

The most remarkable parallels between the Old Testament and
the Gilgamesh Epic—in fact, the most remarkable parallels between
the Old Testament and the entire corpus of cuneiform inscriptions
from Mesopotamia—are found in the deluge accounts of the Babylonians and Assyrians, on the one hand, and the Hebrews, on the
other. With the study of this material we therefore enter a field
which, a priori, should prove most fruitful in our examination of
the genetic relationship between the Mesopotamian records and our
Old Testament literature. Here, if anywhere, we should expect to
find evidence enabling us to decide the question whether any part
of the Old Testament has been derived from Babylonian sources. It
is therefore with special interest that we shall make the following
inquiry.

The Authors of the Flood

The Book of Genesis, consonant with Hebrew monotheism, attributes the sending of the deluge to the one and only true God
recognized in the Old Testament, while the cuneiform tablets represent a multitude of divinities as engaged in bringing about this
fearful catastrophe. In the Sumerian inscription from Nippur it
is stated that the deluge was decreed by the assembly of the gods.
But their decision, even though evidently approved by all, at least
formally, did not receive the wholehearted support of all the divinities of the pantheon; for Nintu, the goddess of birth, deplored
the approaching destruction of the human family and wailed like a
woman in travail, while Enki, the god of wisdom and the benefactor
of humanity, took counsel in his own heart to save at least his
favorite, Ziusudra, whom he subsequently informed of the purpose
of the gods and to whom he also imparted a plan of escaping the
impending fate of mankind. According to the eleventh tablet of
the Gilgamesh Epic, the flood was decreed by "the great gods."
There was Anu, their father; warlike Enlil, their counselor; Ninurta,
their representative; Ennugi, their vizier; and Ea, the Enki of the
Sumerians (cf. lines 14-19). Moreover, we learn that Ishtar, the

224

goddess of propagation, also had an important voice in the council
of the gods, for, after the storm had broken loose in all its fury,
she lamented: "In truth, the olden time has turned to clay, because I commanded evil in the assembly of the gods! How could I
command (such) evil in the assembly of the gods! (How) could I
command war to destroy my people!" (lines 118-21). However, after
Utnapishtim's sacrifice on the mountaintop, both Ishtar and Ea
stigmatized Enlil as the real author of this unwarranted catastrophe
(cf. lines 156-85). Here, as well as in the Sumerian version, it
was doubtless Enlil who was principally responsible for the deluge.
He had received the supreme power and function of Anu, the highest
god of the early Babylonian pantheon, and now he probably imposed
his will upon the other gods, who did not dare to oppose him seriously and who therefore more or less acquiesced in his decision.[1]

The Reason for the Flood

As the cause for the cataclysm, the Old Testament emphasizes
the moral depravity of the human race. Man could have averted
this unparalleled destruction of life if he had conformed his ways
to the will of his Maker, but instead of that he followed his own
inclinations. The whole bent of the thoughts of his heart was
never anything but evil. The earth was corrupt before God and was
filled with violence because of man, for all flesh had corrupted
its way upon the earth (Gen. 6:1-13).

In the Gilgamesh Epic the reason for the deluge is not nearly
so apparent as it is in the Book of Genesis. The opening lines of
the flood story contained in the epic state simply that the heart
of the great gods prompted them to bring a deluge (Tablet XI:14).
From this passage one might get the impression that the flood was
due to divine caprice. But according to Ea's speech toward the
close of the account, where he reprimands Enlil for this thoughtless and unjustifiable destruction, the flood was sent because of
the sin of man. Unfortunately, this does not give us any clue as
to the nature of man's offense.

An answer to this question is given in the fragmentary Atrahasis Epic. Starting out much like Genesis, chapter 6, the epic
states that, when the people had multiplied and, apparently, had

---

[1]L. W. King, Legends of Babylon and Egypt in Relation to
Hebrew Tradition (London, 1918), p. 64.

become prosperous, they became so noisy as to deprive Enlil of his sleep.[2] In an attempt to quiet them, Enlil sent plague after plague. But, in the final analysis, it was all of no avail; mankind became more numerous (and evidently more noisy) than before. In utter exasperation, Enlil at last sent the flood to destroy them all and to put an end to their unbearable noise. The case is analogous, in a sense, to Apsû's struggle against the younger gods, whose incessant noise disturbed his slothful rest and finally prompted him to decree their annihilation,[3] and to a passage in the Irra Epic, where Anu says to Irra, concerning the seven gods whom Anu had placed at Irra's disposal: "When the tumult of the people of the earth has become (too) painful for thee, and thy heart moves thee to set the snare, to kill the black-headed (people), to lay low the beast of the plain, (then) let these be thy raging weapons and let them go at thy sides."[4]

In the Book of Genesis the deluge is a righteous retribution for the sins of the ungodly, while pious Noah and his family are spared, with the full knowledge and the express purpose of Him who sent the flood. The biblical story thus exemplifies the pronouncement of the prophet Ezekiel: "The soul that sinneth shall die. The son shall not bear the iniquity of the father, neither shall the father bear the iniquity of the son; the righteousness of the righteous shall be upon him, and the wickedness of the wicked shall be upon him" (18:20 [cf. Deut. 24:16; II Kings 14:6]). But in the cuneiform inscriptions the destruction is intended for all alike, for the just as well as for the unjust, without any exception whatsoever. This is particularly clear from the words with which Ea reproached Enlil: "On the sinner lay his sin; on the transgressor lay his transgression!" (Tablet XI:180). This line from the epic shows unmistakably that not all were sinners. Yet had it not been for Ea's intervention, Enlil, in his rashness, would have destroyed

---

[2] The manner in which the Atraḫasis Epic begins is, incidentally, a point in favor of treating Gen. 6:1-4 not as a separate fragment but as the introduction to the story of the deluge, regardless of whether the biblical account is dependent on the Babylonian or whether both have a common origin.

[3] Enûma elish, Tablet I:21 ff.

[4] Text published by Edward J. Harper in Beiträge zur Assyriologie, II (1894), 499:8-11, and by Erich Ebeling, Keilschrifttexte aus Assur religiösen Inhalts (Leipzig, 1919-23), No. 168: 39-42.

all human and animal life without discrimination and thus would have
defeated the very purpose for which, according to the Babylonian
creation stories, mankind and the animals had been created, viz.,
to supply the wants of the gods. Whether Enlil, like Jupiter in
Ovid's Metamorphoses (i. 250 ff.), had planned a new creation of
men after the deluge is not indicated in any of the Babylonian
flood stories at our disposal. But, whatever may be said about
the wisdom of Enlil's scheme, there was little justice in it.

The Hero of the Flood

The name of the deluge hero varies with the different recensions. The Sumerian account calls him Ziusudra, which means something like "he who laid hold on life of distant days," the reference being to the immortality which after the flood was bestowed
upon the hero. In the Gilgamesh Epic he bears the name Utnapishtim.
This is obviously a free rendering of the Sumerian Ziusudra and is
today commonly translated with "he saw life," i.e., he found or
obtained everlasting life.[5] Here again the name is, of course,
symbolical of the role played by the deluge hero. In another version the hero is referred to by the name of Atraḥasis, meaning "the
exceedingly wise." In the excerpts from Berossus he is called
Xisuthros, Sisuthros, Sisithros, and Seisithros, all of which probably go back to an original Zisuthros, corresponding to the Sumerian
Ziusudra. In the Bible his name appears as Noah, meaning "rest."
The Book of Genesis makes no attempt to establish a relation between the name and the experiences of the central human figure in
the account of the flood.

Utnapishtim was the son of Ubara-Tutu, the Otiartes, or, rather,
Opartes of Berossus. According to Berossus, the deluge hero was
the tenth prediluvian king in Babylonia. Also in the Sumerian in-

---

[5]However, this translation is not beyond criticism; for if
this is the real meaning of the name, we should expect the form
Utnapishtam (or Utanapishtam), i.e., the second element should stand
in the accusative (as in Utamisharam), instead of the genetive. On
the basis of the Sumerian equivalent and the genetive ending in Babylonian and Assyrian, one would, in this particular instance, expect
the element uta to be a substantive or nominal formation of some
kind. Perhaps the name means something like "the finder (or ob-
tainer) of life" (cf. B. Meissner, Babylonien und Assyrien, II
[Heidelberg, 1925], 113).

scription he is referred to as king; there he occupies also a
priestly office, viz., that of the administrator of the temple provisions of a certain god. In the Gilgamesh Epic, Utnapishtim is
not vested with any royal power or intrusted with any priestly office; from it we learn simply that he was a citizen of Shurippak
(Tablet XI:23) and a man of considerable wealth (XI:70 ff.). Noah
was the son of Lamech and the tenth prediluvian patriarch (Genesis,
chap. 5).

Utnapishtim dwelt in the city of Shurippak (or Shuruppak),
which was one of the oldest cities in southern Babylonia and which
today is represented by the mounds of Fâra, about eighteen miles
northwest of Uruk. Shuruppak is listed also among the five ante-
diluvian cities enumerated in the Sumerian Nippur version. In the
Hebrew account no city at all is mentioned in connection with the
hero of the flood.

As indicated before, Noah escaped destruction because of his
godliness. He was a righteous and faultless man among his contemporaries; like Enoch, he walked with God (Gen. 6:9) and thus was
in the most intimate relation with God. This made the performance
of the will of God self-evident. When, therefore, he was ordered
to build the ark, he showed no signs of doubt or unwillingness but
obeyed and carried out the command. The piety of the deluge hero
is emphasized also in the Sumerian account; there he is called the
administrator of the temple provisions, and there it is stated that
he prostrated himself in reverence and humility and that he daily
and perseveringly stood in attendance at the shrine. After the
flood he again prostrated himself in adoration and offered an abundant sacrifice. This characteristic can be inferred also from the
Gilgamesh Epic; for upon Ea's announcement of the impending catastrophe he showed reverence to his divine overlord, he hearkened to
the voice of his god, and carried out his instructions; after the
flood he offered up a sacrifice to placate the gods. Finally,
Berossus states that Xisuthros "obeyed" the instructions of his
god and that he was translated to the society of the gods because
of his piety.

The Announcement of the Flood

The manner in which the impending cataclysm was announced to
the deluge hero in the Babylonian stories differs widely from the
way in which it was revealed to the Old Testament Noah. According

to the Sumerian version, Ziusudra had an extraordinary dream, "such
as had not been (before)." Apparently, in view of its singular
character, he conjured by the name of heaven and earth either to
determine the meaning of the dream or to receive divine assurance
that his interpretation of it was correct. Thereupon he heard a
voice which bade him take his stand beside a wall and then told
him that by the decree of the assembly of the gods a flood would
be sent to destroy mankind. The remainder of the communication,
which in all probability dealt with the construction of the boat,
is unfortunately broken away. In the Gilgamesh Epic, Ea begins
his disclosure of the things to come by addressing himself to a
reed hut, probably the dwelling of the deluge hero; but then, turning to Utnapishtim, he tells him to tear down his house and build
a ship according to certain specifications, to abandon his possessions, and to save his life and to take into the ship the seed of
all living creatures (Tablet XI:19-31). This warning took place
while Utnapishtim lay asleep in the reed hut, for, when Ea was taken
to account by Enlil for having divulged the secret of the gods, he
tried to justify his course of action by asserting that it really
was not he who had revealed the divine resolution but that he had
shown a dream to Utnapishtim and that from this dream "the exceedingly wise" had guessed the plan of the great gods (Tablet XI:170-
87). Also Berossus states that Kronos, i.e., Ea, appeared to the
deluge hero in a dream and warned him of the impending doom. The
Atrahasis Epic (Fragments II and III) exhibits certain features
both of the Sumerian version and of the flood account embodied in
the Gilgamesh Epic. Utnapishtim was not told expressly, in the
Gilgamesh Epic, that a deluge would be sent in which all mankind
was to perish, but he was told enough so that he could draw the
necessary conclusions. This revelation was made not only without
the knowledge of Enlil, the real author of the flood, but it was
also quite contrary to his plan, according to which "no man was
to live through the destruction" (Tablet XI:173).[6]

In Genesis, on the other hand, Noah apparently received a
direct communication; there is no indication that the will of God
was conveyed to him through the medium of a dream. Furthermore,
the disclosure was made by the Lord himself, and was therefore in

---

[6]King, op. cit., pp. 69-76; A. Ungnad and H. Gressmann, Das
Gilgamesch-Epos (Göttingen, 1911), pp. 192-94.

full accord with his purpose. The God who caused the flood also
saved his faithful servant by informing him of the approaching
catastrophe and by ordering the building of an ark. However, all
available accounts agree that the impending peril was divinely
announced to the hero of the deluge.

The Period of Grace

According to Gen. 6:3, man was granted a period of grace extending over one hundred and twenty years, during which he had an
opportunity to amend his sinful ways and to avert the threatened
destruction (cf. I Pet. 3:20).[7] There is no mention in the biblical
text that the intended punishment was announced to Noah's contemporaries. But that this was done may be taken for granted; for, had
it not been disclosed to mankind, there would have been little meaning in giving them a period of grace, particularly since they were
apparently permitted to go unpunished during all this time. And
since Noah was the only person who had found favor in the sight of
God, it is an obvious conclusion that he was intrusted with the
task of communicating the decision of God to his fellow-men (cf.
II Pet. 2:5).[8]

In the Gilgamesh Epic there was no thought of granting mankind an opportunity to repent. There the planned destruction of
the human race was a zealously guarded secret of the gods. It was
such an inviolable secret that even as great a divinity as Ea did
not dare to communicate it directly to his favorite, Utnapishtim,
but felt compelled to resort to a subterfuge, by warning the latter
in a dream from which he could guess the contents of the gods' decree. And when Utnapishtim, in his dream, inquired of his divine
overlord what he should answer his fellow-citizens when asked about
the purpose of the building and provisioning of the boat, Ea instructed him to deceive them, lest they should learn the truth and
likewise escape. Utnapishtim was to tell them in effect: "I have
learned that Enlil hates me and that I may no longer dwell in your
city. I will therefore go and live with Ea, my lord. Then Enlil
will turn to you with his grace and favor and pour an abundant

---

[7]See Eduard König, Die Genesis (Gütersloh, 1919), pp. 333-34,
and Franz Delitzsch, Neuer Commentar über die Genesis (Leipzig,
1887), pp. 151-52.

[8]H. L. Strack, Die Genesis (Munich, 1905), p. 25.

blessing upon you, which will begin with a wheat-rain on a stormy
evening" (Tablet XI:32-47). Thus, as L. W. King[9] has put it,
Utnapishtim is "ordered to allay any misgivings that his fellow-
citizens may feel by assuring them beforehand that the signs of
the deluge are marks of coming prosperity, and not of destruction."
Virtually the same deception is recorded in the extract from
Berossus, where we read: "If he [i.e., Xisuthros] should be asked
whither he was sailing he should say: 'To the gods, in order to
pray that it may be well with mankind!'" That the gods (at least
Enlil) never intended to give mankind another chance becomes even
more apparent from the quarrel which ensued among the gods after
the flood. When Enlil found out that a number of people had survived the flood, he was filled with anger, for it had been his
determined purpose that all should perish and that no one should
live! There is no indication that other means of correcting mankind had been tried before but without success. On the contrary,
to judge from the way in which Ea remonstrated with Enlil for not
having resorted to less drastic measures, such as sending wild
beasts, or a famine, or a pestilence among mankind to diminish their
numbers, and from the fact that Enlil had nothing to say in reply
to Ea's censure, it would seem that this was the first attempt on
the part of the gods to curb the wickedness of man; for otherwise
Enlil could have pointed out that other means had been employed
before but that all had failed and that his action, consequently,
was not as thoughtless as maintained by Ea (Tablet XI:170-96).

According to the Atraḫasis Epic, man was granted several periods
of grace before Enlil determined to destroy the human race by means
of a flood. There the decision to cause a deluge was preceded by
a number of severe plagues which Enlil sent at different intervals
for the purpose of inducing humanity to refrain from making so much
noise. He first sent a dire famine, which lasted about six years
and assumed such dimensions that parents ate their own children and
that one house, or family, devoured the other. Since the people
reverted to their former ways after the plague was over and after
they had recovered from its effects, Enlil sent another famine,
accompanied by a failure of childbirth, to diminish the numbers of
the human race. At this juncture the wise man Atraḫasis interceded

---

[9]*Babylonian Religion and Mythology* (London and New York, 1899),
p. 130.

with Ea and in some indeterminable way effected relief. But soon
the noise of mankind was as great as before, so that Enlil called
a council of the gods in which it was resolved to send a pestilence
among men in order to put an end to their unbearable noise. Once
more Atraḥasis pleaded with Ea on behalf of groaning mankind and
apparently was again successful in his effort to bring about a
removal of the plague. When also this punishment failed to effect
a lasting change, Enlil afflicted them with another famine attended
by a cessation of births. However, despite all these visitations,
the human family had not learned their lesson; for when the plague
had been removed, and they were able to breathe freely again, they
became as noisy and hilarious as before. Seeing that all his attempts at correcting the ways of mankind had failed, Enlil resolved
to destroy the whole human race by sending a flood. And once the
complete annihilation of man was decided upon, there was no more
grace; for also according to this version, Enlil tried to keep the
coming of the deluge a secret of the gods, as we can see from Fragment II, in order that no human soul might escape destruction.

The Ark

Another interesting point of comparison is the ark which the
hero of the flood constructed. Like the hero himself, the ark is
known by a number of different terms in the various flood stories.
The Sumerian recension designates it as a _magurgur_, which means
"a very great ship," "a giant boat."[10] This word occurs also in
the Semitic Babylonian deluge fragment from Nippur, where it corresponds to the Semitic phrase _elippu rabitu_, used two lines previously in that text and signifying "a great ship or boat."

The Gilgamesh Epic calls this craft by the general term _elippu_,
"vessel," "ship," "boat." Once it also uses _êkallu_ (Tablet XI:95),
a word which, derived from the Sumerian language, literally means
"a great house" and occurs in reference to palaces and temples.
This term is employed as a poetic designation for the ark, giving
"an indication of its large size, with its many stories and compartments."[11] In the passage under discussion I have translated it

---

[10] A. Poebel, _Historical Texts_ (Philadelphia, 1914), p. 58.

[11] Morris Jastrow, Jr., _Hebrew and Babylonian Traditions_ (New
York, 1914), p. 330, n. 1.

somewhat freely with "the mighty structure."[12] Berossus refers
to the deluge boat as σκάφος, πλοῖον, and ναῦς, all three of which
mean "ship," or "boat."

The Old Testament word for the ark is tēbâ. Outside of the
biblical flood story, this term occurs only in Exod. 2:3/5, where
it is applied to the reed vessel in which the infant Moses was
saved. The Hebrew tēbâ is hardly related, as has been suggested,
to the Babylonian ṭebîtu, denoting a deep-drawing freight ship (for
in that case we should expect הבֵּת instead of the actual הבָּת), but
rather to the Egyptian ḏb't, meaning "chest," "box," "coffin."[13]
In the Septuagint and the New Testament, Noah's ark is called
κιβωτός, "box," "chest," "coffer"; this term is applied also to
the chest (Hebrew אֲרוֹן) placed at the entrance to the temple by
Jehoiada, the priest (II Kings 12:10-11), and to the ark of the
covenant (cf., e.g., Exod. 25:10 ff. and Heb. 9:4).

These comparisons show that as there is no etymological connection between the name of Noah and the Babylonian names for the hero
of the flood, so there is none between the Hebrew term for the ark
and the Babylonian designations for the same vessel.

The Old Testament deluge ark was made of gōfer wood. The
meaning of this expression, found only in Gen. 6:14, is quite uncertain, although it is generally held to refer to some kind of
resinous wood, such as pine or cypress. The Hebrew gōfer is hardly
derived from the Babylonian and Assyrian gipâru, which in some passages appears to denote some kind of tree or shrub. Gipâru is a
loan-word from Sumerian. Consequently, if gōfer were etymologically
related to gipâru, it would likewise have to be a loan-word, either
from Sumerian directly or from Babylono-Assyrian. In that case,
however, we should expect a form something like gifār in Hebrew.
As a loan-word from Babylonian, the term gōfer would presuppose a
form like gupru (cf. Babylonian kupru and Hebrew kōfer), which has

_____

[12]The term bîtu, "house," as a name for the ark, does not occur
in the Babylonian versions of the deluge, contrary to the opinion
formerly held by some scholars, whose view was based on an erroneous interpretation of Tablet XI:24, which they rendered: "Construct
a house, build a ship!" The corresponding passage in the Atrahasis
Epic (Fragment II) has very plainly: ú-bu-ut bi-ta bi-ni e-li-ip-pa.
This can mean only: "Destroy (thy) house, build a ship."

[13]For references see A. Salonen, Die Wasserfahrzeuge in Babylonien (Helsinki, 1939), p. 48, n. 2.

actually been found in two or three passages, but in the sense
of "table."[14] In the preserved portions of the Babylonian deluge
traditions nothing is said about the kind of wood that was used
for the construction of the boat.

Utnapishtim's vessel had seven stories and was divided ver-
tically into nine sections, thus having sixty-three compartments
(Tablet XI:60-62). Its roof was like that of "the subterranean
waters," i.e., it was as strong as the earth, which holds the subterranean waters in their place (Tablet XI:31).[15] According to
the Semitic Nippur fragment, the boat was topped with "a strong
cover." It had a door (Tablet XI:88.93) and at least one window
(XI:135). Noah's ark, on the other hand, had three stories and
consisted of numerous unspecified cells, or compartments. It had
a door in its side and an opening for light below the roof (Gen.
6:16). The Hebrew term used to designate the opening for light
is ṣōhar. This word has been equated with Arabic ẓahrun and Babylonian ṣîru, both meaning "back," and has been taken to refer to
the roof of the ark.[16] But if ṣōhar really meant "roof," the addition "above" or "from above," in Gen. 6:16, would be quite super-
fluous, inasmuch as it is self-evident that the roof is "above."
Moreover, the specification "to a cubit" would be meaningless.[17]
From these considerations and the references to a window in Gen.
8:6[18] and the main Babylonian account of the flood, it is reasonably
certain that the term in question denotes an opening for light.
This opening was one cubit in height and, according to the prevalent
explanation, extended all around the ark, interrupted only by the
posts supporting the roof. This interpretation seems to be favored
by the wording of the text: "Thou shalt make an opening for light

---

[14]Once it occurs in the Gilgamesh Epic, Tablet II, col. ii,
33 (Old Babylonian version).

[15]H. V. Hilprecht, The Babylonian Expedition of the University
of Pennsylvania, Series D, Vol. V, Fasc. 1 (Philadelphia, 1910), p.

[16]Wilhelm Gesenius, Hebräisches und aramäisches Handwörterbuch
über das Alte Testament, ed. Frants Buhl (Leipzig, 1915), pp. 675-76,
Hermann Gunkel, Genesis (Göttingen, 1910), p. 142; Otto Procksch,
Die Genesis (Leipzig, 1913), pp. 447-48.

[17]See König, op. cit., pp. 344-45, and Hebräisches und aramäisches Wörterbuch zum Alten Testament (Leipzig, 1931), p. 383.

[18]I take ḥallôn to denote either the same thing as the ṣōhar
or a part thereof.

for the ark and to a cubit shalt thou make it complete from above."
This passage seems to indicate that Noah is to construct an opening for light completely around the ark.[19]

The Old Testament ark was coated inside and out with pitch,
or bitumen, to make it watertight. Bituminous materials figure
more prominently in the main Babylonian account than they do in
the biblical. Utnapishtim poured six (var.: three) shar of pitch
into the furnace, or pitch pot, and three shar of asphalt. The
purpose is not stated, but there can be no doubt about it—he melted
these substances and then calked the boat therewith. This is quite
clear from Berossus' statement: "Some get pitch from the ship by
scraping (it) off." The word for pitch, as we shall see later on,
is the same both in Genesis and in the Gilgamesh Epic. In addition
to these materials, Utnapishtim used three shar of oil, which the
basket-carriers brought. Of this oil, one shar was used presumably
to saturate the water-stoppers; the other two shar the boatman
stowed away, for unspecified purposes (Tablet XI:65-69). The use
of oil is not mentioned in the biblical narrative.

Noah's ark, as evidenced by its dimensions and the names by
which it is designated in Greek and Hebrew, was of flat-bottomed,
rectangular construction, square on both ends and straight up on
the sides. Such a craft is represented on bronze coins from the
Phrygian city Apameia, which already at the time of Caesar Augustus
bore the cognomen Κιβωτός, distinguishing it from other cities of
the same name in Bithynia and Syria. To the right these coins,
dating from the reign of Septimius Severus (A.D. 146-211) on down
and betraying doubtless Jewish influence, picture an open chest
swimming in the water and bearing the inscription ΝΩΕ or simply
ΝΩ. In the chest are seen the deluge hero and his wife, both ap-
pearing from the waist upward. On the raised lid of the ark a dove
is perched, while another comes flying toward the ark with a twig
in its claws. To the left the same pair of human beings are seen
but standing on dry ground and raising their right hands in adoration.[20]

---

[19]A. Dillmann, Genesis, trans. W. B. Stevenson, I (Edinburgh,
1897), 272; Delitzsch, op. cit., p. 171; S. R. Driver, The Book of
Genesis (New York and London, 1904), p. 88.

[20]H. Usener, Die Sintfluthsagen (Bonn, 1899), pp. 48-50; Sir J.
G. Frazer, Folk-lore in the Old Testament, I (London, 1918), 156-57.

The length of Noah's ark was "three hundred cubits, its
breadth fifty cubits, and its height thirty cubits" (Gen. 6:15).
Since the cubit is here given without any qualifying addition, it
probably represents the ordinary Hebrew cubit, which supposedly
corresponded to the distance from the tip of the middle finger to
the elbow and measured about 18 inches. According to this standard, the ark was 450 feet long, 75 feet wide, and 45 feet high,
and had a displacement of approximately 43,300 tons.

Utnapishtim's boat, on the contrary, was an exact cube, the
length, width, and height each being 120 cubits. Since the Babylonian cubit was equal to about 20 inches, 120 cubits correspond
to about 200 feet. The Babylonian vessel, accordingly, had a displacement of about 228,500 tons. The shape and the manner of construction of Utnapishtim's boat are strongly reminiscent of the
guffa, a kind of coracle made of wickerwork and coated inside and
out with bitumen. But, contrary to the view expressed by King,[21]
it is by no means identical with this circular craft, which is
still in constant use on the lower Tigris and Euphrates. Tablet
XI:30 and 57-58, which instructs Utnapishtim that the length and
the width of the boat should be equal and which then gives the
exact height of its walls and the exact length of each side of its
deck, refers to a quadrangular craft. King's argument that the
boat's interior division of each story into nine vertical sections
"is only suitable to a circular craft in which the interior walls
would radiate from the center" overlooks the possibilities that
the compartments may have extended from side to side,[22] or that
Utnapishtim may have built in four walls, two of which ran in one
direction and two in another, crossing at right angles to make nine
square rooms on each floor.[23]

Berossus speaks of a boat over 3,000 feet long and more than
1,200 feet wide. The height of this fabulous vessel is not given.

There is thus a decided variance between the dimensions of the
boat as contained in the Babylonian traditions and those given in
Genesis. But all accounts agree that the hero of the deluge was
divinely ordered to construct the vessel in which—to borrow a

---

[21]Legends ...., pp. 80-81.

[22]Paul Haupt in Beiträge zur Assyriologie, X, Heft 2 (1927), 8.

[23]A. Schott in Zeitschrift für Assyriologie, XL (1931), 16.

phrase from the Babylonian versions—"the seed of all living creatures" was saved from the waters of the great flood that covered
the earth. Moreover, the Atraḫasis Epic (Fragment III) would seem
to indicate that the god who disclosed the imminent calamity even
drew a plan of the boat. The detailed instructions which Noah received amounted to about the same thing. According to Tablet XI,
Utnapishtim himself appears to have drawn up the necessary plans.

The Occupants of the Ark

Upon the completion of his craft, Utnapishtim loaded aboard
it all his gold and silver and whatever he had of "the seed of all
living creatures," and caused all his family and relations, "the
game of the field, the beasts of the field, all the craftsmen,"
and the boatman to go up into it (Tablet XI:80-85 and 94-95). The
craftsmen (or learned men) were taken aboard undoubtedly for the
same reason for which, according to Berossus, Xisuthros was ordered
before the deluge "to set down in writing the beginning, middle,
and end of all things," and to bury these writings in Sippar—in
order to preserve the divine revelations concerning the origin of
the world and to transmit the arts and sciences, human culture,
and civilization to the postdiluvian race.[24]

The last preserved line of column v of the fragmentary Sumerian
account shows that Ziusudra took at least sheep and cattle with him
into the boat, for after the flood he killed an ox and offered an
abundant sacrifice of sheep. According to the Atraḫasis Epic, the
deluge hero put into the ark his grain, his goods and chattels,
his family, his relations, the craftsmen, "[game] of the field
(and) beasts of the field, as many as eat herbs" (Fragment III).
The preserved portion of the Semitic Nippur fragment refers only
to "the beasts of the field" and "the fowl of the heavens." That
Utnapishtim likewise took birds with him into the ark is apparent
from the fact that after the landing of the ark he sent out a dove,
a swallow, and a raven to ascertain to what degree the waters had
fallen (Tablet XI:145-54). Berossus relates that Xisuthros went
aboard the ship with "his relatives," his "wife and children, and

---

[24]H. Zimmern in Eberhard Schrader, Die Keilinschriften und das
Alte Testament (Berlin, 1903), p. 548, n. 5; Poebel, op. cit.,
p. 44, n. 3.

his close friends" and that he stored up in it "food and drink"
and "put into it also living creatures, winged and four-footed."
A reference to the storing-up of food supplies is perhaps found
also on Tablet XI:64: "I provided punting-poles and stored up a
supply." These documents seem to indicate that the Babylonian
hero of the flood took only <u>herbivorous</u> animals with him.

In contrast with the great number of people who were saved
according to the Babylonian diluvial traditions, the biblical ark
carried only eight persons, viz., Noah, his three sons, his wife,
and the wives of his sons. With respect to the preservation of
animal life Noah received the following instruction, according to
Gen. 6:19-21: "Of every living thing, of all flesh, thou shalt
bring two of every (species) into the ark to keep (them) alive with
thee; they shall be a male and a female. Of the birds after their
species and of the beasts after their species, of all the creeping
things of the earth after their species; two of every (species)
shall come unto thee to keep (them) alive. And thou shalt take
unto thee of every (kind of) food that is eaten and shalt gather
(it) unto thee; and it shall be food for thee and for them." In
Gen. 7:2-3 this general rule is amplified and a distinction is made
between clean and unclean animals: "Of all clean beasts thou shalt
take unto thee seven pairs, the male and its mate; but of the
beasts that are not clean (only) two, the male and its mate; likewise, of the birds of the air seven pairs,[25] the male and its mate,
to keep seed alive upon the face of all the earth." The story then
continues: "And Noah, with his sons, his wife, and the wives of
his sons, went into the ark, because of the waters of the flood.
Of the clean beasts and of the beasts that are not clean, of the
birds and of everything that creeps upon the earth they went to
Noah into the ark in pairs,[26] the male and (its) mate, as God had
commanded Noah" (vss. 7-9).

A question frequently asked in this connection is how the
gathering-in of the animals took place. According to the Atraḥasis
Epic, Fragment III, the animals came by divine guidance, for Ea
told Atraḥasis: "[Game] of the field (and) beasts of the field, as

---

[25]König, <u>Historisch-comparative Syntax der hebräischen Sprache</u>
(Leipzig, 1897), § 316, <u>b</u>.

[26]See Gesenius, <u>op. cit.</u>, under צ׳נם; and Dillmann, <u>op. cit.</u>,
pp. 275 and 277.

many as eat herbs, [I will s]end unto thee." This appears to be
the import also of Gen. 6:19-20: "Of every living thing, of all
flesh, thou shalt bring into (lit.: cause to come into) the ark
two of every (species) to keep (them) alive with thee: they shall
be a male and a female. Of the birds after their species and of the
beasts after their species, of all the creeping things of the earth
after their species; two of every (species) shall come unto thee
to keep (them) alive." The natural meaning seems to be that these
creatures would come voluntarily to Noah and that he should then
put them in the ark.

The Day of the Beginning of the Flood

"In the six hundredth year of Noah's life, in the second month,
on the seventeenth day of the month, on that very day all the fountains of the great deep (tĕhôm) were broken open, and the windows
of the heavens were opened" (Gen. 7:11). In trying to determine
the time of the year when the flood burst upon mankind, we are at
once confronted with the problem of identifying "the second month."
Scholars have debated this point from the earliest times, and still
there is no unanimity among them. Some hold that the months are
here reckoned from the commencement of the agricultural year among
the Hebrews, which started in the autumn (cf. Exod. 23:16; 34:22),
so that "the second month" would refer to the second harvest month,
known as Bûl or Marcheshwan and corresponding to the latter part
of our October and the first part of November, when the rainy season in Palestine began.[27] Others, counting the months of the year
from the spring (cf. Exod. 12:2), understand "the second month" as
the second spring month, called Ziw or Iyyar, which corresponds to
the latter part of April and the early part of May, when the Tigris
and Euphrates, following the melting of the snow in the mountains
of Armenia and Kurdistan, reach their highest point of inundation.[28]
The evidence is so meager on both sides that it is rather difficult
to reach a definite conclusion on this matter. According to Berossus, the date which the gods had set for the commencement of the

---

[27]Thus Dillmann, op. cit., p. 253; Delitzsch, op. cit., pp.
175-76; and Driver, op. cit., p. 90.

[28]Thus Gunkel, op. cit., p. 146; König, Die Genesis, p. 351,
n. 3; John Skinner, A Critical and Exegetical Commentary on Genesis
(New York, 1910), p. 168; and Procksch, op. cit., p. 449.

flood was "the fifteenth of the month Daisios." This month is
derived from the Macedonian calendar and corresponds approximately
to our May.[29] The available cuneiform material is silent on the
point in question.

The Causes of the Flood

The causes which the Genesis version assigns to the diluvial
catastrophe are torrential rains from heaven and the eruption of
the subterranean waters (7:11-12). The destructive forces listed
on the Sumerian tablet are the amaru, meaning "rainstorm," "rain
flood," or "cloudburst,"[30] and mighty winds. These two elements,
accompanied by thunder and lightning, are mentioned again in the
Gilgamesh Epic, where they are referred to under the designations
shamûtu kibâti, "destructive rain," shâru, "wind," mehû, "tempest,"
"southstorm(?)," râdu, "downpour," abûbu, "rainstorm," or "rain
flood," and imhullu, "evil wind," or "storm." In addition, there
is a reference to the breaking of the dikes of the canals and reser-
voirs, which was caused by the violent rise of the rivers (Tablet
XI:90-131).

Berossus, in his description of the deluge, employs the term
κατακλυσμός , "flood," "inundation." In the sense of "flood" or
"deluge," this word is used of the Deucalionic flood, caused by
heavy rains.[31] In the Septuagint and the New Testament it almost
invariably corresponds to the Hebrew mabbûl, by which the deluge
is designated in the Hebrew Old Testament.[32] The excerpt by Abydenus attributes the catastrophe to "copious rains" (πλῆθος ὄμβρων).
This is supported, moreover, by his statement that, "after the
rain had subsided" (ἐπεί τε ὕων ἐκόπασε), Sisisthros released a
number of birds to test the conditions of the outside world.

King, in his effort to defend the position that the deluge
was caused by the annual overflow of the Tigris and the Euphrates,

---

[29]See Pauly-Wissowa, Real-Encyclopädie der classischen Alter-
tumswissenschaft, Vol. VIII (Stuttgart, 1901), cols. 2014-15.

[30]Poebel, op. cit., p. 54.

[31]Apollodorus The Library 1. 7. 2 and 111. 8. 2.

[32]In Ps. 31(32):6, Nah. 1:8, and Dan. 9:26 (Theodotion) it is
the equivalent of אֶצֶף or אֶצֶף , "outpouring," "flood," "inundation."

argued that abûbu should properly be rendered "flood," adding:
"In itself the term abûbu implies flood, which could take place
through a rise of the rivers unaccompanied by heavy local rain."[33]
However, there does not appear to be any decisive evidence that
abûbu was ever employed to denote also an inundation caused by the
rivers unaccompanied by heavy rains; to designate a river-flood, or
a high tide of water, the Babylonians used mêlû or edû. But even
should such evidence be available, it still does not alter the
fact that the Babylonian versions very definitely attribute the
deluge to a heavy storm. This phenomenon is emphasized with special force in column v of the Sumerian version and on Tablet XI:
90-131 of the Gilgamesh Epic. Neither of these passages sounds
anything like a description of an inundation due merely to an overflow of the rivers. According to the latter passage, the flood
was caused principally by "the raging of Adad," the god of storm
and rain, who had nothing to do with the periodic rising of the
rivers in Mesopotamia. On Tablet XI:131, where it is said that
"the flood (abûbu) ceased" simultaneously with the quieting of the
sea and the cessation of the storm, the abûbu quite obviously signifies the heavy downpour of rain and not the inundation caused by
it and at that time still covering the earth.[34] In like manner
mabbûl in Gen. 7:17: "The flood (mabbûl) came[35] upon the earth
forty days, and the waters mounted," evidently refers to the unprecedented stream of rain coming down from above, without including the resultant inundation, which continued for a long time afterward, as we shall see shortly.[36]

Toward the end of the last century, the eminent geologist Eduard
Suess,[37] of Vienna, endeavoring to rationalize the Babylonian flood

---

[33]Legends ...., p. 70, n. 2.

[34]P. Jensen in Reallexikon der Assyriologie, I (Berlin and
Leipzig, 1932), 11-13; A. T. Clay, The Origin of Biblical Traditions
(New Haven, 1923), pp. 152-56.

[35]With this meaning of מַבּוּל cf., e.g., Gen. 7:10: "And it came
to pass after the seven days that the waters of the flood came upon
the earth"; Jer. 3:3: "The spring rain has not come."

[36]In other passages, however, both mabbûl and abûbu undoubtedly
have a wider meaning (cf., e.g., Gen. 9:28 and the Gilgamesh Epic,
Tablet I, col. 1, 6).

[37]The Face of the Earth, trans. Hertha B. C. Sollas, I (Oxford,
1904), 17-72.

story and realizing the insufficiency of the inundation theory
alone, advanced the view that the deluge was caused chiefly by gigantic sea waves produced partly by seismic disturbances "in the
region of the Persian Gulf, or to the south of it" and partly by
a cyclone or hurricane, which, arising from the Bay of Bengal,
crossed India and then traveled north through the Persian Gulf
and, at the height of the annual inundation, during the period of
the most violent shocks of the earthquake, which caused the subterranean waters to burst forth from the fissured plain, swept over
the Tigro-Euphrates area, damming back the waters of the rivers
and driving before it stupendous masses of water from the sea, accompanied by torrents of rain. The deluge as a whole, however,
Suess contended, came from the sea; the rain and the subterranean
waters, as well as the regular overflow of the rivers, were "merely
accessory elements."

In support of this view, Suess invoked both the biblical and
the main Babylonian flood story, from which he believed the former
to have been borrowed. To prove his contention that the deluge re-
sulted in part from an earthquake, he appealed to the mention of
the breaking-up of the fountains of the deep in the biblical text
and to a number of features derived from quite untenable translations of the Babylonian material. With his arguments drawn from
the Babylonian material, we need not concern ourselves in this instance. Elaborating on the biblical statement, Suess declared that
the "rising of great quantities of water from the deep is a phenomenon which is a characteristic accompaniment of earthquakes in the
alluvial districts of great rivers."[38] Again: "Such phenomena
have never been observed on any great scale except in extensive
low-lying districts, where subterranean water is present, nor would
they be explicable under any other conditions."[39]

Since one of the earthquake zones in the world runs along the
east and north of the Persian Gulf and stretches across Mesopotamia,[40] the Babylonians could perhaps have connected the deluge with

---

[38]Ibid., p. 31.

[39]Ibid., p. 33.

[40]F. de Montessus de Ballore, Les Tremblements de terre, géo-
graphie séismologique (Paris, 1906), pp. 209-14 and Map I (cf. also
J. Milne, "Catalogue of Destructive Earthquakes," in Report of the
British Association for the Advancement of Science, 1911, esp. p.
731).

terrestrial convulsions; but in all the extant diluvial traditions
from Babylonia—whether composed in Sumerian, Semitic Babylonian,
or Greek—there is not the faintest trace of such a phenomenon.
According to the biblical narrative, on the other hand, the flood
was evidently accompanied by a most violent earthquake.[41] But
whether the import of the story is that the breaking-up of the
fountains of the deep occurred only in the alluvial plains of the
earth is quite a different question. Since the Genesis account is
full of the miraculous or the supernatural, and since according to
it the flood was universal, the statement, "All the fountains of
the great deep were broken up" (7:11), obviously carries the implication that the subterranean waters gushed forth everywhere, irrespective of the condition of the terrain.

Suess's further assertion that the flood as a whole was of
marine origin rests, in part, on a change imported into the Hebrew
text. Following J. D. Michaelis and others, Suess modified the
vocalization of the Hebrew phrase hammabbûl ma(y)yim, "the flood
(of) waters" (Gen. 6:17 and 7:6), making the words read instead
hammabbûl miyyām, which the proponents of this alteration translated
"the flood from the sea."[42] The biblical text was thus, so it
seemed, in perfect accord with his position. However, the proposed
emendation is rendered improbable by similar expressions in Gen. 7:7
and 9:11 15, where ma(y)yim cannot be changed to miyyām, and, as
observed by K. Budde,[43] is ruled out by the consideration that instead of miyyām the Hebrew text would have to read min-hayyām.[44]

Finally, the idea of a cyclone, serving as a further support
for his view that the deluge was produced primarily by a raging sea,
was inferred by Suess from the course taken by the ship in the main
Babylonian story; for he observed that after the flood Utnapishtim's
craft, traveling against the natural current of the water in Babylonia, is found over two hundred miles north of Shurippak, its
starting-point. In this, Suess saw conclusive evidence for a cyclone
originating in the vicinity of the Andaman Islands, in the Bay of

---

[41]So in Ovid Metamorphoses 1. 283-84.

[42]Suess, op. cit., pp. 38-39.

[43]In Theologische Literaturzeitung, Vol. XVI (1891), col. 247.

[44]Or mêhayyām, as in Isa. 19:5.

Bengal.[45] These cyclones, or hurricanes, are among the most terrific in the world. "Travelling more or less westwards or north-
wards," to quote the words of another geologist, W. J. Sollas,[46]
they "sweep over the waters of the bay of Bengal, and raise the sea
into waves mountains high, which every now and again rush over the
low-lying lands of the Ganges delta, overwhelming the unfortunate
inhabitants by the myriads." But, as Sollas continues, "these
storms do not, as a rule, travel towards the Persian gulf, and the
North Arabian sea is singularly free from them." Suess himself is
unable to point to a single instance where one of these cyclones
is known to have entered the Persian Gulf. This is a serious blow
to his theory. To remove the difficulty, Suess assumed that for
once such a storm lost its way, so to speak, and actually traveled
through the Persian Gulf and reached the Mesopotamian Valley. Since
the Babylonian deluge version imbedded in the Gilgamesh Epic speaks
of a heavy storm and since the severest atmospheric disturbances in
Babylonia arise in the south, it seems to be a natural conclusion
that the boat was driven by a violent storm from the southern sea,
which kept the boat from drifting into the Persian Gulf and, instead, drove it from Shurippak all the way to Mount Niṣir, about
270 miles north.[47] But the storm need not have been the kind suggested by the famous geologist. Furthermore, there is no evidence
that the storm was believed to have caused an inundation from the
sea.[48] On the contrary, the fact that Ea, the god who presided at
least over the waters at the northern end of the Persian Gulf,[49]
is nowhere mentioned as having taken part in the actual causation

---

[45]Op. cit., pp. 38 ff.

[46]The Age of the Earth (London, 1905), p. 315.

[47]According to the Sumerian recension (col. v), "all the mighty
windstorms blew together."

[48]On Tablet XI:131: "The sea grew quiet, the storm abated, the
flood ceased," the word "sea" apparently refers to the sea of waters
produced by the deluge, as it does in line 138 and in all probability
also in line 132.

[49]Cf. H. C. Rawlinson, The Cuneiform Inscriptions of Western
Asia, Vol. III (London, 1870), Pl. 12, Slab 2:30-34; also R. Campbell
Thompson in Cuneiform Texts from Babylonian Tablets, etc. in the
British Museum, Vol. XVII (London, 1903), Pl. 42:25: la-aḫ-mi tâmti
sh[u-ut] dé-a, "laḫmu's of the sea bel[onging] to Ea."

of the deluge makes it doubtful whether the thought of an incursion
of the sea was really in the minds of the Babylonian mythographers.
It is therefore manifest that the incursion of the sea, if this
element was at all present, can have played only a secondary role
and that the real source of the flood was rain.

The Duration of the Flood

Modern biblical criticism, as is well known, sees in the Genesis account of the deluge a blending of two main, in several respects irreconcilably contradictory, sources put together by a
redactor. According to the one source, called P (or the Priestly
Code), the flood began on the seventeenth day of the second month
(7:11) and ended on the twenty-seventh day of the second month of
the following year (8:13-14), the whole occurrence thus extending
over a period of one year and eleven days. But according to the
other source, called J (or the Yahwistic Narrative), it rained for
forty days and forty nights (7:12), at the end of which Noah opened
the window of the ark and sent forth four birds at intervals of
three successive periods of seven days (8:6-12), whereupon he removed the covering of the ark and found that the face of the ground
was dry (vs. 13b); accordingly, the duration of the flood was only
sixty-one days.

With this view I cannot agree. However, this is not the place
to enter upon a detailed discussion of the problems involved; a
few words will have to suffice. I do by no means deny that a number of different documents may have been utilized in the composition of the biblical flood story, for the Scriptures themselves
indicate unmistakably that the sacred penmen employed written records and the like in the preparation of their books. But, in spite
of the claims that have been made, I am not at all convinced that
the biblical material can be resolved into its constituent elements
with any degree of certainty. Moreover, I am not in sympathy with
the common practice of treating the alleged remnants of each supposed document as if it constituted the whole, with the result that
the Genesis account of the deluge, with which alone we are at present concerned, fairly teems with discrepancies. It must be apparent
to every unprejudiced reader that the Genesis version of the flood,
as divided by modern biblical criticism, shows several important
gaps in the portions assigned to J and P. Therefore, if we had

access to the complete text of the supposed documents denominated
J and P (assuming, for the sake of argument, that such documents
ever existed), we might see at once that there were no discrepancies
at all between the two. But even without such access, it has been
demonstrated repeatedly that the alleged contradictions in the
Genesis narrative are capable of a simple and reasonable solution
if the story is left as we find it in the Hebrew text.

A good illustration of this we have in the point under examination—the duration of the flood. If we leave the biblical text
as it stands and treat the story as one whole, the numerical data
on the duration of the deluge are in perfect harmony, as shown by
the following.

According to 7:11, the flood began in the six hundredth year
of Noah's life, on the seventeenth day of the second month, coming
seven days after Noah had received the command to enter the ark
(7:1-4.10). For forty days and forty nights it rained upon the
earth (vs. 12). It is not said anywhere that after this period
the downpour stopped altogether. On the contrary, the rain and
the gushing-forth of the subterranean springs continued; for it
is clearly stated that the fountains of the deep and the windows
of heaven were not closed and that the rain from heaven was not
stopped (וַיִּכָּלֵא)[50] until the end of the one hundred and fiftieth
day after the outbreak of the flood, for which reason the waters
kept rising or maintained their maximum height during all this time
(7:24—8:2). But while the flow of the subterranean waters may
have continued with great force even after the first forty days,
the uninterrupted and unrestrained torrential downpour from heaven
must have ceased and the rain must have continued much more moder-
ately, for we read in 7:12: "The rain came upon the earth forty
days and forty nights," and in verse 17: "The flood (mabbûl) came
upon the earth forty days." As pointed out before, the term mabbûl
in verse 17 undoubtedly describes the unprecedented stream of rain
from above, which made the waters mount on the surface of the
earth. From this it seems quite obvious that it was the unchecked
torrential rain or the sheets of water from the sky which ceased
after the first forty days.[51]

---

[50]Cf. Ezek. 31:15 and Exod. 36:6.

[51]Thus Lino Murillo, El Génesis (Rome, 1914), pp. 371-72.

At the end of the 150 days the waters began to decrease (8:3), and on the seventeenth day of the seventh month the ark rested on one of the mountains of Ararat (vs. 4). This was exactly 5 months and 1 day from the beginning of the flood (cf. 7:11). The obvious conclusion appears to be that the 150 days constituted 5 months and that each month, consequently, consisted of 30 days. On the day that the waters began to abate, i.e., on the one hundred and fifty-first day from the commencement of the flood, the ark grounded. The waters continued to decrease until, on the first day of the tenth month, the tops of the mountains became visible (8:5). If a month is reckoned at 30 days, this gives us 74 additional days, yielding a total of 225 days. At the end of 40 days from this date, i.e., the first of the tenth month, Noah opened the window of the ark and sent forth four birds at intervals of three successive periods of 7 days (vss. 6-12). Since the first bird was released on the forty-first day, these figures add up to 62 more days and bring the total up to 287 days. The last bird was sent forth on the two hundred and eighty-seventh day from the beginning of the deluge, or (adding the 46 days of the year which elapsed before the outbreak of the flood) on the three hundred and thirty-third day of the year. We have, accordingly, arrived at the third day of the twelfth month. Twenty-eight days later, on the first day of the following year, in the six hundred and first year of Noah's life, the waters were dried up from off the earth (but the surface of the ground was not yet fully dry) and Noah removed the covering of the ark (vs. 13). A month and 26 days after that, on the twenty-seventh of the second month, the earth was again dry and firm, and Noah left the ark (vss. 14 ff.). These two periods amount to 84 days. Adding these days to the 287, we gain a grand total of 371 days, or 1 year and 11 days, beginning with the outbreak of the flood. There is here no discrepancy whatever.[52]

The year in which the flood came upon mankind, according to the biblical data, apparently consisted of only 360 days, the reckoning being neither by lunar years of 354 days nor by solar years of 365 days. This year, accordingly, seems to have fallen 5 or 6 days short of our calendrical year. However, it may well be that 5 extra days were added at the end of the year, so that 94 instead of 89

---

[52]Instead of "the seventeenth day" in 7:11, the Septuagint, perhaps due to an effort to make the deluge last exactly one year, has "the twenty-seventh day."

days elapsed between the first of the tenth month (8:5) and the
beginning of the following year (vs. 13), the whole period from
the entry into the ark to the disembarkation thus lasting 376 days.
The latter calendaric system would find its parallel in Egypt and
the former in Babylonia. The Egyptian calendar, which is probably
followed in the Genesis story, had 12 months of 30 days each, adding
up to 360 days. But to these were added 5 days at the end, which
produced a rough conformity with the solar year. The Babylonians,
on the other hand, with their lunar calendar of 29 and 30 days to
the month, equalized the difference by a cyclic intercalation of
an additional month. But alongside the real lunar calendar, they
had also, already in early Babylonian times, "a schematic calendar
of 12 months of 30 days each, regardless of the real moon," the
year thus having only 360 days.[53]

According to the Sumerian version, the flood raged for seven
days and seven nights, at the end of which the sun-god came forth
and shed his light over heaven and earth (col. v). In the Gilgamesh Epic it is stated that a destructive rain in the evening began the deluge and was followed at the break of day by a terrific
storm lasting six days and six nights. "When the seventh day arrived, the tempest, the flood, which had fought like an army, subsided in (its) onslaught. The sea grew quiet, the storm abated,
the flood ceased." And after an unspecified number of days, Utnapishtim and those with him left the boat (Tablet XI:90-156). The
excerpt from Berossus is silent on the duration of the deluge.

The Magnitude and Effect of the Flood

The magnitude of the storm and its appalling effect are described in forceful terms in the main Babylonian recension of the
deluge. "As soon as the first shimmer of morning beamed forth,
a black cloud came up from out the horizon." Adad, god of storm
and rain, thundered within it. Irragal, god of the underworld,
pulled out the masts. Ninurta, god of the wells and the irrigation
works, came along and caused the dikes to burst. The Anunnaki,
the judges in the underworld, raised their flaming torches, "lighting up the land with their brightness; the raging of Adad reached
unto heaven (and) turned into darkness all that was light," so that

[53]O. Neugebauer in the Journal of Near Eastern Studies, I
(1942), 396-403.

"no man could see his fellow." The tempest raged in all its fury
and apparently assumed greater dimensions than many of the gods
had anticipated, for, terror-stricken at the frightful cataclysm,
they fled to the highest heaven and cowered like dogs in their
distress! Ishtar, the lovely voiced lady of the gods, cried out
like a woman in travail and lamented: "In truth, the olden time
has turned to clay, because I commanded evil in the assembly of
the gods! How could I command (such) evil in the assembly of the
gods! (How) could I command war to destroy my people, (for) it is
I who bring forth (these) my people! Like the spawn of fish they
(now) fill the sea!" (118-23). Even the Anunnaki, who had helped
to spread terror and destruction among mankind, wept with her.
"The gods sat bowed (and) weeping. Covered were their lips." When
at last, after six days and six nights, the storm had exhausted its
force and the flood ceased, Utnapishtim opened a window and looked
upon the sea caused by the unprecedented storm. What he beheld was
heartbreaking—"(All) was silence, and all mankind had turned to
clay." Moved to tears by the complete desolation round about, he
"looked in (all) directions for the boundaries of the sea. At (a
distance of) twelve (double-hours)^{54} there emerged a stretch of
land." This turned out to be Mount Niṣir, on which afterward the
boat grounded. This mountain had either not been covered at all
by the flood or only lightly so that it reappeared immediately upon
the abatement of the water. But all the rest, at least in that
part of the world, was one vast expanse of sea. The impression
which this story is intended to make obviously is that the flood
was universal and that all the land animals and all mankind perished,
except the occupants of the ark. The other Babylonian deluge traditions convey the same general impression.

According to the Genesis account, the fountains of the abyss
broke open and the windows of heaven were opened; for forty days
and forty nights the waters gushed forth from below and poured down
in torrents from above. "The waters increased and lifted the ark,
so that it rose above the earth. And the waters grew mighty and
increased greatly upon the earth, so that the ark floated on the
face of the waters. And the waters grew exceedingly strong upon
the earth; and all the high mountains under the whole heaven were
covered. Fifteen cubits above (them) the waters rose, so that the

---

^{54}One double-hour is equal to about seven miles.

mountains were covered. And all flesh perished that moved upon
the earth, the fowl, the beasts, the game, every creeping thing
that creeps upon the earth, and all mankind. Everything died in
whose nostrils was the breath of the spirit of life, namely, everything that was on the dry land. Every creature was wiped off the
face of the earth, from mankind to the beasts, to the creeping
things, and the fowl of the heavens; they were wiped off the earth,
so that Noah alone was left and those with him in the ark" (7:17-23).
This account, like the main Babylonian story, plainly asserts the
universality of the deluge.

The Landing-Place of the Ark

The place on which Utnapishtim's boat came to rest is given
in the Gilgamesh Epic as Mount Nisir, which signifies the "Mount
of Salvation," if our reading is correct and if the name is of
Semitic origin. Such a mountain, or mountain range, is recorded
in the annals of King Ashurnasirpal II of Assyria (883-859 B.C.),
according to which it was situated to the south of the Lower Zab
and is probably to be identified with Pir Omar Gudrun, having an
altitude of about 9,000 feet.[55] Berossus names the mountains of
the Gordyaeans, or the Kurds, as the landing-place of the boat of
Xisuthros. These mountains, corresponding to Jebel Jûdî, where
also Syriac and Arabic traditions localize the landing-place, are
in the southwestern part of Armenia. The Genesis account is quite
indefinite on the point under consideration, stating merely that
the ark grounded "on (one of) the mountains of Ararat." The name
Ararat is identical with the Assyrian Urartu, which, broadly speaking, embraced the territory of Armenia. In three of the four Old
Testament passages where the word Ararat occurs, the Septuagint has
simply transliterated it (Gen. 8:4; II Kings 19:37; Jer. 51:27
[28:27 in the Septuagint]), while in the remaining passage the
translators have rendered it with "Armenia" (Isa. 37:38). Since
it is believed that the ark rested on the highest peak in the country
it has long been customary to identify the landing-place with Mount
Massis (or Agridagh), situated a little northeast of Lake Van and

---

[55]See E. A. Wallis Budge and L. W. King, Annals of the Kings
of Assyria, I (London, 1902), 305 ff.; M. Streck in Zeitschrift für
Assyriologie, XV (1900), 272 ff.; and E. A. Speiser in the Annual
of the American Schools of Oriental Research, VIII (1928), esp.
18 and 31.

rising to approximately 17,000 feet above sea-level. Evidently
through a misunderstanding of Gen. 8:4, this elevation has tradi-
tionally been called Mount Ararat.[56]

The Bird Scene

On the seventh day after the landing of the boat on Mount
Niṣir, Utnapishtim released a dove for the purpose of testing the
subsidence of the water. But since the dove found no resting-
place, she returned. After an unspecified interval, he sent forth
a swallow, which likewise returned. Finally he sent out a raven.
The raven ate, flew about, and cawed, but did not return.

The extracts from the account of Berossus also mention the
sending-out of the birds on three different occasions, but they
fail to state how many and what kinds of birds were used for the
experiment. According to the longer and more detailed excerpt,
Berossus says that, as soon as the flood ceased, "Xisuthros let go
some birds..... But as they found no food nor a place to alight,
they returned to the ship. After certain days Xisuthros again let
the birds go; these again returned to the ship, but with their feet
muddy. But when they were let go for the third time, they did not
again return to the ship."

The Book of Genesis describes the episode of the birds at considerable length. Forty days after the tops of the other mountains
had become visible, Noah opened the window of the ark and sent forth a
raven (8:5-7). The wild, omnivorous bird went flying back and forth,
sometimes away from the ark and sometimes back to it again, until
the waters had dried off the earth, but he did not again go into the
ark. He presumably found some carrion meat floating in the water
or deposited on the mountaintops, or some aquatic creatures trapped
on the mountain peaks as the water receded, and this provided sufficient sustenance for the unclean raven with his carrion-eating
propensities. The raven's failure to return into the ark does not
show that he proved himself useless for the intended purpose and
that the experiment was unsuccessful.[57] To the contrary, it was a
good sign; for it proved that the waters had declined considerably
and that even though the outside world was still very unfriendly or

---

[56]Dillmann, op. cit., pp. 282-83; Skinner, op. cit., p. 166;
and König, Die Genesis, p. 354.

[57]Dillmann, op. cit., p. 285.

inhospitable, it was no longer too inhospitable for so sturdy and unfastidious a bird as the raven.[58]

After seven days Noah let a dove fly out, "to see whether the waters had subsided from the surface of the land; but the dove found no resting-place for the sole of her foot, so she returned to him into the ark; for there was (still) water upon the surface of the whole earth. Then he put forth his hand, and took her, and drew her into the ark with him" (8:8-9). The dove, unlike the raven, is a gentle, timid, and more particular bird, which will not feed on carcasses; it loves valleys and dislikes mountains (Ezek. 7:16). Although the waters had abated considerably by this time, revealing many a mountain peak, the dove found no resting-place agreeable to her; so she returned. This was an indication that the lowlands were still covered.

Having waited seven more days, Noah released another dove, which did not come back until toward evening. The second dove had evidently found food and a resting-place, but the conditions of the outside world was still such that the dove preferred to spend the night in the ark. On her return, she brought an olive leaf in her bill. It was not a withered leaf, nor one that had been floating on the water, but "a freshly plucked" leaf (8:10-11). Since the olive tree does not grow at great altitudes, Noah had proof that the waters of the flood had fallen roughly to the level of the olive trees in the lowlands. That the olive tree was found also in Armenia we know from the Greek geographer and historian Strabo (ca. 63 B.C.-ca. A.D. 23).[59]

After another seven days, Noah sent out a third dove, but she never returned (8:12). Also this was a good sign; it showed that the lowlands as well as the mountains were free of water.

A comparison of these stories reveals that they are in agreement on the main points with regard to the bird episode. All agree that the hero of the flood, after the subsidence of the storm, sent out a number of birds to secure information concerning the conditions of the outside world. While the purpose of this experiment is not expressly stated in the Babylonian legends, it can be inferred without difficulty from the course of subsequent events. But the Hebrew and Babylonian versions differ very decidedly in the matter of de-

---

[58]Delitzsch, op. cit., p. 181.

[59]xi. 14.4.

tails. The Babylonian stories speak of three trials, the biblical
of four. Utnapishtim and Noah release one bird on each occasion,
whereas Xisuthros lets go a number of them each time. Utnapishtim
sends out a dove, a swallow, and a raven; Noah releases a raven
and three doves. The biblical account contains no reference to the
swallow, which is well known in Palestine and is mentioned in the
Old Testament under the term sûs or sîs (Isa. 38:14; Jer. 8:7);
perhaps also under the term dĕrôr (Ps. 84:4; Prov. 26:2). Noah
begins with the raven, Utnapishtim ends the experiment with this
bird. By releasing the raven first, Noah, whose wisdom is nowhere
mentioned in the biblical account, displayed greater wisdom than
Utnapishtim, who, notwithstanding the fact that he is called "the
exceedingly wise," sent the raven out last. For what legitimate
conclusions could Utnapishtim draw from the raven's failure to return after he had sent out the dove and the swallow? As is well
known, he deduced from it that the earth was dry enough for the
occupants of the boat to disembark. This was a mistake in logic.
However, as luck would have it, the earth turned out to be habitable
again, and Utnapishtim's reputation was unimpaired.[60] In addition
to these, there are a number of other points of dissimilarity, such
as the biblical reference to the olive leaf and the statement in
Berossus that the second group of birds returned with mud adhering
to their feet, both of which points find no parallels in the other
narratives.

The Exit from the Ark

The disembarkation of the occupants of the deluge vessel receives but a passing notice in the Babylonian cuneiform sources.
From the Sumerian version it can only be inferred, while, in the
Gilgamesh Epic, Utnapishtim contents himself with the bare statement that he "sent forth (everything) to the four winds" when the
raven failed to return. Berossus is somewhat more informative on
this point. By him we are told that, when the last group of birds
did not come back, Xisuthros concluded that land had appeared,

---

[60]The view that Noah dismissed the raven first because he
wanted to get rid of the unclean and therefore obnoxious bird (Lev.
11:15) at the first opportunity (Jastrow, op. cit., p. 361) is
rather fanciful. If this had been Noah's intention, we cannot help
wondering why he did not at the same time send out the raven's
mate.

whereupon he unstopped "a part of the seams of the ship and perceiving that the ship had grounded upon a certain mountain, he
disembarked with (his) wife, (his) daughter, and the pilot"; all
the others, who had remained behind, disembarked later, when Xisuthros and his companions failed to return.

The Genesis account treats the subject under examination with
considerable circumstantiality. Almost two months after the waters
of the flood had dried up, God said to Noah: "Go forth of the ark,
thou and thy wife, thy sons and the wives of thy sons with thee.
Bring forth with thee every living thing that is with thee, of all
flesh, including the fowl and the beasts and every creeping thing
that creeps upon the earth, that they may breed abundantly on the
earth, and be fruitful and multiply on the earth" (8:16-17). In
obedience to this command, "Noah went forth, and his sons and his
wife and the wives of his sons with him. Every living thing, every
creeping thing, every fowl, (and) everything that moves on the
earth went forth out of the ark according to their families" (vss.
18-19).

It will be observed that Noah did not leave the ark until the
ground was again fully dry and, so we may infer, until the plants
had again grown sufficiently to support the parent-stock of the
new world. The situation is different in the Babylonian versions.
Since the flood, according to Babylonian traditions, was only of
short duration, the ground and the plant life upon it were not
thought to have been disturbed seriously. We notice, furthermore,
that, while the Babylonian deluge hero, guided by the principle of
self-help, disembarked on his own motion, Noah waited patiently for
the express command of God to leave the ark. As he had entered the
ark at the command of God, so he remained in it until he received
divine orders to leave it. Utnapishtim, on the other hand, had
entered the boat upon the instruction of a friendly deity (Tablet
XI:86 ff.), but he disembarked at his own discretion. The biblical
story is pervaded by the spirit of complete submission to the will
of God and complete dependence on him, while the Babylonian traditions reveal something of the spirit of self-determination and self-
reliance, recalling those well-known lines of William Ernest Henley:
"I am the master of my fate; I am the captain of my soul."

The Sacrifice

In both the Babylonian and the Genesis accounts the deluge
hero performed one or several acts of worship after his escape
from the waters of the flood.   Ziusudra prostrated himself before
the sun-god and offered up an ox and an abundant sacrifice of sheep.
He again fell down and worshiped when Anu Enlil made his appearance.
The Sumerian story would seem to represent the sacrifice and at
least the first adoration scene as having taken place on board the
boat, while it was still floating on the waters.   However, since
this version constitutes probably an epitomized form of the deluge
tradition, we cannot be certain about it.   In all the other narratives the sacrifice and the act of prostration took place after the
landing from the vessel.   Utnapishtim offered a sacrifice, poured
out a libation on the peak of the mountain, and burned fragrant
materials—"(sweet) cane, cedar, and myrtle."   According to Berossus,
Xisuthros prostrated himself to the ground, built an altar, and
sacrificed to the gods.   The biblical version closely parallels
the Babylonian counterparts.   Noah built an altar unto the Lord
and offered burnt-offerings "of every clean beast and of every clean
fowl" (8:20).   The sacrifice was great, corresponding to the importance of the occasion.

The purpose of the offerings is naturally similar in all accounts.   Since the Babylonian hero escaped against the will of the
assembly of the gods, who had decreed the complete extermination
of the human race, he had reason to fear the wrath of the gods,
particularly that of Enlil, the instigator of the deluge; hence it
is an obvious conclusion that his sacrifice was one of propitiation.
However, as far as Utnapishtim's attitude toward Ea was concerned,
the offering was no doubt an expression of gratitude.   The propi-
tiatory character of the sacrifice is brought out quite clearly in
the biblical narrative, where the ascending essence of the burnt-
offerings is called a "soothing odor," or, literally, an "odor of
tranquilization" (8:21).[61]   One purpose of Noah's sacrifice, as
seems to be indicated by what follows, probably was to appease the
wrath of God which had been kindled by the sins of mankind and which
Noah had just witnessed.   But at the same time it was undoubtedly
an offering for the expiation of his own sins and those of his

---

[61]With this meaning of reah hannihoah cf., e.g., Exodus, chap.
29, and Leviticus, chap. 1.

family. For even though Noah is characterized as righteous and
faultless among his contemporaries (6:9), and even though 8:16-17,
where he is told to leave the ark, contains no trace of any divine
displeasure toward him or those with him, Noah was not absolutely
perfect in the sight of God (cf. 8:21), and he was therefore in
need of a sacrifice of atonement. On the other hand, since he had
been delivered by the express will and help of God, there is no
doubt at all that his sacrifice was a manifestation of deepest
gratitude as well.

When the Lord "smelled the soothing odor" of the burnt-offerings and perceived the humble and grateful disposition of Noah's
heart and mind, his wrath in general subsided, and he resolved
henceforth to bear with the sins of mankind and never again to
visit the earth with a universal flood or to interrupt the course
of nature as long as the earth endured (8:21-22).

A rather repugnant parallel to the last part of this episode
we find in the main Babylonian deluge tradition. When "the gods
smelled the sweet savor," they "gathered like flies over the
sacrificer." Since through the extirpation of humankind, with the
exception of the occupants of the ark, all sacrifices had ceased,
the gods had not been fed for some weeks and now were hungry. In
view of the opportunity of feasting again, all the gods and god-
desses present apparently forgot their grievances against mankind
and were glad that Utnapishtim had survived. Ishtar "lifted up
the great jewels which Anu had made according to her wish (and said):
'O ye gods here present, as surely as I shall not forget the lapis
lazuli on my neck, I shall remember these days and shall not forget (them) ever! Let the gods come near to the offering; (but) Enlil
shall not come near to the offering, because without reflection he
brought on the deluge and consigned my people to destruction!'"
(Tablet XI:163-69). When at last Enlil arrived, he was unaffected
by the sacrifice. A quarrel ensued among the gods, in which Ea was
accused of being responsible for Utnapishtim's escape by having revealed the secret of the gods. But Ea turned from defender to ac-
cuser, condemning Enlil's rash and indiscriminate destruction of
the human family and upbraiding him for not having resorted to more
reasonable measures to induce mankind to mend their ways. Enlil was
moved by the reproach and had nothing to say in reply. Obviously,
this was a silent admission that he had gone too far. His silence,
together with the blessing which he subsequently pronounced upon

Utnapishtim and his wife, doubtlessly implied also a resolve that
the earth should never again be devastated by a catastrophe like
the flood.

Divine Blessings

Enlil's apparent change of heart is followed by a scene of
rare beauty and great solemnity, contrasting sharply with the preceding episode. Enlil went up into the ship, took Utnapishtim by
the hand, and caused him and his wife to go aboard and to kneel
down; then, standing between them, he touched their foreheads and
blessed them: "Hitherto Utnapishtim has been but a man; but now
Utnapishtim and his wife shall be like unto us gods. In the distance, at the mouth of the rivers, Utnapishtim shall dwell!" (Tablet
XI:193-95). According to Berossus, also their daughter and the
boatman were translated to the society of the immortal gods. The
Sumerian legend, on the contrary, speaks of only Ziusudra's apotheo-
osis, probably taking for granted that his wife shared in the same
honor. Upon Enlil's bestowal of divinity and immortality on Utnapishtim and his wife, the gods took them and caused them "to dwell
in the distance, at the mouth of the rivers" (line 196).[62] In the
Sumerian version the flood hero was transferred to Dilmun. Some
scholars have expressed the view that Dilmun was a country situated
somewhere on the eastern shore of the Persian Gulf,[63] while others
have identified it with the Bahrein Islands (in the Persian Gulf),[64]
and still others with these islands and the neighboring coastland.[65]
On the basis of the Sumerian text we are probably justified in assuming that by the expression "the mouth of the rivers" in the Gilgamesh Epic was meant originally the general area where in ancient
times the Tigris and Euphrates flowed into the Persian Gulf through
separate mouths. But that the phrase in question cannot refer to

[62] That also Utnapishtim's wife was taken there, is clear from
Tablet XI:202 ff.

[63] Jensen in Zeitschrift für Assyriologie, XV, 225 ff.; Poebel,
op. cit., p. 62; S. N. Kramer in the Bulletin of the American Schools
of Oriental Research, No. 96 (December, 1944), pp. 18-28.

[64] W. F. Albright in the American Journal of Semitic Languages
and Literatures, XXXV (1918/19), 182-83; King, Legends ...., p. 86,
n. 2; Salonen, op. cit., p. 53, n. 1, where numerous references to
further literature on this point are found.

[65] E. Burrows and A. Deimel in Orientalia, No. 30 (1928), pp.
3-31.

this region in the present form of the epic is clear from the fact
that the epic pictures Utnapishtim as living in a faraway country
and that Gilgamesh has to make a long and perilous journey over a
virtually impassable mountain range and across a wide and dangerous sea before he arrives there. Scholars therefore incline to the
view that in the course of time, as the Babylonians became better
acquainted with the southern part of the land, the home of blessed
Utnapishtim was transferred from "the place where the sun rises,"
as the Sumerian version puts it, to a part of the world somewhere
toward the setting of the sun, beyond the Mediterranean shore, and
that this region was then designated as "the mouth of the rivers."[66]
The excerpt from Berossus fixes the place of Xisuthros' postdiluvian
residence in heaven, adding that the flood hero was translated to
the realm of the gods because of his piety.

The biblical account likewise speaks of a blessing imparted
to the deluge hero, but it is of an altogether different nature.
The blessing consists, in part, in the power—first conferred on
man at the time of his creation and now bestowed anew on Noah and
his sons—to multiply and fill the earth and to exercise dominion
over the animals. Added to this is an extension of man's right over
the animals, legalizing the eating of their flesh. However, in order
to prevent man's degeneration to the level of barbarism and savagery,
he is forbidden to eat their blood or the flesh with its blood.
Moreover, while man is permitted to slaughter the animals for his
consumption, he himself, being created in the image of God, may not
be slain with impunity either by man or beast (Gen. 9:1-7). The
blessing pronounced on the Babylonian hero included his removal from
the ken of mortal man, but Noah remained in the company of those who,
together with him, had escaped the waters of the great flood and
lived for many years afterward.

The Conclusion of the Covenant

To date no real parallel has been discovered in any Babylonian
diluvial tradition to the covenant which the Lord made with all
flesh, including the animals, that the earth would never again be

---

[66]Jensen, Assyrisch-babylonische Mythen und Epen (Berlin, 1900),
pp. 506-7 and 576; Das Gilgamesch-Epos in der Weltliteratur, I
(Strassburg, 1906), 36-37; Poebel, op. cit., pp. 62-63. A different
view has been expressed by Albright in the American Journal of
Semitic Languages and Literatures, XXXV, 161-95.

destroyed by a flood, or to the rainbow, the symbol of the covenant. However, Enlil's presumed resolution that there should be
no recurrence of such a catastrophe comes close to the biblical
story of the covenant. Jensen,[67] moreover, raised the question
whether a parallel to the rainbow might not be found in the scene
which portrays Ishtar as lifting up her azure-blue necklace and
swearing that, as she would never forget these jewels, so she would
never forget "these days," evidently meaning the starvation days
of the flood followed by the glorious day of the sacrifice (Tablet
XI:162-65). Jensen's idea, which he had advanced with much reserve,
was subsequently adopted by Otto Weber[68] with a high degree of confidence, while R. W. Rogers[69] went another step further and accepted
it as an established fact. But while Ishtar's oath probably implied
that she would never again consent to so terrible a destruction of
life and that the necklace was to serve as a reminder of her oath,
as the rainbow is to remind the Lord of his promise to all flesh,
the picture drawn in the Babylonian passage looks drab alongside
what we find in the biblical story. The parallel becomes even less
impressive when we consider that in the Mesopotamian version it was
not Enlil, the head of the pantheon and the real author of the flood,
who swore the oath, but Ishtar, a subordinate deity. It is interesting to note that as ardent a Pan-Babylonist as Heinrich Zimmern[70]
declined to accept Jensen's idea.

A New Creation of Humans after the Flood

The final column of Fragment IV of the Atrahasis Epic records
that Ea and Mami (or Mama), with the help of fourteen women, created fourteen human beings after the deluge. The reason for this
new creation of human life was not that all mankind had perished
in the flood, for Fragments II and III indicate quite definitely
that this was not the case; in fact, the fourteen women partici-
pating in this act probably were themselves survivors of the flood.

---

[67]Assyrisch-babylonische Mythen und Epen, pp. 503-4.

[68]Die Literatur der Babylonier und Assyrer (Leipzig, 1907),
p. 84, n. 1.

[69]The Religion of Babylonia and Assyria (New York and Cincinnati, 1908), p. 205, n.

[70]In Schrader, op. cit., p. 550, n. 2.

The purpose obviously was a speedy repopulation of the earth.

The new creation appears to have taken place in the following manner. Ea, the god of incantations and one of the creators of mankind, recited an incantation in the presence of Mami, the goddess of birth. At Ea's request, Mami then recited this same incantation over a lump of clay, whereupon she pinched off fourteen pieces of this clay and placed seven of them to the right and seven to the left and a brick (or brickwork) in between, probably as her symbol. She then called fourteen women who evidently had given birth before. These, apparently looking upon the pieces of clay, of which Mami seems to have modeled fourteen human beings, gave birth to seven boys and seven girls.[71]

There is, of course, no parallel to this tale in the Genesis account of the flood. But there is a certain parallel in the Greek deluge tradition of Deucalion and Pyrrha, who were divinely directed to cast behind them "the bones of the great mother," i.e., the stones of the earth, to renew the human race, with the result that the stones thrown by Deucalion became men, while those thrown by Pyrrha, his wife, became women.[72]

The Problem of Dependence

After the detailed examination of the points of contact between the Mesopotamian and Hebrew accounts of the flood it remains to inquire into their historical or genetic relationship. That the Babylonian and Hebrew versions are genetically related is too obvious to require proof; the only problem that needs to be discussed is the degree of relationship. Here, as in the case of the creation stories, three main possibilities have been suggested: first, the Babylonians borrowed from the Hebrew account; second, the Hebrew account is dependent on the Babylonian; third, both are descended from a common original.

The first explanation finds little favor among scholars today, since the earliest known tablets of the Babylonian legend are, upon any view of the date of the Book of Genesis, considerably older than

---

[71]Jensen, _Assyrisch-babylonische Mythen und Epen_, p. 547; Ebeling, _Tod und Leben nach den Vorstellungen der Babylonier_ (Berlin and Leipzig, 1931), p. 174, n. _d_.

[72]Apollodorus _The Library_ 1. 7. 2, and Ovid _Metamorphoses_ 1. 348-415.

the biblical narrative. The oldest dated tablets are the first two
fragments of the Atrahasis Epic, which were inscribed in the reign
of Ammizaduga, the second-last king of the First Babylonian Dynasty.
But, as attested by the scribal notation "a new break," on Fragment
I, even the oldest available tablet is a copy of a still older
original. Moreover, if the Atrahasis Epic is based on Tablet XI,
as suggested above (p. 107), it follows that the deluge version
imbedded in the Gilgamesh Epic must antedate even the oldest recension of the Atrahasis legend. All this is in perfect harmony
with the fact that in all the Babylonian versions of the flood
Enlil is still the chief god, while Marduk, who already in the days
of Hammurabi was well on the way to supremacy among the gods,[73] is
not even mentioned on a single deluge tablet. We shall probably
be safe in placing the date of the earliest written Babylonian account of the flood at the end of the third or the very beginning
of the second millennium B.C. However, since priority of publication does not necessarily imply priority of existence, the argument derived from the age of the Babylonian account to disprove the
originality of the Hebrew cannot be regarded as conclusive; the
deluge version which we now call the Hebrew account of the flood
may well have existed in some form or other many centuries before
it assumed its present form.

The most widely accepted explanation today is the second,
namely, that the biblical account is based on Babylonian material.

One of the foremost arguments advanced in support of this explanation is the contention that the coloring of the biblical account is distinctively Babylonian. A. H. Sayce declares: "The
whole conception takes us back to the alluvial plain of Babylonia,
liable at any time to be inundated by the waters of the Persian
Gulf, and is wholly inapplicable to a mountainous country like Palestine, where rain only could have produced a flood."[74] And Driver,
following Zimmern, asserts: "The very essence of the Biblical narrative presupposes a country liable, like Babylonia, to inundations;
so that it cannot be doubted that the story was 'indigenous in Babylonia, and transplanted to Palestine.'"[75]

_____

[73]Meissner, op. cit., II, 46.

[74]The Early History of the Hebrews (London, 1897), p. 125.

[75]Op. cit., p. 107.

But this view, for which many more authorities could be quoted,
finds no confirmation in the biblical text. In the biblical record there is not the slightest indication of an inundation caused
by the rising of the rivers or the swelling of the sea. As we have
observed, it mentions only torrential rains from heaven and the
bursting of the subterranean fountains. Moreover, the first of
these two elements is anything but characteristic of climatic conditions in Babylonia, while the second is by no means unknown in
the West.

The average annual rainfall in Babylonia, amounting to about
six inches, is quite inconsequential; were it not for the irrigation canals and the flooding of the rivers, Babylonia would be a
barren desert. This condition has prevailed in Babylonia since
time immemorial. In Palestine, by way of contrast, the mean annual
rainfall is about four times as heavy, while in Syria it is from
about six to eight times as heavy.[76] However, Friedrich Delitzsch,[77]
accepting the theory proposed by Suess, argued that when the Babylonian flood story had traveled to Palestine, the Hebrews, owing
to the totally different conformation of their soil, "forgot that
the sea had been the main factor." This assertion on the part of
Delitzsch amounts to an attempt to prove one assumption by means of
another. Although the deluge, according to the Gilgamesh Epic,
was accompanied by a storm of extraordinary magnitude issuing
probably from the Persian Gulf, there is no evidence, as we have
seen, that the Babylonian tradition refers to an inundation from
the sea; while, conversely, the idea of a flood caused by the descending rains is brought out in unmistakable terms. Had the deluge been due at least primarily to an incursion of the southern
sea, the Babylonian mythographers should have made express mention
of this point, instead of ignoring it and placing so much emphasis
on the downfall of rain. To meet the last-named difficulty, G. A.
Barton[78] assumed that the rain, followed by a disastrously high
overflow of the rivers, was stressed because it happened to be un-

---

[76]Clay, The Origin of Biblical Traditions, pp. 75-78 and 150-59;
M. G. Ionides, The Régime of the Rivers Euphrates and Tigris (London
and New York, 1937), esp. pp. 24-36.

[77]Babel und Bibel (Leipzig, 1902), p. 31.

[78]In the Journal of the American Oriental Society, XLV (1925),
28.

usually heavy. This, of course, proves nothing but is a concession
that such a rain does not reflect climatic conditions characteristic of Babylonia; an exceptionally heavy rain may occur anywhere
and, therefore, does not point to any place in particular.[79] The
fact of the matter is that not even in the Babylonian flood stories
do we have a true reflection of climatic conditions in Babylonia.
For instead of ascribing the flood to the annual inundations caused
by the rise of the rivers following the melting of the snows in the
mountains of Armenia and Kurdistan, the Babylonian deluge traditions mentioning the cause of the cataclysm all agree that the real
force of nature producing this unparalleled destruction was rain,
even though Babylonia's annual rainfall is insignificant, as we
have seen.

As for the springs of water, mentioned in the Genesis account,
they figure much more conspicuously in Syria and Palestine, owing
to the physical structure of the land, than they do in Babylonia.
Palestine is appropriately described as "a land of brooks of water,
of fountains and depths (tĕhômôth) that spring out of valleys and
hills" (Deut. 8:7).[80] In Babylonia, on the contrary, "springs do
not gush from the earth,"[81] i.e., normally. Furthermore, if, according to Suess, an earthquake in an alluvial region, such as
Babylonia, causes a larger volume of water to burst forth than a
terrestrial upheaval of equal magnitude would produce in an area
like Syria-Palestine, must the story on this account have originated in a low-lying district? Since Syria-Palestine is a land
of fountains, could not an earthquake of highly extraordinary violence—for it is a highly extraordinary seismic phenomenon that we
must assume in either case, if we want to rationalize the flood
story—cause sufficient subterranean water to erupt in this region
to meet the description in Genesis? The fact that such eruptions
have so far been observed on a large scale only in extensive low-
lying parts of the world is no proof that under certain conditions
they could not take place in the land of the Hebrews and their
northern neighbors. Finally, is it not significant that not even

---

[79]Cf. Clay's rejoinder to Barton, ibid., pp. 141-42.

[80]A Dictionary of the Bible, ed. James Hastings, II (New York,
1903), 62; G. A. Smith, The Historical Geography of the Holy Land
(26th ed.; New York and London), pp. 76 ff.

[81]Clay, The Origin of Biblical Traditions, p. 157.

the main Babylonian diluvial tradition, the most detailed of all
the Mesopotamian accounts of the flood, contains as much as an
allusion to the breaking-up of the fountains of the deep, particularly in view of the fact that it makes mention of such common
manifestations as thunder and lightning?

In support of the view that the Genesis narrative reverts to
the Babylonian account, attention has been called also to the bird
episode. But we have seen that on this point, as in many other
instances, the data of the biblical record are at a decided variance with those of the Babylonian versions; there are differences
in the kind and number of birds and in the order in which they
were released. Furthermore, as R. Andree has observed, the general idea of sending forth birds on the high seas for the purpose
of obtaining information is met with also elsewhere in ancient
literature and is not as extraordinary as it may seem at first.[82]
Pliny reports that the seafarers of Ceylon "take no observations
of the stars in navigation" but "carry birds on board with them
and at fairly frequent intervals set them free, and follow the
course they take as they make for the land."[83] It will also be
recalled that the Argonauts sent forth a dove to determine whether
or not they would be able to make their way to Pontus between the
twin Cyanean rocks in their quest for the Golden Fleece.[84]

Another argument for the priority of the Babylonian record
has been derived from Gen. 8:21, which states that, as the Lord
smelled the soothing odor of Noah's sacrifice, he determined that
he would never again destroy all life by means of a flood. The
first part of this passage has been said to be in literal agreement
with Tablet XI:159-60: "The gods smelled the savor; the gods

---

[82]Die Flutsagen (Braunschweig, 1891), pp. 131-32.

[83]Naturalis historia vi. 24. 83 (trans. H. Rackham in the
"Loeb Classical Library").

[84]Appolonius Rhodius Argonautica ii. 317-407 and 528-610.
Plutarch (ca. A.D. 46-120) Scripta moralia: de sollertia animalium
13 relates that, according to the mythologists, Deucalion dispatched
a dove from the ark to ascertain the condition of the weather; the
return of the dove was a sign to him that the storm continued, while
her failure to come back meant fair weather. But, attractive as
this observation may appear at first reading, one can hardly base
an argument on it, because the probability is that this idea, if not
the Deucalionic flood story in general, emanated from Babylonian
sources.

smelled the sweet savor."[85] But—to begin with one of the least
significant points—while the agreement between the two passages
is undeniably close, the one cannot be regarded as a verbatim translation of the other. Rendered literally, the Babylonian lines
read: "The gods smelled the odor; the gods smelled the good odor."
Gen. 8:21a states: "And the Lord smelled the odor of tranquilization." The wording is not quite the same. Moreover, there is not
a single etymological correspondence between the terms employed in
the one version and those used in the other. But the main consideration against the above contention is the fact that Gen. 8:21a does
not contain an element foreign to the Old Testament but one which
is identical in thought and language with numerous other passages.
Exactly the same phraseology is found in Lev. 26:31: "I will not
smell the odor of your (offerings of) tranquilization." Much the
same phrase occurs again in Amos 5:21: "I will not smell (the
offerings) in your solemn assemblies," and in I Sam. 26:19: "Let
Him smell an offering." The same idea we meet again in the ever
recurring phrase of the ritual "a sweet savor unto the Lord," or,
literally, "an odor of tranquilization unto the Lord" (cf. esp.
Leviticus, chaps. 1 ff.). Nor can it be demonstrated that this concept first entered the Hebrew mind with the flood story. The argument based on Gen. 8:21 to prove the Babylonian origin of the biblical deluge account has no foundation whatever.

Perhaps the most important point which has been urged in favor
of the explanation that the biblical story rests on Babylonian ex-
emplars is the use in both accounts of bituminous substances for
calking the vessel. Utnapishtim employs pitch (kupru) and asphalt
(ittû) to make his boat watertight, while Noah uses only pitch
(kōfer) for the same purpose.

The mere reference to the use of mineral pitch in both narratives, for the purpose of rendering the boat impervious to the
waters of the flood, is not particularly remarkable, for surface
deposits (which alone enter into consideration) of bituminous ma-

---

[85]Gunkel, op. cit., p. 71; S. Oettli, Der Kampf um Bibel und
Babel (Leipzig, 1902), p. 20. A similar passage may perhaps be
found on a tablet from Ras Shamra. C. H. Gordon, The Loves and
Wars of Baal and Anat (Princeton, etc., 1943), p. 33, has rendered
the lines in question as follows: "The gods eat the offerings(?),
the deities drink the offerings(?)." For the original see Ch.
Virolleaud, La Légende phénicienne de Danel (Paris, 1936), p. 187
and Pl. V.

terials occurred in various parts of the ancient world. The three
most important bitumen regions known in antiquity are found in
Mesopotamia and in Iran (or Persia). Beginning with the eastern-
most, they are the zone on both sides of the river Karûn, north
of the Persian Gulf; the zone between the Tigris and the Zagros
Mountains; and the zone around Hit and Ramadi, on the western bank
of the lower Euphrates. Of these, the last-named area, where seep-
ages and streams yield bitumen in a form virtually ready for use,
was the most important center in ancient times. Also in Syria and
Palestine there were rich surface deposits of bitumen, especially
in and around the Dead Sea, whence bitumen was exported to Egypt,
which is poor in this material. A reference to such deposits in
the Dead Sea area is found in Gen. 14:10: "The valley of Siddim
(consisted of) pits (upon) pits of bitumen." Unfortunately, we
still know very little about the application of bitumen in ancient
Palestine. About all that can be said on this point with any degree of confidence is that bitumen was used for mortar as far back
as the latter part of the third millennium B.C. Whether the Pales-
tinians in antiquity employed this material as a waterproofing
medium in the construction of their ships or boats remains a problem whose solution must await further evidence.[86]

However, what is indeed remarkable about this point of contact
is the term by which this material is designated in the flood story.
Elsewhere in the Old Testament, pitch, or bitumen, is expressed by
ḥēmār (Gen. 11:3; 14:10; Exod. 2:3) or zefeth (Exod. 2:3; Isa. 34:9).
But here, in Gen. 6:14, and nowhere else, it is called kōfer, corresponding to the Babylonian and Assyrian kupru, Arabic kufr, Aramaic
kufrâ, and Armenian kupr.[87] However, on the strength of this one
word it cannot be concluded that the biblical account was derived
from the Babylonian; nor can it be maintained on the basis of this
passage that the term in question entered the Hebrew vocabulary with
the story of the deluge.[88] The bitumen industry presumably originated in Babylonia, the land of bitumen par excellence, where this

---

[86]R. J. Forbes, Bitumen and Petroleum in Antiquity (Leiden,
1936), esp. pp. 11-30 and 53-90, and "Neues zur ältesten Geschichte
des Bitumens," in Bitumen, Vol. VIII (1938), Heft 6 and 7; Salonen,
op. cit., pp. 146-49; J. P. Harland in the Biblical Archaeologist,
V (1942), 21-22.

[87]Zimmern, Akkadische Fremdwörter (Leipzig, 1915), p. 60.

[88]Cf. Dillmann, op. cit., p. 270; Driver, op. cit., p. 87.

substance served a great variety of purposes from time immemorial
(as building material, a waterproofing medium, etc.), and presumably spread from there to other parts of the world, to Assyria,
Arabia, Syria, Palestine, and Armenia. If this is correct, it
would seem likely that the name of the substance spread with the
industry or the use of the material. If bitumens were spoken of
more frequently in the Old Testament than they are (only in five
passages), or if we had more Hebrew literature of the Old Testament period, we might perhaps find the word kōfer in numerous
passages outside the flood story and utterly unrelated to it. Had
the biblical account been derived from the Babylonian and had the
term under discussion not been known to the Hebrews from any other
source, they would in all probability have replaced kupru by a word
with which they were familiar, choosing for this purpose either
ḥēmār or zefeth.[89]

It is obvious from all this that the arguments which have been
advanced in support of the contention that the biblical account
rests on Babylonian material are quite indecisive.[90]

Finally, there is a third way of accounting for the analogies
between the Hebrew and the Babylonian versions of the deluge, viz.,
that they revert to a common source of some kind. This source need
not at all have sprung from Palestinian soil but may very well have
originated in the land of Babylonia, where, indeed, the Book of
Genesis localizes the home of postdiluvian mankind (11:1-9) and
whence Abraham emigrated to Palestine (11:27—12:5). Such a source
is a very distinct possibility, especially since we know that a
number of different deluge versions were current in the Tigro-Euphrates area; but for the present, at least, this explanation can
be proved as little as the rest.

---

[89]In passing, we may make mention also of the view that mabbūl,
the Hebrew term for the flood, is derived from the Babylonian abūbu,
"rainstorm," "rainflood," "flood" (Gunkel, op. cit., p. 63; Procksch,
op. cit., p. 448). Suffice it to say that this idea lacks evidence
and that it has gained but little acceptance.

[90]The arguments relating to the date of Genesis, the integrity
of the sacred writers, and the biblical doctrine of inspiration,
which are frequently adduced in certain circles to disprove the
second explanation, are identical with those advanced against a dependence of the Old Testament creation material on Enûma elish and
have already been treated at some length in my book The Babylonian
Genesis. I shall therefore pass them up and refer the reader to
that study.

Concluding Remarks

As in the case of the creation stories, we still do not know how the biblical and Babylonian narratives of the deluge are related historically. The available evidence proves nothing beyond the point that there is a genetic relationship between Genesis and the Babylonian versions. The skeleton is the same in both cases, but the flesh and blood and, above all, the animating spirit are different. It is here that we meet the most far-reaching divergencies between the Hebrew and the Mesopotamian stories.

The main Babylonian flood legend, in particular, is "steeped in the silliest polytheism," to quote the words of Dillmann.[91] The gods are divided in their counsel, false to one another and to man; they flee in consternation to the highest heaven and cower like dogs in their distress; they quarrel and lie and gather over the sacrificer like a swarm of hungry flies! In the Babylonian accounts the moral or ethical motive is almost completely absent. As we read the first few lines of the flood story on Tablet XI of the Gilgamesh Epic, we get the impression that the cataclysm was caused by the caprice of the gods, for no ethical reason at all; however, toward the end of the story we are told, quite incidentally and by implication only, that the flood was due to the sin of mankind. Wherein the sin consisted is not indicated. According to the Atraḥasis Epic, the flood was sent because mankind with their noisy, hilarious gatherings disturbed the sleep of Enlil. Some such idea may also have been in the minds of the authors of the flood tradition in the Gilgamesh Epic. In none of the other Babylonian legends do we find any reason at all for the deluge, an omission which may, however, be due solely to the imperfect state in which they have come down to us. At any rate, in the Babylonian stories it is nowhere emphasized that the gods were actuated by moral ideals or that the flood was a divine visitation on human corruption. Rather, considering that the gods were intent on destroying the whole human race without discrimination between the just and the unjust, it is apparent that the gods were prompted more by caprice than by a sense of justice. It is true, the deluge hero was saved by a friendly deity because of his piety; but that was done clandestinely, through trickery, and against the decree of the gods in council.

In the biblical story, on the other hand, the flood is sent by

---

[91] Op. cit., p. 262.

the one omnipotent God, who is just in all his dealings with the
children of men, who punishes the impenitent sinner, even if it
means the destruction of the world, but who saves the just with
his powerful hand and in his own way. In Genesis the deluge is
clearly and unmistakably a moral judgment, a forceful illustration
of divine justice meting out stern punishment to a "faithless and
perverse generation" but delivering the righteous. What a serious
view the biblical account takes of the moral depravity of the prediluvian race of men can be seen also, as remarked by Gunkel,[92]
from the fact that in it no tears are shed, as on Tablet XI:116-25
and 136-37, over those who perished in the flood; theirs was a just
and deserved punishment. In the Hebrew document the ethical motive
is so strong that God is portrayed even as regretting the very creation of man;[93] while in the Babylonian, the gods, with the possible
exception of Enlil, regret the destruction of man. Although God
resolves not to send another flood, he is nowhere represented as
regretting the diluvial catastrophe. Irrespective of whether or
not the Hebrew account is to some degree dependent on Babylonian
material, also this piece of biblical literature was "written for
our learning" (Rom. 15:4), in order to rouse the conscience of the
world and to give hope and comfort to the God-fearing.

---

[92] Op. cit., p. 71.

[93] Jastrow, op. cit., p. 362.

PHOENIX BOOKS
in Sociology

PHOENIX BOOKS
in Anthropology

PHOENIX BOOKS
in Archeology

PHOENIX BOOKS
in History

PHOENIX BOOKS
in Philosophy

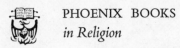

PHOENIX BOOKS
in Religion

PHOENIX BOOKS
Literature and Language